About the Author

Sue was educated at Oldborough Manor Secondary School, Maidstone. She achieved several passes at 'O' Level, then went on to Technical College gaining 2 'A' Level passes. After several failures in the job market she joined her father's Law firm on a temporary basis, but six years later qualified as a Legal Executive. Upon her father's retirement she joined the Chief Prosecuting Solicitors Dept. of the Kent County Council, which later became the Crown Prosecution Service.

Dedication

To Jackie Farr [nee Hails]: Kent Sports Development Officer for Disabled People; who was the instigator in my being able to turn my life around.

To my parents who transported me everywhere and who had to tolerate at times a 'gibbering idiot' whilst I was staying with them.

Also to the Johnston's Golden Labrador Dog, Shassie, who was always by my side when times were grim

Finally, to Clive [Barbara's husband], and their daughter Lynne, for their expertise with the computer.

Sue Pepper

LIFE AFTER DEATH

AUSTIN MACAULEY
PUBLISHERS LTD.

A CIP catalogue record for this title is available from the British Library.

ISBN 9781786932440 (Paperback)
ISBN 9781786932457 (E-Book)
www.austinmacauley.com

First Published (2017)
Austin Macauley Publishers Ltd.
25 Canada Square
Canary Wharf
London
E14 5LQ

PART 1

MY LIFE BEFORE

Chapter 1

There is life after death after all. When I had the misfortune to contract Multiple Sclerosis I thought my life had come to an end. A bloody great big door had slammed shut in my face and I could see no way of opening it.

I feel I should at first explain what my life was like before this happened.

I played sport very hard, in fact I used to do everything very hard. Metaphorically speaking I was a tough nut.

I used to compete at badminton in the Premier League and Division one. The competition being mainly County standard. These matches were held during the week, always after work and played until their conclusion usually in the early hours of the morning. I participated in both mixed and ladies doubles, playing on both Tuesdays and Thursdays. These were the club nights.

However matches were on Fridays, if played at home and at any other day of the week if we had to play away.

Before I started my day I used to go to the local swimming pool at Tenterden, at first 3 times a week then 4 times a week and used to swim about 100 lengths of a 25 metre pool in roughly a hour.

Rush home, have breakfast, rush to work, slave for the Prosecution for anything between 10 to 12 hours every day non-stop, have lunch on the run, take all the abuse from judges, police officers [some], witnesses, defendants, and defence witnesses and their hangers on, and not turn a hair. They seemed to know more about my private life than I did.

Was this the start of my problem? I had already stopped playing hockey at weekends and also umpiring it as again I was fed up with the abuse, and being cold and wet through each and every Saturday. Did I really give up my time for that? I found I was beginning to get more and more tired. Something had to give.

Did my problems start several years ago when I noticed I had difficulty breathing? My system used to indicate I needed to take a deep breath, but when I tried I found it was impossible, then all of a sudden I took a deep breath. Strange.

I never bothered with seeing my doctor about this, perhaps I should have done in hindsight, but we can always be wise with hindsight can't we.

I noticed my vision was blurring and as I already wear glasses I thought my specs needed changing. I went to have an eye test but this was not at all helpful as I was told my present prescription was adequate. I was rather amazed.

I then started to have further difficulties with my breathing and this resulted in coming down with bug after bug after bug! I am of course referring to the 'flu'. I had so many I was warned about my sickness leave at work.

Whilst I was off with the flu suffering with a temperature, shivers, etc. My HEO [Higher Executive Officer] telephoned me at home and ordered me back to work the next day as one of my cases was in Court and I was the only one who could deal with it. I suppose she rang me because she probably thought I was swinging the lead, although I was off with a medical certificate.

Not knowing any better I went into work the next morning feeling like 'death warmed up' spreading my germs all over the place, dutifully dealt with the problem and came home again. Suffice it to say I was off even longer.

Having received my warning I went back to the 'Quack' and informed him of my predicament, whereupon he referred me to a General Specialist.

My 'Quack' also informed me to take up swimming. I could not think of anything more boring than ploughing up and down a pool ad nauseam. This I was supposed to do 3 times a week.

The first time I got into the pool at Maidstone I sank after managing 2-3 strokes, this was a cross between 'doggy paddle' and something that could be called breaststroke, but I persevered and then to my surprise I had done a length. Then I thought, perhaps I could do another length. I wonder if I could do 2 lengths straight off. I did. I progressed and within 6 months I was completing 1500 metres.

By this time I was ploughing up Tenterden pool. Now a challenge reared its ugly head. Could I possible get a team together to swim the 1991 BT National Swimathon? The distance being, 5000 metres or 200 lengths of Tenterden pool, which is 25 metres in length.

Three girls from the office Catherine Winter, Jo Smith, and Louise Smith all volunteered. We decided to split the distance between us with each of us trying for the 60 lengths except Jo who had not been swimming long who completed the remainder of the distance of 20 lengths.

We did it and in a respectable time of 2hrs. 29mins. Our first attempt.

At this stage I was also singing having been a member of the St. Mildred's Church Choir for a number of years. Following on from my experiences with 2 Operatic Companies, I was persuaded to join the Tenterden Choral Society. This I did most reluctantly as I would no longer be able to specialise in my favourite form of music, being the works of Gilbert and Sullivan.

Providence was to take a hand. With all the problems of my nose and breathing difficulties. It transpired I needed an operation to remove a bone in the bridge of my nose.

This was due to a clash with my ladies' doubles partner at the time who broke my nose. She walloped me with her racket, quite by accident she said!

I was no longer able to play badminton as much as I had been. I was also suffering from extreme tiredness, and therefore I thought my age was going against me and therefore I needed to slow down. I was only in my mid-thirties and now looking back I realise it was not my age, that was affecting me. I joined the Society, under the direction of Tony Allen, and was asked to do some solos and duets for some of the lighter concerts. I am glad to say I was still singing, my favourite medium, although on a smaller scale, and not in costume.

Unfortunately, my nose problem deteriorated to such a degree I had to give up playing any sport. That is no badminton, tennis, squash, hockey, or even sailing. I was so tired all the time, after having slaved for the C.P.S. [Crown Prosecution Service], my employers. They really did make sure they got every last amount of energy you had. After about 10-12 hours solid you were not fit for much. However I still persevered. Not realising there was anything seriously wrong. I just thought I was overworking.

The general specialist who I went to see realised there was something wrong but not in the general sense. Ha, I hear you say, this girl has gone crazy. Well not quite, but I will say he referred me to an Ear Nose and Throat Specialist.

He immediately ordered X-rays of my nose and upon looking at them he said "there's your problem, a bone growing the wrong way."

This was completely blocking the nasal passages and had to be removed.

This duly performed, and removed, I thought that would be the end of the problem. How wrong I was. All the colds and flu's stopped but my breathing problems still carried on. I ignored it.

Great I thought, I can get back onto the badminton court, and the tennis court, squash I only played to keep fit. I attempted it, but somehow I was not as good as I was. I was weak, tired, slow, concentration and co-ordination off. I decided to give up. How could I still stay with the game I loved? I thought back to my Hockey umpiring days and decided to see whether I could become a badminton umpire. I attended the course, and passed and was duly appointed a Probationary Umpire.

One thing led to another, and I became a line judge for the World Badminton Championships to be held in Birmingham at the National Indoor Arena, during May/June 1993.

Chapter 2

I attended the 8th World Badminton Championships and 3rd Sudirman Cup as a line judge. These were held at the National Indoor Arena between 25th May 1993 and 6th June 1993.

The championships are split into 2 competitions. During the first week teams play for the Sudirman Cup whilst the individual competitions are held during the second week.

I had been requested to either attend the fortnight or to attend the first week. As there was no financial assistance I was only able to work during the first week.

I greeted this task with some trepidation as never before had I been so close to world famous sports people. They had only been pictures and names in papers and magazines.

On the first morning of duty I was supplied with my uniform which consisted of a short sleeved navy blue polo shirt, provided by the sponsors to Manchester 2000 Olympic bid. The shirts were only provided in either large or extra-large sizes, fortunately I was given a large, and whilst some girls were given the extra-large; imagine what a size 10 looks in extra-large! Then given my identity badge which we had to wear at all times whilst at the arena.

Briefings were given to us all by Dr John Alexander who was our control, together with the tournament referee Mr Neil Cameron.

A line judge's word is sacrosanct and cannot be overruled by the umpire. The only thing that can happen is a line judge could be removed from the court, fortunately this did not happen. We were informed if we felt unwell whilst on court, we were not to wait until we collapsed, but inform the umpire between rallies and leave the court as quickly as possible, and not to use the service judges' bin as this could be rather messy with the shuttles.

There is only one word which is said by a line judge and it is *OUT* with both arms extended horizontally. This had to be said loud enough so the umpires and players could hear it. Two other signals are also given during play and they are:-

[1] Right arm forward indicating in

[2] Hands over the eyes indicating unsighted

No verbal sounds are made with these signals. We only call for the line to which we are assigned to.

Line Judges assembling for their briefing.

Up until the semi-finals all the line judges were formed into teams of 4 which meant only the 2 base lines and the 2 side lines could be covered. All other line calls are given by the umpire.

My very first match was between Peru and Malta, and fortunately a ladies singles. I was so nervous when making my first call my arms were shaking, but I quickly gained my confidence.

The concentration of continually looking at a line is immense. The game cannot be watched, but the peripheral vision informs you of where the play is and how close the players are. Several times whilst covering base lines I thought the players were going to land on top of me. I would not have really minded because some of the male competitors were very good looking with wonderful physiques, the best one being a Russian.

During the first week there were not too many disputed calls, but one girl was very badly sworn at by a member of the New Zealand team, [male I have to say]. His language was so appalling the umpire had to officially warn him, but as this did not stop him, she docked him some points. He lost the match and his behaviour was reported to the team manager, whereupon he did not play in the team competition. I expect he was allowed to play in the individual event during the following week as this was a separate tournament.

The Belgian men's singles player disputed one of my calls, whilst he was playing a Scotsman. The Belgian was convinced one of my calls was wrong indicating the shuttle was 1/4 inch out. I stuck to my guns insisting the shuttle was in. This one call played on his mind to such a degree he lost the match.

The first Friday evening 28th May 1993 saw the first of the semi-finals played between Korea and Denmark. I was assigned to the front service line in the mixed doubles, and for the first time all lines were covered by line judges. As there were five matches:-

Men's and Ladies' Singles

Men's and Ladies' Doubles

Mixed Doubles

This meant 50 line judges were needed to be available as there are 10 lines per court.

I was surprised at the state of the shuttles, as the players seemed to replace them after every rally. If there was one strand of the feather that had fractionally come adrift, it was changed. The match was won by Korea, who were the holders of the Sudirman Cup and they were therefore defending the Championship in the final.

Saturday 29th May 1993, the second semi-final between Indonesia and China was played, but there had to be resolved the 5th/6th place playoff between England and Sweden. The losing team being demoted out of the world elite Group 1 to Group 2.

England started, as usual on their current form, badly, and lost their opening two matches. I was fortunate to be assigned to the men's singles which featured Darren Hall, England's number 1 and the Swedish number 1 Jens Olsson. I was, for this match to cover the base line. Behind me were the whole of the English Team who could see what I was seeing. I had one close call of *OUT* when a shot from Darren landed 1/4 inch beyond the base line.

A chorus of "Bad luck Dell" echoed around the arena.

England eventually won the match 3:2 and therefore remain in Group 1.

The second semi-final between Indonesia and China started play on the adjoining court and lasted into the early hours of the morning. I was assigned to the centre service line otherwise known as the sleep line, of the ladies' doubles, which was the longest game I have ever seen, it lasted just about 2 hours, with Indonesia the eventual winners.

Unfortunately, the Chinese girl suffered a serious injury to her leg, towards the end of the second game, where the Indonesian pair squared the game. I feel that if the injury had not occurred then the whole game would probably have lasted at least 3 hours.

A line judge's job just does not end with the line judging. At 22.30 hrs the court moppers [who were school children] just departed and Jan [a fellow line judge] and I were asked to court mop for the final match, a men's doubles, but never had to claim our fame as no sweat needed to be mopped.

Sunday 30th May 1993, dawned wet as usual, and we arrived at the arena for 12.00 hrs. for the final, between Korea and Indonesia, which started at 13.00 hrs. I was on match 4, the side line for the Ladies' Doubles final. Again a marathon, which lasted 1hr 45mins, and is what badminton is all about.

Pressure, excitement, and expectations were immense from all parties, players, officials, and spectators alike. Korea became the eventual winners, successfully defending the championship, by beating Indonesia 3:2 after over six hours of high level badminton.

A line judge's duty started at 08.30 hrs. when we all had to report to the arena, for play started at 09.00hrs. We finished our duty when play ended usually at about midnight or in the early hours of the morning.

Our group of 4 ladies were only given two afternoons off during the whole time when play was scheduled.

Although the hours were long, the stress and the strain arduous, we all thoroughly enjoyed ourselves, with many new friendships being forged. It was a real pleasure to meet umpires from all around the world, and I now understand why the language in my umpire's handbook has to be adhered to so rigidly. One Chinese umpire could not speak a word of English, except the language in the handbook. All tournaments, wherever held in the world are umpired in English, as English is the international language for badminton.

One of the nicest gifts given to me was a handmade Indian doll in National dress, by the Indian umpire. He gave one to all 4 girls in our group. At the end of my tour of duty, I was presented with a medal on behalf of the International Badminton Federation to thank me for giving up my time to help stage this premier event.

Chapter 3

Now, by this stage I was still swimming, having completed two BT National Swimathons as an individual. Both in 1992 and 1993 I managed the full distance of 5000 metres. Which is 200 lengths of Tenterden pool a 25 metre pool. Not a pretty stroke, one I think I made up myself!

Life carried on in the same way as before. But by now I was umpiring my badminton rather than playing it, although I was still keeping my hand in on the court. So to speak!

I had also started to have singing lessons to see if this would improve my breathing problem, as the techniques for singing are working with the diaphragm. This seemed to help for a time but I noticed I was beginning to become dizzy. I could be standing talking to someone and I would start swaying on my feet just as if I was drunk. Very strange for someone who is teetotal, and allergic to alcohol. I could not understand it.

Also I was beginning to get, I can only describe it as a fluttering in the thigh muscles of the right leg. It just seemed like a piece of cotton was dangling and rubbing against my leg, but when I looked there was nothing there.

I was also getting more and more tired and crotchety, and still only thought I was overworking.

For some time now the prosecution department had been taken over by the Civil Service, from the Kent County Council. It was hell. With less and less staff, more and more work, although we were kept being told the crime rate was going down. I did not believe this as there seemed more and more work. Several of us were taking work home to do in the evenings and at weekends as there did not seem to be enough time in the day for fitting it all in. I always maintained what did not get done during the time I was there stayed undone. I refused to take work home. After 10-12 hours of non-stop 'aggro' I thought my own time was my own. In fact the so called management, if they could, would have you at it 24 hours per day 7 days a week. Several of the staff would go in on a Saturday. If I was to do this how on earth would I get my housework, cleaning, washing and the garden done with only one day at the weekend. I live on my own.

'Our wonderful management' who I think had nothing better to do with their time used to dream up more and more forms for what seemed a pointless number of statistics and seemed more concerned that the forms were not being filled in rather than worrying about whether cases were being prepared properly, and on time for when the case was listed in court.

So many times we got by with a wing and a prayer. It was no wonder the Judges were rude, but it was not our fault, as there seemed there were not enough hours in the day. However, sometimes after listening to a harangue from a Judge and this was all on the Court record, it transpired the Judge was in the wrong but he would never apologise to you so therefore the criticisms would remain on the record.

It can also be seen why the Police became angry as they were in a similar position to us, with a load of senseless forms. They used to think we would 'throw our hat' in too quickly.

By this stage I was working on very large cases, armed robberies, where the perpetrators did not care who was in the firing line or where, manslaughters, illegal immigration rings involving anything up to 20 defendants, car rings also involving a great number of defendants and high valued vehicles. Serious assaults and of course, my speciality *FRAUD*. I loved it. This meant dealing with mortgage fraud which was abundant. Also large scale company fraud. On entering my office, if you could find the way in, I was weighed down with paper.

I had the preparation of these cases for trial at the Crown Court, co-ordinating of attendance of a vast amount of witnesses, preparation of bundles of documents to go before the jury, ensuring that all the barristers in the case, and the judge together with the court usher all having the same set.

Attendance with counsel, usually at his chambers in London for conferences, which were usually held between 16.30 hrs - 17.00 hrs and until they finished, anything up to 3 hours later. By this stage I had already done a full day in the office before leaving to travel to London. By the time I got home it was anything up to 23.00 hours. I was knackered. We did it for the love of it, or so the management thought.

I was not normally allowed to meet any dignitaries who visited the office as when asked for my opinion they got *my* opinion, not the opinion they wanted to hear. However on one occasion I happened to be in the office when the Attorney General visited in an official capacity. I was researching about Criminal Bankruptcy, upon a foreigner, who had assets in this country. My desk looked as if a bomb had hit it. Law books and papers everywhere. Not only that, boxes of papers of cases that I was currently working on filled my room.

"It's nice to see that you can work under pressure," he said.

That was the only thing that man said to me after finding out what I was doing.

I felt I wanted to pick up my stapler and throw it at him. After this spurious remark I then put my head down and carried on.

I am of the opinion that C.P.S. management could not organise a "piss up in a brewery" or "a fart in a bean factory," unless the appropriate forms in quadruplet were completed and submitted some weeks before the event. I may be doing them an injustice, but I doubt it!

Chapter 4

At the world Championships in Birmingham, I met Duncan!

Upon my return home, I was very tired and needed an extra week off work to recover. I received from him a complete list of the results of the Championships for both the Sudirman Cup and the individual tournament, together with a thank you card with a message saying he would like to meet me, and he would be a "perfect gentleman."

I travelled to Kelvedon [where he lived] and met him at the station one Sunday. He had been to work. We had lunch and found we had some items in common, especially our love for the game of badminton.

One thing led to another and we started to see quite a lot of each other. He used to send me flowers, ring me nearly every day, and either I would travel to Kelvedon for the weekend, or he would travel to Tenterden for the weekend. Whenever I had to meet him he was always late. Whether I was seeing him in London where he worked, or at the railway station in Headcorn. He worked for British Rail on the Health and Safety side, but still managed, always to be late.

During June of that year [1993] we went to Wimbledon for the Tennis Championships. We queued for nearly 8 hours until we got in. In the blazing sun all day. We had a great time and met some marvellous people who, like us, were waiting to get in. It is not often in this country an umbrella is used to shield yourself from the sun. We got in, and it was crowded. I was by this time tired and needed to sit down. We managed to get seats on Court 3 where we stayed for the rest of the day's play. As this was a Friday we had the weekend to recover. Thank goodness.

Duncan did not drive saying as he was so tall [6ft 4ins am I allowed to use the Imperial measurement now we are governed by [Brussels]?]. He did not feel comfortable driving any vehicle as they did not seem large enough for him. I now think this was an excuse so he could be taken everywhere by someone else and not have to contribute to the expenses. He never had to pay to use the trains, as this was a perk. I have now met many people who are not only tall but are taller and they do not seem to have that problem.

Also we found we had a liking for classical music, and I was singing at Northiam Church for the Choral Society. I was performing a solo, not from the Gilbert & Sullivan repertoire, but a piece from 'Oklahoma' written by Rogers and Hammerstein.

At the end of the concert Duncan gave me a ticket for the whole of Promenade Season at the Royal Albert Hall. This enabled us to pick and choose which concerts we wanted to go to. I forget just how many we attended but it was in the region of between 10-15. My favourite was Beethoven's 'Ninth' [The Choral Symphony]. Duncan's favourite was Holst's 'The Planets'. We also attended the last night, for the 'party performance'. This was the second last night performance I had attended.

In October of that year we went on holiday together, to the Greek island of Kos. It was a disaster. We chose the hotel because it was described as a perfect place for quiet, rest, and relaxation. It was anything but!

The Greeks seemed to use it as a clubroom, and the noise at the highest rate of decibels lasted until about 03.00 hrs. How anybody was supposed to relax with that row going on I can't imagine. There was one particular Greek brat who only had one word of conversation and that was 'Ahhhhhhhhhhh' screamed at the top of his voice, until the early hours of the morning. I think he was only about 8 or 9 years of age. I thought children of that age should be in bed. I must be very old fashioned.

We complained incessantly, not only to the hotel staff, who pretended they could not understand English, but also to the Tour Rep. We were not the only ones to complain. I felt I was being treated as a nuisance. After the sort of job I do, and the type of life I lead, and with the description of the hotel, was it too much to ask to have a decent night's sleep?

I did not feel Duncan was completely in support of me, as unfortunately for me, he could sleep through an air raid and not notice it. However during the day we took ourselves off into the country and I noticed things were beginning to go seriously wrong with my health. I found I was beginning to get more and more tired, my walking speed was slowing down, I was beginning to shake a lot. My legs and arms especially. I needed the holiday to regenerate my batteries, and prepare me for the rigours of work.

Duncan found it very difficult to walk with me as he was always in too much of a hurry, as he put it, to see what was round the corner.

At the airport on our way home we submitted a formal complaint, and upon our return home we submitted a claim for the return of our money. Bearing in mind this was in October 1993, it was not resolved until June 1995, and by only going through A.B.T.A.

Things went on as much as before, but by now the badminton season had started. When I travelled to Kelvedon on the Friday night, after battling my way through the Dartford Tunnel and along the A12 to Kelvedon, it used to take me anything up to 2 hrs. to get there. Was Duncan home from work? Like hell he was. I was always kept waiting. I think he thought it was his way of having a joke.

Then on the Saturday, he never asked but assumed I could read his mind, as we went to his badminton club at Epping [over an hour's drive away]. I did used to enjoy it. He used to coach the juniors, whilst I went through with them what was required if they were ever umpired. We used to get back to Kelvedon in the early hours of Sunday morning. I then used to have to drive home during the afternoon. I felt I spent all the weekend behind the steering wheel. He just did not seem to think. He never offered to help pay for the expenses, but if I was to ask then he would. I did not want to ask all the time. Would it have been too much for him to offer and even pay for a fill up?

On one Saturday when I was in Kelvedon, he decided he needed to go shopping, did he ask, no. He just took it I would know what he wanted, have me drive to the Super store where he promptly filled my car boot with tins of dog /cat food and then drive home again.

I do not drive all the way to Kelvedon to see Duncan – only to be made to traipse through a Super store because he does not drive – to be used in that manner. He did however offer to take me out to lunch. Was this to placate me, or was it because it was now very late, and we would not have had much time to get ready to travel to Epping?

He was constantly telling me I came first in his affections. Yes well of course I did, he was using me. On some occasions we used to travel to see his father, a lovely old boy. However the two of them just used to sit side by side in the armchairs and not say a word. I used to play with his two cats, just to see if I could lighten the atmosphere.

Duncan did not like to be idle, he always had to be busy. He could not, or would not sit and relax. Even when he came to me for the weekend, I had to keep finding him jobs to do. It was very tiresome. When he did sit down there was no conversation with him, as he just closed his eyes and went to sleep. Talk about a bore. If I suggested anything it seemed it had to be done there and then.

Chapter 5

On some occasions when I used to go to Kelvedon, after battling with all the commuter traffic, Duncan used to tell me he had to work over the weekend. This was unavoidable, he said, and as he was paid overtime for these extra duties he said they helped to pay for all the badminton tournaments. He seemed to forget I used to pay my own way with them. The only time he paid for me was when we had to travel by train which was not very often as I hated the trains. As I've said before, he travelled free on the trains.

During these particular weekends, I was at a loose end in a strange house. I had no key, so I could not go out; there were no books to read, or papers, except very old and out of date ones. What could I do? I never knew what time he would come home, but I knew nothing would stop him from attending his badminton club in the evening.

I used to guess he would arrive home at about 16.00 hours. He never told me when he was coming home. I therefore used to prepare lunch for about this time. Oh yes, he always had lunch in the house, and always made a point of telling me what we were having. Was this a hint?

Also lying around was his washing, it had been done, but there were clean shirts strewn all over the place. As I had nothing to do, I, like a mug, used to do his ironing for him. He was always very thankful, I bet he was, probably left it out on purpose, hoping I would do it for him.

I generally managed to guess when he used to come home, all smiles of course. He inevitably had a lift to work on these occasions by a colleague. He did, of course, used to do the washing up, but this left a great deal to be desired, and I'm glad they were not my things as they would have had to be done again.

Then it was all mayhem to get to Epping for his badminton club.

When he used to come to me for the weekend I used to do whatever washing and ironing he wanted. I used to say I had mine to do, so I might as well do his at the same time.

Chapter 6

When Duncan came down for the weekend, I was unable to have my swim first thing on Monday morning as he had to be at the station [Headcorn], which is on my way to the office in Maidstone by 07.15 hrs. This meant I was in the office by approximately 07.30 hrs. This did not mean I left any earlier at the end of the day. I was still lucky to be away by 18.30 hrs. Home by about 19.30 hrs depending on the traffic.

I was now working on *Special Casework.* This did not mean a promotion; it was just a sideways move. The work load increased as I was now preparing cases for the Magistrates' Court, as well as appearing in the Crown Court. The nature of the work meant it was larger, more complicated and complex, and of a more sensitive nature.

As Magistrates' Courts' work was a little unfamiliar to me, I found the girls who regularly worked in this area very helpful. I had no assistance and had to find time to perform all the duties. Christmas 1993 was looming, and I decided to take some annual leave, as the Crown Court shuts down for a period of time. The magistrates' courts still sit, but in a reduced capacity.

I asked Duncan down for Christmas, but he said he would prefer to be on his own, with his pets. [a dog and two cats]. I scotched that idea, as I could drive to Kelvedon and pick him and his pets up. This he agreed to. We arranged I would be at his place by about 18.00 hrs. on the last working day and we could pack the car up and then drive home, same day. He asked me to collect his dog from the dog sitter and he would see me at home.

I picked Lucy [a bearded collie] up and waited for Duncan outside his house. I had no keys to get in, and therefore had to wait in the car in the cold for him to arrive. Suffice it to say he was late. No thought or consideration for me at all. He just greeted me with the usual stupid childish grin on his face, and no explanation. He did not even apologise.

He then farted about for what seemed an age and we finally left Kelvedon about 21.30 hrs. arriving home at about midnight. He did not seem to realise I had driven to Kelvedon that evening, and was driving home the same day. I was knackered. Again he did not offer to pay for the petrol costs. At the end of the holiday period I drove him, and his animals back to Kelvedon.

There were some eruptions as my cat objected to the intrusion. She certainly showed who was boss and although Sophie and Sweep [his two cats], tried to usurp her authority, it did not work. Calam [my cat] spat, hissed, clawed her way round them. With the dog she just did the same, and at feeding time it was quite comical.

Duncan fed his two in the spare room, whilst the dog had hers in the kitchen. The bowls used to be put down roughly at the same time, but my cat went to Lucy's bowl and poor Lucy just used to look at me with her great big eyes and ask 'where do I go from here, she's eating my food?', I used to pick mine up and move her to her bowl, and I promptly got sworn at for my trouble.

It was coming up for my birthday and Duncan promised something special. What occurred was nothing. Absolutely nothing. He had forgotten. No card, no telephone call, nothing. I left it 2-3 days before ringing and he tried to say that he had not forgotten. However at the office the next day a presentation of flowers arrived with the inscription 'Sorry it's late, I didn't forget. Happy belated Birthday wishes, lots of love Duncan'.

He came down to Tenterden that weekend as my parents were taking us out for lunch at the local Chinese Restaurant.

The badminton season was well upon us now. We were travelling up to Glasgow for the Thomas and Uber World Team Championships, where we had both volunteered as line judges.

Unbeknown to me Duncan was also in the Arena party. Which meant he was also involved in the laying out of the courts, and that all the equipment and chairs were in the right places. If a chair was a fraction of an inch adrift Duncan would have to move it. Despite the fact line judges themselves move their own chairs whilst preparing themselves for whatever line they are covering.

It was extremely cold in Scotland, with snow on the ground, and the team from Barbados going 'cock a hoop' as they had never seen snow. They had heard of it but had never actually seen it.

The South African Team competing for the first time were very polite to the officials, and treated us line judges as if we were human beings. If they disputed any calls, they would always apologise to the line judge concerned at the end of the match.

This was borne out when I was assigned to judge the far long line during the men's doubles match. I was moving my arms to indicate out when I was landed upon by a 6 ft. 6ins. hunk of South African male. I was spread-eagled under him. 'Coo' I thought, 'make the most of this it probably won't happen again'.

My chair went one way, I went the other, my glasses ended up by the advertising board, but fortunately still in one piece. Everyone on court went quiet until they heard shrieks of laughter, coming from you know who, then they all joined in.

He got himself together, picked me up from the floor, replaced my chair, retrieved my glasses, and led me back to my chair.

At the end of the game, the umpire asked me if I was going to file a report, as this could have constituted an assault on a Court Official, which would ultimately mean he and his partner would have been disqualified from the rest of the tournament. I said no, as it was clearly an accident. He was concentrating on the shuttle, and I was concentrating on the line. The umpire agreed with me. I had not realised that line judging could be so dangerous.

They were staying at the same hotel, and upon seeing me enter the bar area, he approached me as he was concerned about being disqualified but had not heard anything. I informed him it was clearly an accident and I would not be taking the matter any further.

The chivalric behaviour could not be said for one Polish competitor. He did not like one of my calls and was promptly and firmly dealt with by the Umpire who was Norwegian. The player turned his back on the umpire and told me to clean my glasses, by making a hand movement across his eyes. I just looked at him with complete contempt.

The Kelvin Hall, where the event took place, was not exactly a very healthy arena. There was a lot of food poisoning, and colds going round. As my system was not in a very healthy state, although I did not realise it at the time, I succumbed quite badly. I was very nauseous, and I had the 'flu' and could not complete my duties.

On the last night of the tournament all the players and officials were invited to a dinner where H.R.H.

Prince Edward [the patron of the Scottish Badminton Union] was attending. I was determined to go although I knew I could not eat anything. Duncan, of course had two meals, mine, after I had picked out all the plain food, as well as his. I managed to last till about 22.30 hrs, and I then had to leave.

Duncan rang me at about 23.00 hrs. to say he was on his way up as the Prince had now left. Bearing in mind the dinner was in the Hotel in which we were staying, he did not come back to the room until 03.00 hrs the following morning. You can imagine how I felt. So much for his so called caring nature, by always putting me first.

We had a very early start the next morning, to get the train back to London. At breakfast, he just got up from the table whilst I was still eating or trying to, without telling me where he was going, and when I finished, I found he was settling the bill. Why he could not have told me, heaven only knows.

We had a taxi to the station, and upon arrival Duncan then ran off, carrying his bags, to board the train. I did not know that that was what he was doing. I trudged after, carrying my bags and boarded the train. I have to say I was still suffering with a temperature. Again so much for his caring nature. I should, however, point out I always paid my way with all the bills. I did not want it on my conscience that I was sponging off him.

Chapter 7

Whilst I was at Glasgow, sitting on the front service line in a Ladies Doubles match between Jo Wright and Gillian Gowers for England and a Danish pair, I was very nearly decapitated by one of the Danish girls.

She was becoming cross because they were losing. The players, as in tennis, have their bags by the umpire's chair. The seat for the front service line is also by the umpire's chair, so that area is quite crowded when the tournament reaches the latter stages.

She broke a string and threw the offending racquet towards her bag, picking up another racquet in one movement. She unfortunately missed her bag, and I had to take evasive action to avoid being hit. I ducked! The Danes lost after a close fought battle. Again she threw her racquet at her bag narrowly missing me in the process. Again I ducked! This time she was warned by the umpire, but by now it was too late, as the game had finished.

I must be one of the few line judges in the world who can upset all 4 players on court! I was covering the right side line [the long line] in a men's doubles match very late in the evening, after having been on duty since 08.30 hrs that morning.

Play had been continuous with only a small amount of time allowed off for meal breaks. I was, as you can imagine, very tired, I was beginning to have difficulty with my vision. It was blurring, and also I was seeing double. Was this again a sign the *M.S.* Was trying to come out? I ignored the problem, as I just thought I was overworking, and just tired.

However, back to the game. When shuttles are hit at the speed and power that international players can exert, it is sometimes very difficult to ascertain exactly where the cork base has crossed the line, or indeed if it has crossed the line. Anything landing on the line, even by a fraction of an inch is in. This particular shuttle was smashed with all the power this player could muster and went skidding along the floor at the far end of my line. I was convinced it was in, but with the behaviour of all 4 players it must have been out. I stuck with my decision, but this had a profound effect on me, as I must have been wrong.

Fortunately this was the last match of the day, and I could therefore go back to the hotel for as much sleep as I could possibly get to start duty early the next morning.

Before I attended Glasgow, I had applied to enter the next B.T. National Swimathon, to be held in Tenterden during the early part of March 1994. As the hotel we were staying in had a swimming pool, although very small, I made use of it before breakfast most mornings.

45

However, my training was upset because of the 'flu' and the food poisoning.

I was hoping to cover the whole distance of 5000 metres or 200 lengths in a time of roughly two hours. If I achieved this, this would have been my quickest time.

I returned to work, although I was still feeling unwell, and began to hear rumours of a big shift in personnel, and office moving. I asked the Special Casework Lawyer what was going on, but he did not seem to know. I therefore wrote to the Chief Crown Prosecuting Solicitor of Kent, who was supposed to be in charge and asked what was going on. I thought it better to put it in an official letter rather than seeing him personally.

It was now coming up for Valentine's Day, but both Duncan and I would be in Norwich for the National Championships. These are held over the weekend, which meant I was only going to need the Friday and Monday as annual leave from work.

Regrettably, one of the deputy Chief Crown Prosecutors of Kent, who had retired, died earlier that week, very suddenly. He was also one my lecturers, when I was studying for my Institute of Legal Executives' exams at Maidstone college. My parents who also knew him, [because Dad was a practising Solicitor in Maidstone] attended the funeral which was held in Tenterden Church.

Mr. Ron Webb together with his wife Muriel had recently moved to Tenterden and used to attend the

Choral Society concerts and attend the Church services regularly. I therefore became friendly with them. Ron was very well liked, and I got on very well with both of them. The Church was very full with representatives from the legal profession. Duncan realised how upset I was, and offered to come down to keep me company. I said no, as my parents would be in Church, but I would also be singing in the Church choir.

After the service, I drove to Kelvedon, where I was to meet up with Duncan that evening. By now I was used to being kept waiting. I would have thought, however, after the traumatic day he might have put himself out to be on time, but no. It was cold, and by the time of his arrival I was frozen, and needed to have a hot bath to really warm up.

The following morning we went to Norwich by train and attended the tournament. Although I had not volunteered for any duties, I soon became involved with the line judges and managed to keep busy, and keep my mind off Muriel's sadness, although my thoughts were always with her.

We had a good time at the tournament, and Duncan as usual was doing every job that came his way. He did however concentrate on working the main score-board, as I have said before; he has this 'thing' about pressing buttons, as well as moving chairs.

When we had to leave the hall to walk the short distance back to the hotel, he could not or would not walk beside me. At about midnight in the dark, I wanted someone by my side. Was I being unreasonable? I used to try and joke with him that I would buy a dog collar and lead, but this seemed to fall on deaf ears.

On Monday 14th February 1994, [Valentine's Day], I gave him a card and a present, which was quite expensive. I wished now I had not bothered. He did not even bother to open it, or the card, just threw it in his bag and forgot about it. He did not bother with anything for me. His excuse was he was too busy and he had been in Glasgow and Norwich. That did not ring true with me, as I was also in Glasgow and Norwich, and also have a full time job. I managed to find the time, so why could not he! Perhaps I expect too much out of life, as I maintain if you want to do something badly enough you'll always manage to find the time. He just did not seem to care. He had no thought of me as a person.

Chapter 8

Upon my return from Norwich I found my work had piled up to such a degree, I was going to have to start taking it home. This I deplored doing, as I always endeavoured to get it all done whilst in the office.

I found I was becoming more and more tired, going to bed and not sleeping and waking up as tired as I was when I went to bed. My legs started to spontaneously shake, or go into spasms whilst I was supposedly resting. My breathing difficulties had not improved, so I therefore stopped my singing lessons.

I found I was having difficulty in concentrating, so thought it best to come straight home and rest as much as I could. I also had to give up the Church Choir, as I found the commitment very tiring. Further, I also gave up the Choral Society, so I could at least have that time at home.

In fact, I had by now given up everything, except badminton. I was also supposed to still continue with my umpiring duties at the weekend, but I found I kept losing my concentration.

I was also becoming very clumsy. I would put something down, where I thought the table was, but it seemed to manage to fall on the floor. When putting an item away in the cupboard it fell off and hit me. I was also becoming dizzy.

I had been warned, by one of the International Umpires my level of concentration needed to improve. I knew that, but it seemed to be affecting me in everything. I did not know what to do.

I was still trying to swim in the mornings, as the Swimathon was nearly upon me. I wanted to increase my training in the morning to between 120 and 150 lengths. This should not have been too much more as I was regularly doing 100. I had managed it in previous years, so why not this?

Duncan was not being very helpful. His phone calls were getting less frequent. I could not travel to Kelvedon as often as I had done as I was too tired to make the trip and therefore was a danger on the road.

I then ate something which upset my tenuous hold on my digestive system. I thought the food poisoning bug which I picked up in Glasgow had not completely disappeared. I became rather ill again.

I had to cry off the Swimathon, and found I could not even have swum a length on that Saturday, let alone 200. I'm glad I was not participating in a team, as I would have had to let them down. I do not like letting anybody down as when I say I will do something, I strive to complete whatever the task is. Duncan was supposed to come down for the weekend, but as I had cried off the swim, and was not very well he decided to find something more worthwhile to do.

I was desperately trying to catch up at work, as I had booked special leave for later on in March, to line judge at the *All England Badminton Championships*, again to be held at the National Indoor Arena Birmingham.

I had also expected to receive a reply from the Chief Crown Prosecutor with regard to my memorandum which I wrote before I went to Norwich. As I had not received one, I wrote a reminder, and requested a reply.

I managed to catch up on my work, I don't know how, but I had been given an assistant who was only a temporary, because there was some spare money in the budget. She was a godsend. A very quick learner, and would tie over the special casework whilst I was away.

I kept asking Duncan about accommodation whilst we were in Birmingham, but he never spoke to me about it. I was determined he was not going to use me solely for a taxi service, so I booked the car in to the local Rover dealers for a major service, and a few other problems to be sorted out. I was, however, driving up there with him.

As I had not been informed about the accommodation I telephoned The Badminton Association of England, and spoke to Maryanne, who dealt with all bookings for officials. She informed me it was all booked, and we were staying at the Park Hotel. I felt a real berk.

Why could he have not told me.

Maryanne asked, "Has Duncan not told you?"

"You know Duncan," I replied, and left it at that.

On the last working day, I travelled to Kelvedon where I was to stay the night, having to wait for Duncan to return. As usual he was late.

He had not even started to pack, and I yet again had to show him how to pack a suitcase. He just did not seem to remember from one time to the next. Did he appear to be this helpless for the sake of it, knowing full well I would do it for him. More fool me.

On the following morning I was hoping for an early start, as I had a long journey ahead of me. If I had waited for him to pack his suitcase we would probably still be hanging around Kelvedon now. So for quickness I did it for him. We were also going to Crufts which was being held at the National Exhibition Centre, Birmingham, during the weekend. I was knackered.

At Crufts which I thoroughly enjoyed, I felt the classes should distinguish what the breeds are. For example if the breed is a working group then part of the points to the best dog should be, seeing it working, and not just being made 'pretty, pretty'. It seems such a waste. The same with the gun dogs, etc.

The only part I really enjoyed was the obedience trials. Owners leaving their dogs in the collecting ring and then going off, I suppose to have a cup of tea, then to return, and find FIDO still sitting there. There were demonstrations given by the Police dogs, and the dogs for the blind. All of which I found interesting.

When we left there it was a quick dash back to the National Indoor Arena as Duncan wanted to report in, and we were kept working quite late.

It was cold and I was tired. Duncan was doing the usual, every job he could find. He found it difficult to have lunch, or any meal breaks with me, as he always seemed to have a job to do. I was restricted to my duties as line judge, but he could fit in with anybody and did so, except with me. Was I beginning to become a burden to him?

I was now unable to keep going for as long as I used to. I was so tired. The disease *M.S.* was now I think starting to come out, although I still did not realise it. We had no transport, as the car was being mended, so Duncan used to arrange lifts when convenient for him, or we used to use the transport provided. He never introduced me to the people he arranged lifts with.

Late one evening when we came out of the pizza place to walk back to the hotel, bearing in mind we were in the centre of Birmingham, he just ran off, around the corner and left me standing there. What was I to do? I carried on walking albeit not very quickly and found him at the hotel holding the door for me.

I was flabbergasted.

"Don't you ever do that to me again," I said, "anything could have happened to me out there, and you wouldn't know. You really don't care about me do you?"

He then gave me all the waffle about being first in his affections. I left it there.

During the later stages of the tournament one of the umpires approached me to inform me of the details of the umpire's dinner.

"What umpire's dinner?" I asked.

"Oh, has he not told you, Duncan has bought two tickets."

"Now why should he tell me, I just provide the transport," I said, and then continued, "don't worry I'll sort it out."

I was given the details, and upon accosting Duncan he informed me we were going to the Umpire's Dinner. Perhaps the cat was out of the bag, and he meant to take somebody else.

Upon our arrival back at the hotel at about 01.00 hours, one morning I found I could not stay up for a drink in the hotel bar as I was really tired. I then retired and Duncan said he would have one and follow shortly.

His one drink and him following shortly occurred at 04.00 hours. I was worried sick, I did not know what had happened to him. He said he had met up with some mates who he had not seen since the previous year, and went back to the Holiday Inn [their hotel] to continue his drink. So much for me coming first in his affections. He then complained he was tired the next day. Tough.

I noticed, as had happened in Glasgow, my vision was beginning to blur in the evening, whilst on duty. I did not want a repeat of the incident, so I changed from line judge duty to scoreboard duty.

I picked the car up when it was ready at the end of the week, went to the Umpire's dinner, which we all enjoyed, and then back to the hotel for the long drive back to Kelvedon and Tenterden the next morning.

I had asked Duncan to navigate, as I thought he could map read, he told me he could, but I was forgetting this was a road map and not a train map. When I arrived at a junction I asked which way, I found he was asleep. So much for his assistance. It is just as well I had studied the map and have a good sense of direction. We were going back another way as we were exiting Birmingham from a different direction to which we had entered.

I dropped Duncan off at home and then came onto Tenterden directly.

Chapter 9

I arrived home from Birmingham late on the Sunday, having been driving all day. At least it felt like it. I then had all my washing to do, to prepare me for work the next day. I even attempted a swim in the morning – as I had not swum for a week – and wished I hadn't. I only managed a few lengths. It seemed to be going from bad to worse.

When I know I'm going to be in the office, I usually wear a trouser suit, whereas if I'm in Court then I have to be ultra-smart, and this consists of a skirt suit. As I had had a week off, I presumed I would be in the office and therefore dressed accordingly.

Upon my arrival I found I had been slung out of my office, and thrown in what I can only describe as a rat hole, which had formerly been the smoking room. I also found that my Special Casework Lawyer had arranged for me to attend a conference in London, during the late afternoon and early evening. How was he to know this would be convenient, how did he know I did not have a commitment that evening? Had he been entrusted with a crystal ball? I had been asking for one for some time, but no such luck.

The Chief Crown Prosecutor of Kent, must have known about the move before I went to Birmingham. These things do not happen overnight, as they involve the upheaval of a great many of the personnel. Was it that I was not informed because as only one of the "plebs," I don't count. I'm only an E.O., not very important, and therefore without a brain. I am not supposed to have any feelings either. Or is it that if I had been informed I would have objected. Well I would have, but it would not have done me any good, but at least I could have made sure the rat hole was clean. It stank. I am a non-smoker and everybody in the office knew how much I hated the smell of smoke. I had enough problems with my breathing without them making it any worse.

I felt violated. Someone had gone through my desk. Someone had gone through my personal possessions. My temporary help had finished. I did not know when she was finishing before I went to Birmingham. I had papers all over the place. I could not find anything.

I also had a lot of paper exhibits in the many cases I was dealing with. What would have happened if any of them had gone missing? The judge and the police would have been down on me like a ton of bricks. We would have lost the case or cases. I would have been blamed. How could I explain it all happened whilst I was off on leave, I was not told it was going to happen, therefore I had no control over the files and papers. I used every obscenity towards management that I knew. Not that it would do any good mind you, but at least it gave vent to my feelings.

As I was not in the least bit dressed for sorting anything out I decided "stuff them, I'll go to London for the conference."

The next day I went in dutifully dressed in a very scruffy manner and decided to try and sort something out of the debacle. It was very difficult as I could not breathe. I was told not to make a fuss and get on with it. This came from a smoker, who would not notice the stench anyway. Why should I have to put up with it. I complained, and complained, and got nowhere. Even with the window open it was not a great deal of help as it was so chilly.

I complained to the union, but all they said was that the room would be cleaned. I was still waiting for this to happen when I was forced to finish work towards the end of June.

They all seemed to behave like ostriches, bury their heads in the sand and hope the problems would go away. I never did receive a reply to my memo. Perhaps my reply was made upon my return to work.

I knew I was missing some files. These contained all the statements, and interviews of defendants in a large drug production case. I went spare. Where the hell were they?

I went back to my old own room and found them perched on top of a bookcase with the lawyer stating she did not know who they belonged to as the names of the defendants meant nothing to her. Well of course they wouldn't, but did she bother to find out who they belonged to, or even think they could be mine? NO. I still felt something was missing on one of my attempted murder cases, but I could not think what. I felt I had been treated in a very shabby way. After all I had been with the prosecution department some 13 years.

I felt very cramped, and started to suffer with claustrophobia, but was this another sign of the *M.S.* trying to emerge. The management would not take me seriously. I had never been treated in this standoffish manner before.

I told Duncan what had happened, but I felt he did not believe me. He said that staff would never be treated in such an offhand way. I said he wants to be with the Civil Service. Staff don't count. Feelings don't count. We are just mindless morons doing a job, and if we don't like it get out. There are plenty of unemployed people willing to do the job.

I tried to make the best of it, but it was very difficult. I sprayed the carpet with air freshener a number of times, to endeavour to get a fresher smell, but this failed.

It was now near the beginning of April, and therefore Duncan's birthday. I decided to purchase a watch, as he had hinted to me that he did not have a decent one. Was this the reason as to why he was always late? I bought one which was two-tone gold and silver, together with a cufflink and tie pin set. I asked the opinion of one of my male lawyer colleagues and he thought Duncan should be very pleased. I spent nearly £100.

I was meeting him at Headcorn Station on the Friday night at hopefully 18.00 hrs. Again, as usual, he was late, arriving at about 19.00 hrs. I was kept waiting for an hour in the cold, in the waiting room.

On the Saturday night, after having given him his presents, I took him out for a Chinese meal at the local restaurant. I was paying. [I was also hoping he might feel a heel because he forgot my birthday, I should have known better.] During the meal I asked, quite stupidly where our relationship was going. We had been together for about a year.

He said, "Oh I'm not having a relationship."

Imagine my astonishment. I was flabbergasted. Lost for words. I wondered just what we were having. There must have been something. But of course I see it now, I was being used, abused, and taken for granted. I felt like throwing my chopsticks at him. I continued with my meal in silence, paid the bill and walked out. I don't think he realised how much he'd hurt me with that off-handed remark.

We were also committed to attend the European Badminton Championships later that month. I did not now feel like going. However, I could not let them down. It was not their fault. But I had no intention of paying for the flight, or the accommodation, as I would have done in the past. Duncan did not consult me about when it would be convenient to fly out. I knew it would be the last flight of the day, and knew we would return on the first flight of the day, because he would not like to be away from his job.

PART 2

MY LIFE DURING

Chapter 10

The European Badminton Championships were held between 10th and 17th April 1994 at Den Bosch, Holland. We had to fly there and as usual Duncan did not consult me about the times of departure at Gatwick. He just went ahead and booked it. Fortunately he did arrange extra medical insurance.

I had always, in the past paid my way, except when we went to Norwich for the National Championships. I had said I could not afford to attend all the tournaments that he wanted to go to. Therefore he paid for me to attend Norwich with him.

After his degrading remark in the Chinese restaurant at the beginning of the month, I had no intention of ever paying for anything ever again in the future. If he wanted me around then he would have to pay for me as well. In any event I did not really want to go to Holland, but as I was committed I could see no way out.

I drove from my home to Gatwick airport to catch the British Airways flight to Rotterdam at 19.40 hrs. We had arranged to meet at the airport at 18.00 hrs.

When I arrived, I was quite expecting to find I would have to wait for him, but imagine my surprise when I reached the check in desk Duncan was already there. I was astounded. This was a first. Apparently he had been chatting to the ticket clerk for about 10 minutes, so I did not keep him waiting long.

We boarded the flight which was a twin engine jet prop. You know the sort of thing, one with propellers. Mum had said some years ago they have the, "propellers to keep the engine cool."

Upon our arrival at Rotterdam airport we were met by one of the drivers to the tournament, and driven to our hotel. I had no idea where we were staying as Duncan had not considered telling me.

After a car journey of about one hour and several detours we checked into the hotel, only to find there was a wedding reception in full swing. This was the early hours of the morning, so not much sleep for this poor wretched soul. Yes I was absolutely shattered. As usual.

I was beginning to get very fed up of feeling like this all the time. Was it my age. I was only 39. Surely the onset of middle age had not started. It did not seem to affect Duncan, and he is only four years older than me.

The following morning we were taken to the arena, which was about 30-45 minutes' drive away by Nettie Ooms. She was a great person, with a super personality and the ability to put us all to shame with her command of foreign languages. She spoke English, German, as well, of course Dutch. She was fluent. Me, I had enough problems learning English. We met up with a few other English Line judges, and the camaraderie which had been built up over several tournaments re-kindled itself.

The hotel we were staying in was too far away to be convenient for the tournament. We all discussed it among ourselves, me included, surprise, surprise, and it was agreed we would move and stay at a log cabin village on the outskirts of Den Bosch. Apparently some of the teams were also staying there, notably the Welsh, Polish, [remember him, who told me to clean my glasses in Glasgow], and some of the English players. There was a regular bus between the village and the arena. All run by the tournament organisers.

I was now beginning to notice my dizzy spells were increasing from about 2-3 a week to now 2-3 per day. I was starting to become a little worried. I kept thinking this is not normal. Duncan was no help. I spoke to him about it and it seemed all he did was dismiss it. Don't worry me about it, was the reaction I seemed to be getting. I was starting to walk into walls, and doors, and my vision was blurring more and more. This is very off putting when you are talking to someone and swaying on your feet.

Their reaction is, "What's this drunken lunatic doing?"

I can't help it, and I'm not drunk as I'm teetotal. A likely story they think.

Again the tournament is split into two halves, with the team competition played first, followed by the individual competition. I thoroughly enjoyed what I was doing, and although I was unable to speak any foreign language I did not find this a handicap as nearly everybody could speak English.

Both Duncan and I, together with the other English contingent volunteered to line judge at the World Championships to be held in Lausanne Switzerland the following June 1995. Duncan as usual was volunteering for every job going. Especially his childhood mania for moving chairs and pressing buttons at every possible opportunity.

At the party held in the arena on the night before Finals Day, things really came to a head. I had been dancing with one of the Dutch Umpires, and with Yunis Sulleman [a fellow English line judge]. I was by now sitting down having a breather, drinking a glass of water, as my digestive system was beginning to argue with me, when all of a sudden I landed on the floor. I had passed out.

I had remembered looking at my watch at about 23.30 hrs. The next thing I knew I was coming to in the local hospital wired up to every machine imaginable, and looking at the clock at about 01.10 hrs. There is a complete one hour and thirty minutes I do not know anything about. I was undressed, obviously, who took my clothes off I don't know. It certainly was not me. At my side were Duncan, and Yunis.

To be perfectly truthful I would have felt more comfortable if Duncan was not there. Yunis seemed the only one to really care. Duncan made this great play of looking that he cared, but of course there were other people around. The female Dutch Doctor spoke perfect English, as did the nurse. I felt even more inadequate as I could not communicate in their language.

Seeing all the paraphernalia I was wired up to, I thought I had had a mild heart attack.

I learnt afterwards Duncan had taken my handbag and been through it to see if I was an epileptic, or diabetic. Apparently the hospital had asked him.

We had been together for nearly a year, been on holiday together, done the badminton tournaments together, could I really have kept that from him? Am I the sort of person to keep those sort of problems from those closest to me? Of course not, I'm extremely open, and don't mind people knowing what's wrong. I've nothing to hide. It is now obvious to me that I was inconsequential to Duncan. A burden. If he had taken any kind of interest in me as a person he would have known. Wouldn't he?

I also saw another strange face at the hospital, which seemed to be taking an interest in me so I asked, and was informed he was the driver who brought me. Bearing in mind this was a Saturday night, I discovered I was the only one in casualty. Upon my being discharged soon after, someone else was brought in.

Yunis, Duncan and I were taken back to the village, where I was confined to barracks, whilst they all went over to complete their duties for the finals.

There was no food in the log cabin, so I had to plead with Duncan to get me some breakfast from the cafeteria. He very grudgingly did this, as he did not want to waste too much time. Was I being unreasonable? He told me to stay put, but funnily enough I did not want to go out in case the same thing happened again. I seemed to have lost some of my confidence.

I very gingerly started to pack, but I refused to pack for him. When we moved from the hotel to the village, I went up to the room to pack, and discovered Duncan and Mike Curtis [yet another of the English contingent] had had a bet I would pack Duncan's gear as well. Like hell I would. More fool me for having done it in the past. As he was no longer having a relationship, then neither was I!

The following morning we had a very early start, to catch the bus which was to take us to the airport. I had not slept very well; I was very tired, and still very dizzy, but not as bad as I was the previous day.

We had no breakfast, as it was too early for the cafeteria. This was alien to me, as I always consumed it. As far as I was concerned this was the best meal of the day. It picked you up. It started you off. Got you ready for the traumas of the day.

We had half a mile to walk to pick up the bus. I had two bags. I had just come out of hospital; did Duncan carry one of my bags? NO. I will admit however, that he did have two bags himself, but one he slung on his shoulder so he did have a hand free. A so-called big strapping fit lad, I thought he could have taken one of mine. I could not walk very quickly, my speed was getting slower. I had to stop to keep taking a rest. Did he help? Like hell he did. This would have been too much for him. I could not keep up with him. I've only got little legs. My bags seemed like ton weights. He seemed to think it was beneath him to walk with me. He was making me feel so inadequate. I am usually a strong independent woman, but what was happening to me showed exactly how vulnerable I was.

The driver had patiently waited for us, and then proceeded to take us to Rotterdam Airport for our early morning flight. I tried to make conversation with Duncan; I should have been used to his behaviour by now as he just closed his eyes and went to sleep. He was beginning to become a very inconsiderate bore.

At the airport I tried to telephone my parents and tell them what had happened, but I could not make the phones work. Perhaps I should have got Duncan to press all the buttons. He may have succeeded, with his fondness for pressing buttons.

On the flight home, yes, you've guessed it, he promptly fell asleep. Upon our landing at Gatwick airport, I tried again to telephone my parents, and this time I was successful. I said I should be able to drive home. I had no intention of driving Duncan anywhere. I just wanted to get home, and go to bed. In any event he was going back to work that morning. We then went our separate ways.

I collected the car, and drove home, very carefully. Not in my usual harem scarem manner with right toe to the floor wherever possible.

Chapter 11

After my impromptu visit at the Dutch hospital, I was given a letter to give to my Doctor. I was still convinced I had had a mild heart attack.

On the Monday morning, on the day I should have returned to the office, I telephoned them and stated I had been in hospital in Holland, the reason for it, [I collapsed at the tournament], and I would need to see my doctor. This really upset the apple cart. I had a very full week. Two conferences fixed; one in Canterbury and on the following day in London.

I felt I was not believed.

I went to the doctor's as quickly as I could, gave him the letter, which I thought would be in Dutch, but fortunately it was in English. Every test the hospital did was negative, so I had not had a mild heart attack.

This was a relief. There had to be a reason. One does not just pass out for the sake of it. I was quickly certified off sick with a certificate. I was told to monitor any dizzy spells. I was asked what happened when I keeled over. All I could say was one minute I was sitting down, and then falling on the floor. I could not remember anything further until I came round some 90 minutes later. My doctor was flummoxed. Well if he was, you can imagine how I felt.

I had to inform work of the situation and my parents, who were worried, who then came to my home to take me to theirs. I had been away for a week, not seen my moggy for a week, and had washing to catch up with, as well as all the other boring chores of looking after oneself.

At their house I was not allowed to do a great deal, and the dizzy spells seemed to abate. They did not stop completely but just reduced in number and severity.

I did not swim. Mum said I ought to inform Duncan of where I was. Why, says I. He would not care. He showed that last week. However I telephoned him and left a message on his answer phone at home, as to where I was and the number, should he wish to call. I often tried ringing him at work in the past, but this was difficult, as he was often out and invariably did not receive any messages. Much to my surprise he rang me.

I returned home at the weekend, knowing I had to go into work on the following Monday. I tried to have a swim, but failed abysmally, only managing about 20 lengths. I was knackered. There had to be something wrong. This was not normal behaviour.

I dreaded going into the office, as I could not say what I would be faced with. Upon reaching my 'rat hole', my desk was buried under a mountain of paper.

Upon sorting this out, I found a conference had been fixed for me to attend in London that evening. There was absolutely no way, I was going. This had happened once before and seemed to be a regular occurrence, that when I was away, conferences would be fixed for me to attend on my return.

How did they know I would be well enough to return to work on the Monday? Someone in that department has a crystal ball. I informed Counsel's clerk I would be unable to attend and I informed the Police officer of the situation. None of the parties concerned were best pleased by my decision. Too bad! Appointments like these should not be arranged without consultation with all participants.

I was also due to attend the Medway Magistrates Court for a hearing in another case.

Work was really hotting up now. I was becoming heavily involved in a 20 defendant illegal immigration ring, a D.S.S., [Department of Social Security,] fraud which had been simmering and was now coming up to boiling point. Also my drug factory was beginning to fester. The Maidstone East Station, train derailment case was also coming into court soon.

I seemed to be picked upon by one of the H.E.O.s. Remember the one? The one who ordered me back, although I was still on a medical certificate. She seemed to take great delight in using me for a verbal punch bag.

I was always being "got at" for some petty "crime." I failed to fill in one of the boxes on the many forms we had to complete, failed to complete them on time, omitted an address, and made a miscalculation. Bearing in mind there was no assistance and only so many hours in the day. If so much time was being wasted on petty trivia, then no wonder cases where not prepared properly.

I used to dread going into work. When I drove into the underground car park, I always looked to see if her car was already there. When it was, I used to quiver, because she always managed to find something to moan at me about. We were all complaining [that is all of us on our grade E.O. and lower] there was not enough time in the day to fulfil all the duties we had to accomplish.

She had said to another girl, "If it is not done – be it on your own head."

How the hell could we get it all done, if we did not take work home.

I had by now given up everything. I was so tired all the time, although unable to sleep, worried about work, and also worried about my 'non-relationship' with Duncan. Although I was now swaying upon my feet, quite markedly, also shaking in the arms and legs, I still considered it was overworking that was causing this anomaly.

As I could not travel to Kelvedon, Duncan used to ring me on the Thursday evening to say he would be down on the Friday. This did not leave me much time to get extra food in the house.

On one occasion he was supposed to come down on the Friday evening. He telephoned me at 19.45 hours; I could hear a lot of sounds in the background. He was at a party in London.

A colleague from the office was leaving and there was a going away celebration for him. He knew this when he told me he was coming down.

He stated when he rang to arrange the weekend he would be home at about 19.30 hours. I was rather concerned he had not arrived, but took it that this was his customary late attitude.

I knew he was still at the party. He said I was being unreasonable, when I said he should be at home. I thought he was ringing from Ashford station, to let me know he was on his way.

He should never have arranged to come down on this particular weekend. He said he would arrive home at about 23.00 hours. I informed him he would not. I would be in bed, trying to get as much rest as possible, and I was not going to cook him a meal at that time of night. I said I had had enough of his uncaring behaviour, and I wanted to call it a day. I had had enough. Fortunately the food I had got in as an extra could all be frozen. Thank God. Nothing was wasted. He was not to know that though.

He telephoned me on the Saturday after to apologise. He felt guilty so he said. I had made him feel a heel, he said. About time. I knew where I came in his list of priorities. Rock bottom. Although he still tried to maintain I came first.

Chapter 12

Duncan had to keep in touch, because unbeknown to me; he had invited some friends of his to spend the weekend in my house.

They had been down on a previous occasion but this was at my invitation.

Apparently they had managed to book four tickets for dinner on the Tenterden Steam Railway. This cannot be done overnight, as it takes months to get hold of these tickets. I did not know of this at this time.

On other visits, to me he would arrive at Headcorn Station, and I would then drive home, and prepare a meal for us both. Come the Saturday, he, on some occasions would take me for lunch at the Chinese Restaurant.

During one of these lunches, Duncan informed me that Ray had managed to get tickets for dinner on the train for Saturday 18th June 1994. As it was mum's birthday on the 17th June I knew I would be unable to visit her, I hoped she would not mind. I said to Duncan he could invite Val and Ray down for the weekend. I was unaware he had already done so.

I never knew when he was leaving. Was it, as it used to be, first thing on the Monday morning, or did he wish to leave before hand? I never knew. He would not tell me anything.

Then during the Saturday afternoon he would ask if he could use the telephone, I wondered why. He said, to ring for a taxi. What on earth did he want a taxi for? To take him to the station he said. Of course, how stupid of me not to realise this. I should have known he was leaving. I drove to Ashford station and dropped him off.

Apparently he was going to work on the Sunday. Why on earth bother to come down at all, if he was barely going to stay 24 hours. I now see the reason. Because I was so tired all the time, unable to drive for long periods, needed to rest, I was of no use to him now. I had also banished him to the front bedroom. *If he was not having a relationship, then neither was I.*

I also had to keep in touch with him, because of our claim against the tour operator. Our dreadful holiday the previous October. We were getting some offers of settlement, but they were an insult, to our intelligence.

They were still not accepting any blame, it was still our or I should say my fault, for wanting a peaceful time as described in their brochure. I had drafted out many letters for Duncan, and I was quoting sections from the Sale of Goods Act, and the Trades Description Act.

Chapter 13

During the month of May I had to attend Dover Magistrates' Court where the illegal immigrant case was having a preliminary hearing before a Stipendiary Magistrate.

This hearing was to decide whether there was enough evidence upon which to commit all the defendants for trial at the Crown Court. It was necessary to have a Stipendiary, because of the length of time involved at this particular hearing. It was thought the hearing would last a week, with a possibility of a second week.

Stipendiary Magistrates are professional lawyers and are paid, whereas ordinary Magistrates are members of the public appointed, after due process, by the Lord Chancellor's Department. They are not paid. They sit on various days throughout the month. It is necessary to have at least two but the norm is three.

This hearing lasted for three days only, and then Counsel requested a conference to go through the evidence and to formulate the Bill of Indictment. These are the charges upon which the defendants have to answer at the Crown Court. As you can imagine this was a complicated issue, with so many defendants and many illegal entries. All the defendants were committed to the Crown Court.

With my time in Dover, I was therefore unable to get back to the office.

I had also arranged for Counsel to have a ride in a train which covered the route of the Maidstone East Station disaster. I was also invited, but was able to say no. I don't like trains anyway, but it would have been a very late night. I could not afford to have late or busy nights.

I had a mountain of work to catch up on. As well as attend court. After one very heavy session at Maidstone Crown Court, I returned back to the office absolutely knackered.

We were not just covering one court each, but several. If we were unfortunate to draw the short straw and be landed with a dustbin court, we knew we were in for a heavy time.

A dustbin court is one that is made up of many, varied, and complicated cases. Anything up to about 20 cases. Imagine the forms on one of those days. It was horrendous. You just got on with it. There was no use in complaining. It was expected of you to perform all your duties and tasks efficiently and diligently.

Upon my return, and after trying to sort my desk out, which I still had difficulty in finding, I received, and I can only describe it as a bollocking. Yes, it was from that particular H.E.O.

She still could not stop taking her frustrations out on me. It was like a slanging match. I was trying to reply, but as she was my senior, I had no rights to answer back. The way I did answer back was to collapse on the floor. I just dropped the phone, slid off my seat, and fell on the floor.

This, apparently, caused quite a stir. I was not out for long. I think she was quite worried. This was my second blackout. I came round, finished my cup of tea, I was not going to waste that, and then proceeded to drive home.

It was coming up for the late May Bank holiday weekend. Duncan was not coming at all this weekend. Thank goodness. I could at least rest, not do anything and try to recharge my batteries. I did not have to feel guilty because I could not do anything.

As I've said before when Duncan comes he has to be busy all the time, or he just sprawls out in the arm chair and goes to sleep. Never much in the way of intelligent conversation from that corner.

During this weekend, I was making a cup of tea, when I fell onto the floor. I had passed out again. Good job I did not have the kettle in my hand at the time. I was thinking about work. Thinking I would have to start taking it home with me. Thinking about that telephone conversation with *her.* Worrying about my future. Feeling I could not cope. Feeling useless, inadequate, and stupid.

Chapter 14

I was still convinced that there was something wrong with my heart. I did not believe there was nothing wrong.

After my second blackout I noticed my heart rate would not go down, especially if I was resting in the prone position, in bed.

Also I was beginning to get sharp pains in the left side of the chest. These only lasted for a short time. If I just stopped what I was doing they went away.

I went to my doctor's again, and informed him I had had another blackout. I also informed him of the strange feelings I was now experiencing.

He again asked me what happened when I passed out; I could not answer this, as I just fell on the floor.

His response was, "I wish there were witnesses to these."

Did he not believe me? Was I imagining them? I don't think so. I think I did pass out. I'm sure it was happening.

He said he would contact the local hospital to have my heart checked over a 24 hour period.

When I received my letter from the hospital giving details of my appointment, I informed Duncan on his answer machine at home, saying I was to go on this machine on 2nd and 3rd June 1994. I also informed my parents. I had to let the office know as I would be unable to cover any courts for these two days.

My appointment was for 13.30 hrs. It meant of course I could not swim, neither could I have a bath or shower. Electricity and water do not mix. There may have been a big flash if I had. I quite expected Duncan to ring me. He did not. I attended the hospital at the due time and was wired up.

It is like a 'portable Walkman', strapped to the waist by a leather belt. Then there are a load of suction pads stuck to the torso in various places by some sort of gel. These cover both the front and back of the body. All this paraphernalia is kept on all the time. You have to be very careful what you wear, as it really needs to be loose fitting. You sleep with this thing. I had to undo the belt, and lay the contraption by my side, but I could not turn over without picking it up and turn with it. You are very self-conscious of it.

The next morning, I attended work, with this thing duly strapped to my side. I wore trousers and a plain sweat shirt. Nice and big and baggy. I did not care what I looked like. Too bad, if the powers that be were offended. If *she* did not like it, too bad.

She was not my H.E.O. now anyway. *She* should have made her complaints to the gentleman who was.

I went to the hospital the following afternoon to have the equipment removed.

On Monday 6th of June 1994 I started a very long fraud trial which involved three defendants, having been indicted for Fraudulent Trading. I was in my element. This was my favourite form of crime. It meant I would have little time in the office, but I still needed to catch up on a great deal of paperwork. I refused to take any of this home to do at the weekends.

I had vast amounts of bundles to prepare, as the paper exhibits in these types of cases are immense. Fortunately, Counsel had reduced the amount required to the bare minimum, and said any extra copies required could be done during the hearing.

Also during this time, the Maidstone East Station derailment case was coming into court.

Further, it was now coming up to the dinner on the Tenterden Steam Railway. Bearing in mind Duncan had not rung to ask how I got on with the heart monitoring machine, would I get any sense out of him regarding the weekend?

I wanted to know about catering. Were his friends coming on the Friday night? Was it going to be sometime on the Saturday? What was the dress code? Would they require lunch on the Sunday? Was I being unreasonable in wanting to know?

He actually rang me on Thursday 16th June 1994 in the evening. The dinner had been booked for Saturday 18th June 1994.

He told me they were going to a wedding first on the Saturday and would be down directly after.

That would leave me more time to clean the house, he said. How dare he. He has not got the right to tell me how to keep the house. It has nothing to do with him. Was I that dirty? I was incensed. **HOW DARE HE?** He does not contribute to the living expenses anyway. I was furious, and he knew it. He arrived on the Friday evening. I had as usual picked him up from Headcorn Station. I was still simmering.

Come the Saturday, I knew what was going on. A bit late you might think. I had already done the shopping. I guessed lunch would be required on the Sunday so I had got in salad stuff. Being the summer, and hot, I thought that his friends would not mind. They knew I had been unwell.

The dinner on the train was a great laugh, I thoroughly enjoyed myself. This was the first time I had been out in the evening, for ages. I was still very tired. Val noticed I had banished Duncan to the front bedroom. She sensed something was wrong.

During lunch on the Sunday, she asked me what was the matter when the men went to do the washing up.

I said, "Don't let Duncan do it, I'll only have to do it again,"

Val took this opportunity and tackled me. I told her everything that had been going on, or not, as the case may be. She was shocked. She asked Duncan if it was true he'd said he was not having a relationship. He didn't disagree with her. He just looked very sheepish. She was also very cross about my birthday, Valentines' Day, etc. It was then he said he'd been too busy, with work and Norwich. I told him I'd managed it. She then had a right go at him, in front of me.

All he said was, "Yes, Boss." This was the first time I heard this stupid childish phrase from him, "Yes, Boss," was all he could say – "Yes, Boss."

This of course meant that he was not taking the slightest bit of notice. It was going in one ear and straight out through the other, with nothing to stop it in the middle. It was at this time I'd learned that Duncan had invited them to stay, long before I did. Could you imagine what would have happened if they had turned up on my doorstep with their cases in hand and I had not known what was going on.

Ray even cleaned out my kettle for me. Would Duncan have done that if I had not asked him? She was equally amazed Duncan had not asked how I got on with the 24 hour heart machine. It was then he gave this great pretence of concern.

He was told by Val to communicate, all she got for her pains was, "Yes, Boss."

Chapter 15

Who the bloody hell does he think he is telling me to clean my house? Yes, you've guessed it I'm still seething. He had no right to tell me to do that. He knew I was still cross with him on the Monday morning when I dropped him off at the station in Headcorn.

I refused to get out of my car and see him onto the train as I used to. I presumed he caught the train all right. I had not slept at all well over the weekend, and was feeling very tired, so perhaps it was just as well I had not been able to have my swim.

My trial was progressing well, overcoming the usual problems with running a long complicated case. Counsel was well briefed, and able to 'bat' any of the legal arguments brought by Defence Counsel. We were outnumbered three to one. the judge as usual in these cases was taking a neutral stance, as he has to.

I had to leave early as I had an appointment with my doctor to get the results of the 24 hour heart test.

Upon going in, he informed me there was nothing really untoward with the results, just a very minor wobble. He then put me on a mild beta blocker. I was still convinced there was something wrong. Why am I so tired all the time? Why do my legs go into spasms? Why do I have these sharp pains in my chest? Am I imagining all this? Again he asked me to have some more blood tests. I felt like a pin cushion, with all the blood that had been taken out of me at various times. Worse than if I had attended a 'Vampire Session'. [A blood donating session, to the uninitiated.] Duncan knew I was going to the doctor's for my results. Did he ring? *NO HE DID NOT*. However, Val did. She was concerned. Duncan was not.

All through the week I was getting more and more tired, going to bed at 20.00 hours. I was so knackered. I could not understand it. Still no phone call from Duncan.

On the 22nd June, I went to the surgery for more blood to be taken out and was so relieved that I was home by 17.00 hours instead of my usual 19.30 hours.

I was also not eating properly. We had no time at the luncheon recess for anything to eat, as there was inevitably something to be done for resumption at 14.00 hours. If we were able to grab something to eat in the canteen, it had to be shovelled down very quickly as there was work to do. I did not want to attract the wrath of the judge as I seemed to attract the wrath of her. One was enough in the day.

Thursday came and went, with no telephone call from Duncan, so I assumed it was beneath him to come down for the approaching weekend.

He had told me he had been married before, and that she had gone off with another man. I could now understand why. If he treated her in the same way he treated me. He used to tell me he had to do the shopping. Well if he did not tell her what he was doing there was no wonder. He also used to say she did not cook him a meal when he came home from work. Why should she, if she did not know when he was coming home? Why waste food. She apparently did not work. At least that was what I was told.

As it was Mum's birthday the previous weekend, I arranged to go down and give her her present. I only stayed the one day and drove home in the evening.

The 27th June 1994 marked a big turning point in my life.

I went swimming, or tried to, and failed abysmally. I wondered what on earth I was doing there. I was near to tears. I had pins and needles, cramp, and spasms in the muscles, and could not co-ordinate my arms. What the hell was wrong with me?

Upon my arrival in the office, I noticed a bloody great big box on my desk. It contained, you've guessed it another new case. A fraud. I know, I like doing them, but I already had several on the go as it was. I noticed it had been assigned to me by *HER*. I also noticed that the Bill of Indictment was late, and I would therefore need to submit a grovelling letter to the court as to the reasons why.

That box was not there when I left on the previous Friday evening! She must have been very quick to give it to me. Oh shit! How the hell was I going to have the time to sort that out? These cases are not ones that can be done in the matter of minutes.

I was now going to have to start taking work home with me. Oooooh shit! There is no other polite expletive I can use. Well there is, but I will leave that to your imagination. I left it sitting on my desk, and went to court.

We had now completed the Prosecution case, and survived the inevitable points of law, that there was no case to answer, put forward by the Defence.

The Defence case now started, with the first Defendant going into the witness box and giving evidence on his behalf.

The prosecution now proceeded to cross-examine him. Counsel was brilliant. He had such a calm, level way of talking that it could be seen the Defendant was thinking he had got the upper hand. I knew different. I knew the way Counsel was taking it. He was just coming up to a crucial document that bore the defendant's signature, when I passed out. What bloody awful timing. I have no idea what was happening. I was helped out of court by the Police officer in the case, Detective Constable Epps, and one of our lawyers, Mr. John Hazelden.

I assumed the trial and the court room were adjourned. I had no idea. How embarrassing. I was wavering in and out of consciousness. I think John asked me if there was anyone I wished to call. I said yes. My parents. No good getting in touch with Duncan. I gave him the number. Fortunately I did not have to remember the stupid little 1 that we have to use now. If that had been the case, I would not have been able to give John the number as I cannot remember it now.

As I would not come round an ambulance was called and I was taken to the local hospital. A colleague of mine, Marianne Sheldrake, came with me, and stayed until she made sure I was okay, and another colleague, Jill Peters collected her.

When I finally came round, again I was wired up to every machine possible. I thought I'd had a mild heart attack. I already had some little drain and tap placed in the right arm by the ambulance crew, but the doctor was not happy with it. It was not big enough. He wanted to put another one in my left arm, which he did.

I called out, "Jesus that hurts."

He replied "You called?"

Coming from an Asian, I thought this was quite funny. I was again given all the tests together with a scan over my stomach. All were negative. However, the doctors realised there was something seriously wrong.

They were only going to release me if I was not going to live on my own. Marianne had given them all my details. Mum had been in touch. The office had been in touch. They had been informed that I was going to be in overnight. It was thought there was something wrong with my central nervous system. How right they were.

My parents had arrived at the hospital to take me to their home. I was not allowed to live in mine. I have now lost all my independence. I hate this.

What did I do about the car? It was still in the office car park. I did not want to drive. Dad then drove it to my house, where it was left until the tax had run out. I picked up a few bits and pieces packed them into a case, still feeling very groggy, and was driven to my parents by mum together with my moggy.

I had also informed the family opposite, Chris and Ollie Johnston and their two children, Kirsty and Steven, as to what had happened, and asked them if they could sort my post out, and generally keep an eye on the place. They were so helpful and considerate at this time, and have now become firm friends. I did not realise how much I was going to rely on them in the future. I feel they have adopted me, or is it, I've adopted them!

Chapter 16

It must have been very difficult for my parents. Here I was staying with them when once I was a strong, fiercely independent, self-reliant and confident woman. I was now reduced to something like a gibbering idiot. They could not say anything to me without me bursting into tears. I could not drive, so had to be taken anywhere I wanted by one of them. Fortunately they both drive. Although Dad only when he has to, and never when either Mum or I were in the car. The situation now was entirely different.

I found it very difficult to have to ask to use the telephone, as living on my own it's me that pays the bill. As I was in someone else's house it was only right and proper I should ask.

On the following day after my blackout Mum took me to see my Doctor, in Tenterden. This was about a 30 mile drive, or between 45 to 60 minute drive depending on the traffic. The hospital had given me a letter which stated on it the treatment given, and the tests done. All being negative. With the suggestion I be referred to see a neurologist. Remembering his whimsical remark when I attended upon him after my second blackout about there being witnesses, I said this time there were plenty. A court room full in fact. 12 jurors, umpteen lawyers, barristers, three defendants, police officers, witnesses, court staff, members of the public, and of course not forgetting the judge. Was this enough?

What would have been the outcome if this had happened whilst I was crossing the road? He realised the seriousness of the situation, and said that as a matter of urgency he would refer me to a neurologist in the area of my parent's address, to save unnecessary travelling.

I still carried on with my swimming [if it can be called that!] but I had to drag one of my parents to come with me. Mum was terrified I was going to black out in the pool. I knew this would not happen. I was not under any pressure, and I was not in the vertical position. I did not have any dizzy spells whilst I was in this situation.

Mum said I should inform Duncan – why I can't imagine – so I left a message on his answer machine at home.

He was actually able to put himself out and came down on Friday 8th July, but went home the following day. When he arrived he always came loaded with flowers. A bunch for Mum and a bunch for me. The great pretence of caring, but then I was in somebody else's house. I was in company. He never did ask me how I got on with the heart machine.

I was still having to undergo blood tests, and if I felt like a pin cushion before, I must have looked as if I had gone 10 rounds with a porcupine.

On the 11th July I had an appointment with the consultant neurologist at the local hospital. I was not overly impressed. He asked me what had happened; I was surprised at this, as I thought my doctor would have filled him in.

I said about the four blackouts, what work was like, sheer hell, and about the spasms in my muscles, lack of co-ordination, feeling very tired, pins and needles, and bad balance.

I explained that my balance had always been bad, as I seemed to spend more time on the floor when I played badminton, than I did standing up. I always put it down to my brain [yes I have got one] acting quicker than my feet.

Also when I tried water skiing off Mombasa, Kenya, I managed to get to my haunches, but never on my feet, and again when I tried cross-country skiing in Switzerland, I spent more time on the floor, but my balance was never as bad as it was now.

He tried all the tests, regarding my balance and I could not put one foot in front of the other without falling over. I could not stand on one leg without falling over. He then asked me to lay down on the couch and rub my right heel up and down my left leg, and then vice versa.

He never said anything, nor did he give any encouraging help. Mum was convinced that I had a brain tumour. I still thought I had had a mild heart attack. He never said yes or no to anything. The only thing he wanted was for me to have a brain scan, at the local hospital in Hastings.

Duncan knew of the appointment, but he did not ring.

I attended the Conquest Hospital on 21st July for my first brain scan. I did not have to take any clothes off, but I had to remove all jewellery.

It's just like undergoing an X-ray. I had to lie down on a very hard cold moulded bed like structure. My head was placed in such a manner that it could not move, and I had to be in this position for nearly half an hour. Numerous pictures were taken, and at the end of it, as I was getting up, I had a dizzy spell. The consultant radiologist was rather concerned, and asked if I had had many of them. I said they were quite frequent. I now had to move in a field of slow motion, taking a rest whenever I could.

Duncan attended upon me again on 22nd July, and came armed with further presents, this time a jigsaw. A difficult one, as it was the same picture on both sides, but the reverse had been rotated by 90 degrees. The picture consisted of hundreds of cats.

He thought t it would keep me going for some time. He again left the following evening. I finished it in four days, but then I had nothing else to do.

The following weekend was Dad's birthday, and Duncan was invited again. I went to the station to meet him. I wished I hadn't. He was not on any of the trains that I had waited for. I then went back to my parents' home alone. At about 20.30 hours Dad insisted we go to the station and see if he was on the next one. I did not want to bother. Dad insisted. Surprise, surprise, he was on it.

His excuse for being late was that he had to stop and buy some flowers. Okay, but could he have not rung and said he missed the connection. Did not think about it, he says. That's your trouble, you don't think, say I. He maintains that he has now arrived, so what's the problem. The words Val said to him on 19th June had no effect on him. I didn't think they would.

Chapter 17

Over Dad's birthday we visited a vintage car rally which was being held in the grounds of Battle Abbey.

Battle Abbey is not normally open to the public as it is a public school for girls. This was one ancient monument I had always wanted to visit. I now had my chance.

With so many old cars to see, together with a parade of old Rolls Royce's, and Minis. I am not referring to the fashion of miniskirts, but to very small innovative cars that were originally built by Austin, or Morris, which became part of British Leyland, then subsequently Rover cars. Dad was in his element.

There was an original Model T, and a Ford 8 both of which Dad had driven in the past. Dad never took a driving test, having driven in the desert during the war. I am of course referring to the 2nd World War, in case you are thinking I'm referring to the 100 Years' War, or the Prussian wars. I can be very cheeky when I want to. I'm sure Dad won't mind. I always refer to him as the "Old Man" anyway, because he is always going on about how old he is.

I think Duncan would have preferred trains, but he seemed to show some interest, although I don't know how genuine this was.

He did however stay all weekend, as we were all going out to lunch at a local Chinese Restaurant, on the Sunday.

I next attended the specialist on the 1st August 1994 and was informed the scan was negative. That put Mum's mind at rest; I did not have a brain tumour. The next test was to have an M.R.I. brain scan and an E.E.G. at the Princess Anne Hospital, Haywards Heath. He still did not tell me what he was looking for.

These appointments were made and I attended on the 18th August 1994.

The M.R.I. scan is very similar to the set up at the Conquest Hospital, but is deeper.

Again I was informed to remove all jewellery, and led into the chamber. The cold hard moulded bed was there, but the chamber that I went into was larger. The bed was moved electronically but what happened next, I really can't say. To avoid my head moving, it was secured down, so I decided to go to sleep. I was asked if I wanted to listen to any music, and I chose a very soothing tape of Mozart.

An M.R.I scan means a Magnetic Resonance Imaging. A diagnostic scanning technique which gives detailed images of internal tissue by analysing its response to being bombarded with high – frequency radio waves within a strong magnetic field.

After it was all over I then proceeded to the Neurological centre for my E.E.G. [Electro Encephalo Gram].

This is where tiny electrodes are placed on the head to register brain waves. Before these can be put on, the head has to be measured, and various coloured pencil marks made on the scalp. You can imagine what it does for your hair. When all these were attached I was given various instructions to follow by the technician.

There was a light I had to watch, at various places, and in various positions. I cannot remember if I was lying down or sitting in a chair. I seem to think I must have been lying down but I'm not sure. I can't remember.

Duncan again came for the weekend of 19th August 1994 and returned home on the 21st August. He had informed my parents on a previous occasion that when this was all over he was going to take me away. I thought this meant a holiday.

I then sought some advice from the travel agents, because I knew he would want to be busy all the time, whereas all I wanted was to rest. I found what I thought would be the perfect solution. I did not want the same kind of fiasco we had experienced the previous year. Yes we were still arguing with the tour operator, only this time we put in our claim for compensation from A.B.T.A., thinking that this might resolve the situation.

I scoured the brochure thoroughly, looking for the best destinations for us, and tried to discuss this with him. I had no feedback from him. He just did not seem interested.

I went to see my consultant on the 22nd August, 1994 and was informed that all the scans were negative. Was I then imagining all my troubles? Was it psychosomatic? Was it all in my imagination? How could I imagine the blackouts? They did happen, didn't they?

Was it because I did not want to go back to *that place.* Meaning work. I knew if I returned I would end up in a worse state than I was at the present, or I would end up in a mental institution, or they would really finish me off and I would be 6 feet under. I did not relish any of these possibilities.

The next step was to have some more blood tests, and a lumbar puncture. Before all this occurred, I requested to take a month off, and wondered if it would be all right to have a holiday. He agreed.

I returned home, my home, on the 25th August. All during the time that I stayed with my parents, Dad drove me home about once a week to see to the mowing of the lawns, and my post, and generally try to tidy up the garden.

It was during one of these visits I met Joyce. She was Ollie's Mum. The people who were looking after my house had gone away for their holiday, and had asked Joyce, who went into look after their house and feed their cats, to keep an eye on my place. I had only met her about once before. She was extremely kind and helpful, and did not seem to mind the added burden. I now seem to be friendly with the whole family.

During my stay with my parents I realised that several things that I took for granted, were no longer possible. Dad took me to church on several occasions so I could partake of Holy Communion. I could not stand for long, without getting dizzy, I could also not sing, as this also caused me to be dizzy. What was happening to me?

I tried to hide my fears, because I knew how much of a worrier Mum is. A neighbour's rabbit escaped into our garden, and I saw it, ran after it and promptly did a somersault on the back lawn. [Olga Korbut eat your heart out!] The lady who owned the rabbit said that she wished she had had a video camera to record it. I'm glad she did not, I was terribly embarrassed. I was okay though, but the sudden realisation that I could not run, hurt.

Upon my arrival home, I telephoned Duncan and left a message on his blasted answering machine to say I was now home. I quite expected him to ring, and say he would be down the following weekend, as it was August bank holiday. I did not hear a thing. He completely ignored me. When he did next ring, I said that the specialist had said I could have a holiday, and which of the destinations would we be going to. I left the choice to him. I had already given him my list of options. He then informed me he did not want to go away. The bastard.

Chapter 18

How dare he give me a false impression of the fact of no holiday, after I went to the trouble of getting all the brochures, and wasting my time of trying to sort something out that would appeal to both of us? No wonder he did not take any interest when I was trying to discuss it with him when I was at my parents. Another sham. Another false way of showing he cares.

If he did not want a holiday, then I did. Was I being unreasonable? I don't think so. Where can a single woman, who is on her own go, and feel safe. Unmolested. I knew I would need someone to take me. I was not driving. I still did not want to. Mum said she would take me. But where?

The only place I can think of was a health farm.

I had been to two previously.

[1] Henlow Grange

[2] Ragdale Hall.

After my first attempt at the swimathon in 1991, I decided to learn the front crawl. This I did at Henlow Grange. The pool they had was a pokey dark depressing thing, but I did learn the freestyle [front crawl], an improvement on what I was able to do, which was a cross between the doggy paddle and something called the breaststroke, but still not swimming in the proper sense of the word. Also the food and the treatments included in the package were excellent.

Just before I attended the 1993 World Championships in Birmingham, I went to Ragdale Hall. Although the pool was larger and more airy, I was not impressed. It seemed to me all the therapists went around with fixed grins on their faces. I was unsure whether they were really smiling at me because they wanted to, or whether they had to keep this expression up all day. I felt very uneasy. I also felt that the clients did not seem to be as friendly.

However there was one couple I got to know, basically because she wanted to learn to swim. She could not understand how I could keep going. How I was non-stop for 1500 metres, which was 120 lengths in the pool. She took the advantage of the swimming lessons, and at the end of the week was so glad that she could now swim the width of the pool, whereas before she had been frightened of the water.

I now decided to obtain the brochures. I had heard a rumour, whilst I was at Henlow Grange they intended to have an extension, and were going to build a larger pool. I was very sceptical. I knew what rumours were like.

Imagine my surprise. They had had the extension built, and had now got a 25 metre pool. This is the equivalent of a short course championship pool. All the other brochures then went flying out the window!

I booked for a Traditional week, in one of the best rooms available. Sod the expense, I thought.

Included in the package were five facials or neck and shoulder massages, and five full body massages. Unlimited use of the spa facilities, which included the pool, whirlpool, steam room, and sauna. Also unlimited use of the gymnasium and any of the classes run in the fitness studio.

I also booked as an extra for the Aromatherapy. I knew what to expect. I had been pampered like this before. I also knew the food would be exceptional.

I left a message for Duncan on his answering machine. Asking him to get back to me as quickly as possible. I had been given an option for a second person to share my room, at a reduced price, and thought he might like to come. The quickest time that he returned my call was 60-70 hours later. I was wondering if he was ever going to ring. When he did manage to find the time, I told him what I had done, and gave him the option of coming. He said no, after much dithering, saying he could not afford it. The truth will out now.

Why he could not have said this in the first place I do not know. He said he was saving up for the Scottish Open. How stupid of me. I should have realised badminton came first. This was not till the end of

November anyway. I told him when and where I had booked it.

At this stage I then decided not to ring him, or leave any messages on his damned machine.

Several of my friends were worried, because they had not seen me for some time. I had not been to church, and neither could they raise me on the telephone. Don and Peggy Webb had rung my parents whilst I was staying there, and were surprised to find that I was indeed there. Also Muriel Webb had been in touch.

Diana Jorsta an old friend of some 20 years was also worried. She could not raise me at home, and neither had I been round to see them at weekends as I was in a habit of doing. She and I went right back to when we attended the Maidstone Operatic Society Auditions, in 1976. We knew from the moment we met we would be friends. We said at the time, that if we both passed the auditions and meet at the first rehearsal our friendship would be long lasting.

They all rang me whilst I was at my parents.

Upon my arrival home in mid-August, I contacted them all, and they all promised help and support. Nobody at this stage knew what was wrong. Perhaps I was going mad. I don't know.

One of the first things I did was to renew my membership of the Tenterden Leisure Centre. I decided to take out the full membership, as this would enable me to use the swimming pool when it was convenient, and the health suite. I intended to keep up my swimming, as this was all that was left to me. I never thought that that would be all I could do.

It was at this stage I found out I could no longer dig my garden. You can imagine after weeks of neglect, it had gone back to nature. It was badly overgrown. Dad and I had managed to keep the lawns in check though.

Every time I bent down and shoved the fork into the ground, I was very dizzy. Oh blast! What am I going to do, this is ridiculous. Surely there is something wrong with me. This can't be normal – can it? I had to take my time over everything I did. It was like living in a field of slow motion.

During the early part of September, I had to provide the office with a new medical certificate.

Don and Peggy drove me into Maidstone, at the first opportunity, and were given permission to use the office car park.

Don had kindly given me the use of a walking stick, and this now provided me with my third leg. It also helped towards my drunken stance. I was in reception at the office, when the Chief Crown Prosecutor entered. He was now the Branch Crown Prosecutor, as Kent no longer exists. It is now part of C.P.S. South East. This area includes believe it or not, Hampshire. Or should I say Area 13. The B.C.P. [Branch Crown Prosecutor] noticed me, also noticed my stick.

"Hello, Sue," was all he said before he walked out. This was the management. There was no conversation. No thought of asking me how I was, or when it was thought that I was coming back to work, or when was my next medical test, or even what my next test was. Nothing. Was I that much of a non-entity? Did I really work all those hours to be dealt with in such a dismissive attitude? I know that all ordinary CPS employees are only robots. We should never get ill, neither should we need to take lunch breaks, all we should need is the occasional oil change, at the next 30,000 mile service.

Don could not believe his attitude. He asked me who it was.

"The boss," I told him.

"Well, really," Don replies.

He was quite taken aback. All the other members of staff spoke to me, and treated me in the same way that they had always done. Rudely!

Chapter 19

Mum drove me, together with Dad to the health farm on Sunday 11th September 1994. Before I went, I asked Chris and Ollie [the people opposite] if they could keep an eye on my home, and take my post in. I explained where I was going, and I think Chris would have come with me, if she could get away from College. She is a Geology, Geography, and Environmental Science Lecturer, and also studying for an M.A. at the local University. How she manages to fit everything in beats me, but she has the support of the whole family. She asked me if she needed to feed the cat, I said no, as she was at a local cattery.

Dad was convinced that all we are fed on at a health farm is carrot juice and a lettuce leaf. However much I tried to persuade him, he would not believe me.

Upon settling in, I then showed my parents round the facilities. I think they were pleasantly surprised at the extent of the grounds, and the facilities available.

I had a goal that I would manage 100 lengths of the 25 metre pool once, before I left. I had not managed this distance since about January. After having my medical, and confirming I was not 100%, although nobody seemed to know what was wrong, I knew I was in safe hands. I hoped I would not embarrass anyone at meal times if I started to shake. I need not have worried, as my shakes seemed to abate. The only time it happened was in my legs whilst I was in bed.

Everything would have been wonderful if it had not been for the American Boxer Oliver McCall. He was using Henlow Grange for his training camp. It would have been fine, if he knew how to switch off his 'ghetto blaster' at midnight. My room was directly above his. I suppose you could say I'm one of the few women who hate boxers and have slept on top of one. I find boxing totally barbaric and mediaeval. Its pugilism gone mad.

The meals ordered for his entourage were large. Steaming whole chickens and steaks. The smell of this as it passed by us was very off putting. Here we were, on a diet, and having to cope with the aroma. Some of the guests suffered more than I did. I was not following the diet, thank goodness. The food we had was plentiful, healthy and wholesome, and I was not in the least bit hungry. I took the opportunity whilst I was there to rest and relax, and recuperate. Apart from the boxer, it would have been sheer bliss. I felt a lot better, and everyone remarked upon how well I looked, compared to when I arrived.

During the week I was very surprised to hear from Duncan. He rang me to see how I was getting on. I'm surprised he even remembered, and managed to find the time. He said he would ring me when I got home.

On the 16th [Friday], I attempted the 100 lengths. I made it. Although not as fast as I had been in the past, but nevertheless I did it. As the pool was so large I did not stop for the aqua aerobics class. I wanted to achieve my goal, I hoped the instructor would not mind.

As I was nearing the finish one of the clients who was participating in the class moved out of my way, stood well back, hands in the air, saying, "Serious swimmer, serious swimmer."

If only she knew. If only I knew what would happen the following year.

When my parents came to pick me up on the Saturday, they could not believe the change in me. I had booked lunch for them. I was going to convince Dad that it was not carrot juice and a lettuce leaf.

I introduced them to the various people I had befriended during the week, and Mum said she thought that she might like it. Dad was still unconvinced.

He was very dubious about having lunch, but as it had been booked and paid for, he could not think of a way out. Plus, he could not leave until Mum and I left anyway. He was stuck! Lunch as usual was a salad, but it is amazing how many different cold dishes can be generated. We all thoroughly enjoyed our meal. I knew what to expect. Even Dad enjoyed it. This must have been a first.

I complained to the management about the noise generated by the boxer, and about the 'ghetto blaster', and they gave me a voucher towards my next visit. I knew I would be returning, hopefully with my parents in the New Year. I was also given a two for one voucher, which would be an added incentive.

Chapter 20

Upon my return home from the Health Farm, Chris asked if I would accompany her to Tenterden Leisure Centre on the following Saturday. Apparently they were having a free weekend with a bonus of a reduced membership fee. Wish I had known about this before I had renewed mine. Still it's too late now. I will remember about this for next year though.

We walked to the centre and I found I could run. Yes, I ran across the road. Imagine my amazement. I was not now using my stick. It was kept by the front door to remind me what I had been like.

Chris wanted to take part in the aerobics' class. I thought that I would also try it out, not having done any for some time. I took it very leisurely and casually to start with, not wanting to upset any delicate hold that I had upon my constitution. Everything was fine until we had to start moving the head. I quickly realised I could not take any further part in the class. It made me feel dizzy.

As I was dressed in a leotard and tights, I knew a swim was out of the question. Imagine the mess. With the colours of green and red mixing with the chlorinated water. What could I do next? I had used the gym whilst at the health farm, so I thought I would make use of the treadmill.

After all this exercise, together with the use of the cycle machines, and the weights, I felt pleasantly pleased with myself. We did not, however, walk home as Chris managed to ask a friend of her's to take us home. I had not enjoyed myself so much for some time.

Joyce [Ollie's mum], was going on holiday. She went into their house to let the dog out into the garden, and feed the cats in the evening, and generally help Chris with the running of the household. Chris asked me if I could go in, in the afternoon, to let their dog out in the garden.

Now, a large, stupid, demented but very caring dog was to enter my life. It was a female Golden Labrador, whose pedigree name was Shasta of the Weald. She generally answers to anything really, but is better known as Shassie.

After having been over on a couple of occasions, I thought it was silly of me just to let her out in the garden. I wondered if I could take her for a walk in the afternoon. Chris thought that the idea was a wonderful suggestion, and quickly agreed without any hesitation. I, however, on the one hand, was terrified. What if I let her off the lead, and she would not come back? What if she completely disobeyed me? What if she ran off completely? Golden Labradors are always hungry, and Chris suggested that I always carry a biscuit with me.

On our first walk out, she pulled on her lead. She did not realise I could not walk as quickly as Ollie. I have smaller legs for one thing, but then I was generally walking a lot slower than normal. I let her off the lead, when we reached a vast expanse of green at the back of the Tenterden railway. I found some sticks and threw them for her. I need not have worried; she came back to me, and always obeyed me. She was wonderful.

As I was doing this every afternoon, I realised I would have to change my time of my swim. I was in the practice of going around lunchtime as it was not generally very busy at this time. All I wanted was to swim length after length after length. Very boring I know.

I knew that the centre opened at 06.30 hours on every morning except Thursdays. There was no way I was going to resort to being there at that ridiculous hour. I know I was always in the habit of being there then, but I was working then. I'm not now. What time could I go?

I now left home at about 08.00 hours to walk the short distance of about 400 yards to the pool. This took me about 30 minutes. I then unwound after my workout in the Health Suite, in the steam room and the sauna. I needed to relax. It seemed after any form of exercise I was knackered.

Chapter 21

My car had been sitting all this time in front of my house. It had been left untouched from the day Dad had left it after that fateful day in June. It was now fast becoming illegal. I could no longer leave it where it was. I had to get it into the garage somehow. But there's no room. The garage as usual is full of junk. It will have to be cleared out. Somehow. I was not even sure the vehicle would start. The M.O.T. was running out and the tax was running out. The insurance was however still current. Mum and Dad came over and helped me turn the garage out.

Now, would my car start? Surprise, surprise, it did. After some arguing. We reversed it into the garage, and left it all snug, until I felt able to drive again. I still did not want to; neither did I have the confidence to drive.

Work, or should I say Head Office, were now beginning to take notice of my plight as I had been off work since the end of June. The Welfare Officer had arranged to see me during the first week of October. Before she arrived my H.E.O. *[no not her]* telephoned me to suggest I contact Welfare as I had been off work now for three months. I was able to inform him the officer was coming to see me. This was my first communication with Management since I passed out for the final time.

I had also noticed during one of my visits at the Leisure Centre that there was a sponsored swim for the British Heart Foundation being held during the first weekend of October. I wanted to see if I could take part. I wanted to confirm I could still swim under semi-competition standards.

I had no idea how I was going to get there. I could not walk, as it would be dark. Anyway I did not know what state I would be in at the conclusion. I was only going to attempt 50 lengths. This was the maximum allowed for this event. My parents were away on holiday, so I could not ask them. Bit silly really to ask them to fly back from the South of Spain especially. Would make it a very expensive holiday.

I would have to swallow my pride and leave a message on Duncan's blasted answering machine. Although he had said he would ring me upon my return from the health farm, I was still waiting. I had by now been home a fortnight, and he had not rung at all.

When he finally returned my call I asked him to come down especially for this particular weekend, as I wanted to swim. He promised he would come. I had not seen him since mid-August, when I was still staying with my parents. I also informed him the Welfare Officer was coming to visit prior to the event.

My parents went on holiday feeling contented that I would have company at the weekend. They were always worried about leaving me on my own. Although I had lived on my own for some 16 years.

On the 6th October 1994 the Welfare Officer came to visit me. I had met her before, whilst I was in my 'rat hole', and she knew how disenchanted I was with the Department, and how they always expected to get 'blood out of a stone'.

I wondered how I would cope. I hoped I would not embarrass myself. I managed to make a cup of tea, but was shaking so much I had to carry it in one at a time and on a tray. I did not want to spill it. Did not want to chuck it all over her or on my suite. It would have made a dreadful mess.

We chatted about all my tests, and the fact that they all, so far, had come back negative. Also about the tests that were to occur.

I was worried about *her*. I told the officer what had occurred on a previous occasion, when I was forced to return to work, although on a medical certificate. She was absolutely astounded. It was at this stage I realised *she* had no right to do that. I explained I did not know of this, and thought as *she* was my senior, *she* had every right. I was terrified *she* would do the same thing again. If *she* did then I was to contact her [being the Welfare Officer].

This helped to alleviate my mind a little, but I did not want to be put into that position. I could not handle any problems or stress. She could see the state I was in.

I had been off work for over three months and I did not seem to be getting any better. Surely there was something wrong with me.

We also spoke of medical retirement. This I agreed to. I could not envisage returning to *that place* knowing I would end up in the same state or worse. She was going to put in a report, regarding her visit, and also requested that I fill in a form stating that that would be the final outcome. I could not complete this, as my hand was shaking to such an extent I could not hold a pen. She then filled it in and requested me to sign it. The date would be endorsed at a later stage, when it was confirmed what was wrong with me.

I also chatted about all my symptoms, the feeling of tiredness, feeling dizzy, the feeling of not being in control of limbs. She could see how I shook all the time. She was very supportive and helpful. This came as a surprise as the C.P.S. did not seem to care. She did say they drove their staff very hard.

After she left, I needed to talk to someone. As I had not been able to take Shassie out, I noticed Joyce's car was opposite. I hoped she would not mind me chatting to her. I had hoped that when she returned from her holiday she did not mind me continuing to take the dog out. It seemed to benefit all of us, me especially. Joyce was as usual very comforting and did not mind me spouting off about the visit. She just sat there and let me pour it all out. She was wonderful.

Shassie had missed her walk. I could tell. She came bounding up to me wagging, not only her tail, but her whole body. She would have to be contented with going out in the garden.

Duncan was coming down on the day after, so I could also speak to him.

As Duncan was coming down, Mum had already given me some extra food items the previous weekend, so I did not need to do any further shopping.

I waited for the ring on the door bell, with bated breath. Suddenly the telephone rang. Perhaps it's him telling me he's at Ashford station, just waiting for transport to Tenterden. It was Duncan all right, but not from Ashford. He was ringing from Redbridge.

"What the hell are you doing there?"

"I've been asked to help out at the Essex Open," he informs me.

[In case you're wondering this is a badminton tournament.]

"But you are supposed to be here, this weekend."

"I know I forgot," he retorts.

"You didn't forget, it is just that a badminton tournament is more interesting, than watching swimming."

He still tried to maintain that he'd forgotten.

I replied, "Could you not have said, my girlfriend's not very well, and I haven't seen her for some time and she is trying to take part in a swimming event this weekend, and has requested my company, they would have understood."

"I didn't think."

By this time I was angry. I was crying. I was shaking. Oh, how could he be so insensitive?

"If you really want to do this then take a taxi, I'll pay," was his backhanded comment.

"Yes I know where I come in your list of affections, right rock bottom, I'm not using a taxi for a journey of 400 yards. Who the hell do you think I am?" I then slammed the phone down. This was the first time I had put the phone down on him.

The next day he rang to apologise. He still tried to maintain I should get a taxi.

"I don't know what state I'm going to be in, so I don't want a stranger helping me." I replied, "Go back to your bloody badminton tournament, it's more interesting than me."

I was still very angry. Not only is he an inconsiderate bore, but he is now an irresponsible, unreliable, thoughtless, uncaring, dispassionate cretin.

Chapter 22

Life carried on as usual. I was swimming 4 mornings a week, and walking Shassie every afternoon. I then had a couple of friends in for lunch during this period, Peggy Webb and Dee Moore, [from work].

I knew I could not carry on walking Shassie around the green at the back of the railway. By, the old Seeboard shop, there is an Ordnance Survey map depicting all the footpaths. Upon reading it, I realised there was a walk at the back of the Leisure Centre. From the look of the map it appeared to consist of orchards, shrub land and woods. I wanted an area where I could let her off the lead, and not interfere with any livestock. This looked the perfect solution.

I was extremely nervous of doing this, as this would be in a strange environment. She seemed to enjoy it, though. With all the new smells, rabbits and squirrels to chase. She loved it.

I was also maintaining my resolve not to ring Duncan. I thought constantly about his behaviour whilst I was out with Shassie. I became more and more convinced I was not being unreasonable. Did I ask for too much out of life?

The days were flying past. I seemed to be busy all the time, doing enough to keep me going. Shassie was thoroughly enjoying herself. I was getting home contented, and not in the least bit harassed.

With the onset of the weekends, I was, beginning to dread the sound of the telephone. I thought that each time it rang it would be Duncan, to say he would be down. However, this did occur on the 20th October, saying he would be down on the following day. This would have been a fortnight since the aborted swim.

I had heard nothing from him from that Saturday until this particular Thursday. He seemed to make it sound like he was doing me a favour. If he only knew!

On the following Friday, I had to cut short my walk, just in case he arrived early, and was waiting for me on the doorstep. I need not have worried, though. When he did arrive, I cooked a small meal for him, and he was slobbering all over me. Saying that he had not seen me for some time. Whose fault is that I ask?

He never makes any attempt to help clear up, just picks himself up and wanders into the lounge, whereupon he plonks himself down in the armchair and promptly goes to sleep.

I thought the reason he was coming down was not only to see me, but also have a chat. I should have known better.

I had managed to maintain my resolve of him sleeping in the front bedroom. I did not want him anywhere near me.

On the following Saturday, he did not know I had left the house to pick up my paper at 07.00 hours, I had left him asleep. I made him a cup of tea, which he drank when he awoke. It was cold.

Breakfast was consumed, and guess who cleared up, me.

He then picks himself up and sprawls out on the armchair, guess what, he goes to sleep. He must have been awake really, as at 10.30 I said that I'm going to make a pot of tea. He immediately jumps up, pushes me out of the way, and rushes into the kitchen, saying he'll do it. By now I was really pissed off.

"How dare you push me around in my own home? You continue what you were doing, I'll make it. I'm quite capable you know."

Lunch was a roast. I selected a leg of lamb, and all the trimmings. I still had some potatoes that Mum had given me at the end of September, and he can have those. The vegetables were frozen and only needed microwaving. For pudding all I could be bothered with was opening a frozen pie and shove it in the oven.

At 13.30 hours when I'm trying to co-ordinate dishing up lunch, there is a knock on the kitchen door. By now I'm in a state, panicking, shaking, and near to tears. Who the hell was this visitor, what a stupid time to call, what are they after, a free meal!

I open the door and received the biggest shock ever. It was *her*. Oh hell, what does *she* want? *She* never said *she* was coming. *She* saw the state I was in. I'm also as white as a sheet. *She said that she would not come in as I had company but she wanted to see how I was.* I'll bet. What did *she* really want? *She* never does anything without an ulterior motive. There had to be a reason. I was terrified. What if the so called management had asked *her* to see how ill I really was? Was it genuine? Oh God, how could *she* be so thoughtless? Had *she* received a bollocking from Welfare? I don't know?

After managing to consume the main meal, I placed the pudding in front of Duncan whereupon it was consumed in a very short space of time. It went down the hatch as if there was no tomorrow. His next comment almost blew my mind.

"That's the best part of the meal!"

I was lost for words. How could he? It was the only part of the meal I did not have to think about. He saw the state I was in. How could he be so insensitive? He then did the usual, sprawled out in front of the television, in the armchair, and went to sleep. I was left with all the clearing up to do. I felt awful. Not only having to contend with *he*r visit, but also with his degrading remark.

After all I did. *HOW COULD HE?*

The afternoon followed the usual course. Him asleep, and me watching the sport. Oh, I wish he would go. I don't want him here anymore. I'm fed up of being used. I'm fed up of being abused. I was hoping he was going to ring for a taxi to take him to the station, but no such luck. He was staying it seemed. He must have been extremely bored. Nothing to do. Me, not being able to do anything. I was by now completely shattered. I was almost on the verge of breaking down. I did not want him to see this. I then took myself off to bed after making and having tea. I took the opportunity of having an early night.

On the Sunday, I did as usual all the cooking and the clearing up. I must hand it to him, though, he did offer to take me out to lunch. He did not seem to appreciate the state I was in, so I completely scotched that idea.

I could not hold a knife and fork without shaking, and did not want to embarrass myself in public. We went out in the afternoon for a walk. I chose the walk that I took Shassie on. I was actually left in peace early on the Monday morning, and I will state I did receive a cup of tea in bed. I'm surprised he could put himself out for me.

Chapter 23

What do I do about *her?* What do I do about **him?** I expect you are wondering why I keep on bothering with him. There is of course our outstanding claim for that rotten holiday. Or is it because this was the first man who took an interest in me as a person for some time? Or is it I no longer have the strength of character or confidence, or guts to tell him that I can no longer tolerate being used or abused in the way he has been treating me.

I was terrified about *her.* What was *she* going to do next? Would I never feel safe? I had to ascertain why *she* came, why at that particular time of day, why without any prior warning. Did *she* think *she* could catch me out, and put pressure on the management to make me come back to work? *She* had managed it in the past. But the Welfare Officer had seen me. She knew the state I was in.

I decided to ring Dee. She also has *her* as her H.E.O. Perhaps she can find out for me. It transpired she wanted to know if I could do work at home. How on earth it was to get to me, heaven only knows. Did *she* think I could drive into Maidstone a distance of some 25 miles and collect it, and return it when I had done it? I was not driving, I still did not want to. Although I had been advised not to. They employ a driver and he could deliver and collect when convenient. Yes convenient for him or them, but not convenient for me. Dee was very angry. She informed *her* I was off sick, and it should be left that way.

After Dee had informed me, I was even more scared and frightened. What was going to be the outcome of it? I decided to communicate with the Welfare Officer. She had been very kind, considerate and thoughtful. She was also very angry about the visitation and the reason for it.

She suggested that I write to *her* saying my health was in such a state I could not cope with having any visits unless previously arranged. This enabled me then to call off any, if any visits had been agreed. Why could I not come to this conclusion? I managed to pen a letter after several abortive attempts. The writing was all over the place as my hand was shaking, and there were tear splodges on it as I was crying at the same time. I never did find out how it was received. I never had a reply.

I wonder why my H.E.O. had telephoned me, in September, after I returned from the Health Farm. Had *she* pounded on his desk insisting he make me return to work, as in *her* estimation there was nothing wrong with me? He obviously knew better and just suggested the visit by the Welfare Officer.

My moggy, who was now 15 years of age, was due to have her booster injections. She goes by the name of 'Calam'. This name derived from a show I did whilst with the Maidstone Operatic Company. The show – 'Calamity Jane'. I thought that she would be living with a walking disaster so I would name her after one.

How was I going to get her to the vets'? I could not drive, neither could I carry her. I asked Chris if she could take me, and if convenient, when would it be possible? She suggested the Saturday.

In the post, on this day was a letter from the Gas Board. Oh hell, what do they want? I'm up to date with my payments, as I pay by standing order. It's been going out each and every month. I've checked my bank statement.

They wanted to change the way I pay to direct debits. Oh no. I don't like direct debits. I don't trust direct debits. I lose control over my account. It goes to someone I don't know, I don't trust. Oh why can't they let me carry on paying the way I was? What's wrong with the way I pay? They are still getting the money. I got very worked up about this. I was extremely upset. I tried to control it. Bundled up the cat in her box and carried her over to Chris's.

Chris knew immediately there was something wrong. I could not hold back anymore and just burst out crying. Is this really the behaviour of once a very strong-minded, independent woman? Is this normal? Surely there is something wrong with me? I'm not imagining all this uncontrollable emotion – am I?

Both Chris and Ollie were a tower of strength. Chris took complete charge of the situation, bundled me into the car and drove to the vets'.

She came in with me. I could not handle the situation. Everyone thought there was something seriously wrong with my pussy cat. She was only having her booster.

Afterwards, Chris then drove me home, and put the cat in my house, and then proceeded to make a cup of tea. I started to feel much better. The letter from the Gas Board went into the bin. If they don't like the way I'm paying – tough.

Out on my walks with Shassie each and every afternoon I started to notice some very strange sensations. I put my right foot down on the path only to fall flat on my face. That hurts. The ground was not where I thought it was. I had to put my foot further down, and then it made contact with the path. Something was very amiss with my co-ordination.

Shassie always seemed to know when I was not very well. She seemed to sense something was wrong. On these occasions she would not leave my side. I took the lead off her, hoping she would get a run, because if she stayed with me, she would not get any exercise. But she would not!

I was having a great deal of difficulty, during one afternoon, in seeing. It was terrifying. My vision was all blurred. I could not focus. What's happening to me? Surely there is something the matter with me? Why don't the tests reveal something?

I had to cut the walk severely short. I saw a man out with his dog and nearly asked him for help. I did not. I was frightened that he would not believe me. Scared he might think I'm trying to pull a fast one. Scared he might take advantage of me. I was not carrying any identification.

I managed to stumble through, until I reached the recreation ground, and then trudged back to Chris's, where she found me lying down on the sofa in the lounge when she came in from work. Shassie was by my side. I'm sure that dog is psychic.

During the afternoon of one of my walks, I was scared to death. I was minding my own business, thinking about nothing in particular, just about to enter the pear orchard, when suddenly there was a 'whoosh' and a long-haired type of Alsatian dog was glaring at me. I immediately thought, 'Oh shit, it's going to attack Shassie'.

I screamed, and started to shake in my whole body uncontrollably. I was also crying my eyes out.

Obviously the dog's owner heard me and came upon the scene in a rush. There she saw her dog just standing there looking, and mine, also just standing there looking, and me in this uncontrollable state.

She wondered what on earth was wrong. I still had no identification; neither did I have a tissue. I had not encountered this situation before. She gave me her spare tissue, clean, and helped calm me down.

I said, "I'm sorry, but I'm trying to get over a nervous breakdown, I've never reacted like this before."

She was really very worried about me. Her dog, Tara, was completely bemused with this. 'What the hell is that stupid woman playing at?', Tara must have thought. Shassie was probably thinking, 'Oh my god she's gone off her rocker'.

The lady told me that her name was Jan and she was a housekeeper for one of the large houses nearby. Although I tried to convince her I was all right, and I was not having a fit, I don't think she was convinced. We parted after some time, and I hoped that I would see her again. I wanted to convince her I was all right.

Why did I say I was getting over a nervous breakdown? Nobody had said this in the past. The neurologist had not confirmed this. If this was indeed the case why was I not getting any better? I had been away from that environment [you remember, work] since the end of June. The pressure was off me. I should be improving, but I'm not!

Chapter 24

I was now carrying identification with me, in the form of my driving licence. I'm one of the lucky ones who can use this for ID purposes.

What would have been the scenario for someone in my position, health wise, but did not drive? What on earth could they carry as identification? No point in having your credit card that does not say anything other than the name. Does not give an address, or a telephone number. If something was to happen could the help be trusted not to take advantage.

The Civil liberty groups are so concerned with protecting the rights of ne'er-do-wells, etc., they forget the rights of the ordinary law abiding citizen. It would make life so much simpler if there was an identification card. For people in my situation it would be a godsend.

I was also carrying my stick with me wherever I went.

I now met other people out on my walk. Fortunately I did not embarrass myself in the same way as when I met Jan. A dog is a great leveller for starting a conversation. Why do they always have to smell each other's bums? It really is so grotesque. Shassie seemed to get on with any dog she met, irrespective of whether it was male or female.

One such dog she always managed to run into the ground was a bloody great big Briard. I have never managed to ascertain the owner's name, but the dog's is Hudson, or Huddie. He always tries to keep up with Shassie, but fails every time.

Huddie is a likened to a rather large lolloping camel. Shassie manages to change direction very suddenly at the last minute. Huddie just carries on coming and bowls over anything in his way. Usually me. He tries to put the brakes on, but his rear end slews out of control and skids generally into me. I usually end up on the floor. I fall over very easily now.

The owner is most apologetic, and tries to help me up, but I'm laughing so much, in the mud, that he ends up in the mud as well. Huddie, fortunately for the owner, is now well and truly worn out, to say nothing for the respective owners.

Another lady I have met has a Boxer, called Poppy. Very timid and shy, and stays with her owner all the time. Marcus is an English Setter, who takes a similar walk with his owner to me.

It was now a month since Duncan had left. I wondered if he would ring.

The time was fast approaching for the Scottish Open. [Badminton Tournament, needless to say.] We had both been asked to assist. The invitation occurred whilst we were at Glasgow for the World Team Championships in February of that year. There was no chance of me going. I could not get there. Could not drive. Had lost my confidence to take myself off out of my area.

He rang me on the Friday evening. The entire Scottish contingent was asking how I was, apparently. He had to ring. He did not know. He had not been in touch for a month. So how the hell would he know? I just said I was okay. I'm not the sort to whine and moan about any ache or pain I may have. Or how I was coping. He then promised to ring me on the Saturday. I stayed in the whole of the weekend, waiting for this, what transpired, non-existent phone call.

Mum was becoming concerned as I had not heard when I was to have the final test. The lumbar puncture. I had asked in August to take a month off from tests, it seemed a bloody long month. She managed to ascertain I was due to go into Haywards Heath Hospital on the 2nd December.

I needed a new bag of cat food. I did not know how I would react to the minor operation, neither did I know when I would be fit enough to return home.

The pet food shop in Tenterden delivers free of charge to my area, fortunately. All I had to do was get myself to the shop. Easier said than done. It is as far down Tenterden High Street as you can imagine. A long walk. Yes I can still walk, but it is not easy after I have swum, and when I'm carrying my swimming bag. My bag always seemed heavier after I had swum, I don't know why. Having purchased the sack, and on my way home I encountered a man using a walking stick, seeking donations for his charity tin.

"You're a cripple, just like me," He said.

I blew my stack. How dare he refer to me as a cripple? I never look upon myself as one. I told him exactly what I thought of him. I was not very polite and finished with, "I bet I can out swim you though."

Also, as I was crossing on the pedestrian crossing the little green man goes out. What do I do? Do I carry on walking? Do I stop and turn round and return from whence I came? Or do I just stand there in the middle of the road? I decide to carry on. I get hooted at to hurry up.

"Arrogant git," I call after the driver, giving him the 'V' sign.

A fellow pedestrian heard me and said, "I heard that."

"What do you expect, he's a man." .

Why does the little green man always go out when you are only half way across the road?

The Tenterden area was now in the grip of the autumn weather. It was very wet. I think it rained nearly every afternoon. It seemed to know when I was going out with Shassie, and waited, and then the heavens opened. Still it did not deter me. I still went out for my walk. Sod the weather, I thought.

I did not possess a waterproof jacket, but I had the next best thing. I was not going to get wet; neither was I going to get cold. I donned my sailing coat and wellies. If it's good enough for the 'roaring forties' or the 'screaming fifties' then it is good enough for a wet Autumnal/Winter afternoon in England.

It is bright orange with reflective rings round the sleeves. I was not going to be missed in the gloom. Everyone was going to see me coming. When it started to get really cold I then placed my sailing hat on my head, which clashes vehemently with the colour of my coat. I don't care what I look like; at least I'm warm and dry. Ollie was surprised and pleased that I had been able to get out with Shassie, because it saved him getting wet and cold in the dark.

When I collected Shassie, she was always beautifully clean and golden. When I returned she was wet, black, muddy, and smelly [because she always managed to find something to roll in]. What would Chris say? Would she be cross? I invariably thought Chris might get angry. She never did though. Even when Shassie miscued shaking herself and specks of mud landed on Chris's clean washing. I tried to steer her away from shaking near the washing, but sometimes she was quicker than me. Now that's not difficult.

Chapter 25

I was not, I repeat not, going to ring Duncan to inform him I was going into hospital for the final test. I wanted to see if he would notice I was missing from home. He had not bothered to communicate with me since the Friday of the Scottish Open. This was now a fortnight ago. Why should I? He knew I was waiting for a hospital appointment. He should have been more thoughtful. He knew what Val had said in June, just before I had my final blackout. He must have conveniently forgotten. Or, did I not count anymore. Or was it that as I could no longer do what he wanted when he wanted, I was of no use anymore? I could no longer drive, at least not for the time being. I don't know if I'll ever be able to get behind the wheel. Would I ever have the confidence again?

Mum, had a very early start on the 2nd December. I had to be at the hospital by 09.00 hours. She did not want to pick me up on the day before, as I would not have been able to take Shassie out for her final walk. I did not know when I would be able to pick up the threads again, of swimming, and looking after, or should I say Shassie looking after me.

Upon our arrival I had to complete a form. I could not do this. My hand was shaking so much I could not hold a pen. Mum had to complete all the rudimentary bureaucratic nonsense. It seems that wherever you go and whatever you do there are always forms to fill in. Is it not possible to do something or go somewhere without the need for a form?

After my admission, Mum went home.

I then had to start the tests. 'Yuk'.

First off, were my eyes. I had to stare at a screen which flashed black and white square images which were flashing at various intervals. This really gives you a very muzzy head. If I thought that head was bad, I had worse to come.

I was sitting in my room when the nurse came in and spoke about what was to happen next. She was very kind, and quiet, but I could not hold back the emotion anymore. I completely broke down. What the hell is wrong with me? This is not normal? Or is it? Perhaps I am going mad? I don't know? It took about 45 minutes for me to get control of myself.

The doctor who was to perform this piece 'needle pulling' asked if I minded if a team of students watched.

I told her yes I did mind.

Normally, I wouldn't have cared in the slightest who watched, but not on this particular day. Where did I get the strength of character to say this? Perhaps there is still something there? I don't know?

I had to sit on the side of the bed, with my legs dangling over the side, and lean forward. This is not easy when you suffer with dizzy spells, but at least mine are not serious, but they are to me. She then injected a local anaesthetic in the lumbar region of my spine.

A lumbar puncture is where a certain amount of fluid is extracted from the spinal column. Having produced the syringe to make the extraction, she then stuck it into my back. But it would not go. Because of all the sport I had done in the past, together with my swimming, the strength of the muscle tone prevented the syringe from going in far enough. She then had to have a second attempt in a different place. Again more local anaesthetic. This time it was successful. It worked. The fluid extracted was clear. So far, so good. This meant that there was no infection in the spine, in the ordinary course of events.

I then had more blood taken out of my arm. Pin cushion again I thought.

After all this activity, then comes the boring bit. You have to lie down. When they say lie down and rest, they mean it! Also, water has to be drunk constantly. This is to help put back the liquid lost.

Then the headaches start. Every time you move or get up even slightly, it pounds. Really pounds. It feels as if the inside of the head is at loggerheads with everything. It is having a bloody big row with everyone and everything. 15 rounds in a World Boxing Heavyweight bout does not compare with anything like the headaches from a lumbar puncture. Frank Bruno has nothing compared to this!

My parents were allowed to take me home [to their home, I was in no fit state to look after myself] on the same day. I pointed out the doctor who performed this piece of masochism, and Dad was surprised that she looked so young. Nothing more than a schoolgirl he thought.

I was able to lie down on the back seat of the car. I could not sit up. Could not wear the seat belt. I'm glad we did not get stopped by the police, as I was breaking the law.

The next few days were hell. Sheer hell. I could not move without getting a pounding head. Although I was drinking plenty of water. Perhaps that's the reason why there was a water shortage this summer.

All the patients who had had lumbar punctures were drinking the reservoirs dry.

I wanted a bath or a shower. How could this be possible with the battle that was going on inside my head? Mum had to run my bath for me. Fancy having this to do for a grown woman. I know she did it for me when I was a baby, but I'm not one now. Am I? I'm nearly 40. Still it was something I needed, and Mum did not seem to mind. I did, though! Having the bath was sheer bliss, until I had to get out. Hell, that bloody head of mine. I'm beginning to get really pissed off with this. Will it never abate? I refused to take pain killers, of any description. I don't like them. They can become addictive. I wanted to be aware of the pain, so that I would not do anything to jeopardise my recovery. I managed to persevere.

After about 10 days of this, I was able to go home. The moggy had been with me all the time. I think she was now getting used to being put in her box and travelling. She hates the box, and miaoooooooows all the time until she is let out.

Although I was still suffering from headaches, they were bearable. I could cope with them.

On the journey home, I was on the back seat, trying to ignore the cat. You become oblivious to this row after a while. At least I used to be, but not on this particular afternoon.

As it was a Sunday, I thought I could try and have a swim in the morning, and take Shassie out. I wanted to get back to my normal routine.

During the journey I noticed I was becoming very nauseous. Would I be able to hang on until I got home? Oh bugger, life is now becoming extremely difficult. Would I ever get back to my old ways and habits?

Fortunately for me, Mum stopped at a local fruit farm for some apples, and my system then started to settle down. We only had about another 15-20 minutes to go. I desperately wanted to hang on. I wanted to go home. I wanted my independence again.

We made it. I did not embarrass anyone. I lasted. I did not vomit anywhere, or anyhow. Thank God.

Mum and Dad settled me indoors, and then left, after having a cup of tea. Yes, I can still do that small task.

I wanted to let Chris know I could take Shassie out the following afternoon. How would she react? Would Shassie sulk? My cat does, after having been in a cattery. Chris wondered how I was. She could tell I was not right, as I was still very white. I had no colour in my cheeks. I need not have worried, she was happy for me to take Shassie out.

The next thing, what about the dog. She had missed her walks. She came bounding up to me wagging everything as if I was her long lost friend. She knew I was back in the fold, and prepared for our exercise.

Ollie, I learned had had a lumbar puncture sometime before, so we spent some time comparing notes. His headaches only lasted for about 3 days. I was still suffering from them for some 3 weeks later.

Chapter 26

Christmas was looming. The season of Peace and Goodwill to all men was nearly upon us. I neither felt at peace, nor did I feel any goodwill. Especially to *her* or to *him*. *She* was still worrying me. I had received no response to my letter. How had it been received? Need I still be worried about *her.* The office knew I had been in hospital for the final test. I had kept them informed of everything that was going on. *She* was probably of the opinion there was nothing wrong and that I was faking it all. Was I? Did I imagine all the odd sensations that were going on in the body? Did I fake the blackouts?

He was still unaware I had been missing from home. *He* still had not rung since the Friday of the Scottish Open. Good job I did not stay in waiting for the telephone call as promised after that weekend. Why make these promises if they not going to be kept? Surely he could have put himself out to ring when he arrived home? Did I not count anymore? Was I that much of a useless lump now?

Mum had asked if *he* was coming down for Christmas. How the hell do I know, *he* has not rung. *He* has not said what *he* is doing. Mum wanted to know if she should bother with a Christmas present for *him*, as she had done the previous year. I said it was up to her, but I was not going to put myself out. I was not even going to send him a card. If *he* can't be bothered then neither can I. Was I right to think like that? Should I have been more accommodating?

I managed to write my Christmas cards but only to the people who really mattered. I really could not be bothered. Oh hell, what do I do about presents? It means having to think, it means having to put myself out. It means I'm going to have to ask someone to take me. More loss of independence. This really brings home to you how vulnerable you become when you realise just how much you were able to do yourself, and how you just took life for granted.

I hoped Diana and Dave would understand, if I could not get them anything. Chris's family were easy. It was a large tin of 'Roses Chocolates', which were Chris's favourite. I managed to purchase an ornamental clock for my parents from the local jewellers'. I still had others to buy. I did not have the energy to traipse round Tenterden High Street, trying to get ideas.

As end of term was fast approaching for both Chris and her two children, Kirsty and Steven, I wondered if I could accompany them on one of their expeditions to the Sava Centre, at Hempstead Valley, Gillingham. There are a great variety of shops all under the one roof, so I would not need to have to wonder far. Chris was all smiles at this suggestion and informed me when they would be going. I hoped I would not embarrass anyone over my nausea whilst travelling in a car. I still felt very ashamed of this feeling. I had never suffered like this in the past. I have sailed in 40 foot yachts across the English Channel and the North Sea and not turned a hair when the wind was blowing at Force 9 or sometimes 10. Why should I feel like this in a car ? Was it the effect of the lumbar puncture?

All the people who I had met out with their dogs were very concerned about my state of health. They all noticed that there was still no colour in the face, and wondered if I was okay. I informed them what had happened, and they all understood. It took me about a week before I was able to partake of my proper walk. During this first week at home, Shassie had to be content with the large open field at the back of my house. I could not manage any more, neither could I go any further.

Whilst out on my normal trudge, I bumped into Jan. She was out with Tara. We were both pleased to see one another. I wondered if she would want to know me, after my disgraceful and embarrassing behaviour when she first met me. I need not have worried.

We quickly picked up a rapport, and fell into step, and completed the walk together. Tara and Shassie became firm friends. Chasing each other around the orchards. Both trying to outrun one another.

Tara, I ascertained was a long haired, Belgian Shepherd dog. She tried to treat Shassie as if she was rounding her up. Shassie just ignored her and sat on the ground, whilst Tara tried to creep up on her and herd her as if she was a flock of sheep. When Tara was nearly upon her, she then set off, in full gallop, with Tara close behind.

Jan and I discussed our first fateful meeting. I tried to apologise, but Jan just said not to worry. She did tell me that she was very worried about me, and hoped she would see me again. Her first reaction when she heard my scream was that Tara had attacked someone or something. She knew it was not possible, as, although Tara is very vocal, she would not attack anyone.

She does however have a liking for wheels, and will attack cars, but there was no car in the area. Neither had she heard one. Jan was perplexed until she saw the scene in front of her. Bob her husband, was equally worried as Jan was very upset by our previous encounter. They did not know who I was, or where I lived, so they could not assure themselves that I was okay.

We both then realised we took the same walk, and it was generally at the same time in the afternoon. We arranged to meet whenever we could, as Jan was exercising her employer's dog, and had to fit in her walks with her duties at the house.

On one such occasion, I was still feeling very vulnerable and unsure of myself, when we were approached by one of the builders to the new housing estate.

Part of the scrub land had been sold off for development. More green areas going under concrete.

When will it stop? Is not Tenterden crowded enough as it is? The schools and the local amenities cannot cope now. I suppose it will mean more flooding, as water will not soak into concrete.

The man was very abrupt with us, and ticked us off for walking where we were. There were no signs up. How are we supposed to know? Are we mind readers? I always wished I was when I was in *that place*. I asked where we could walk, and he informed us in a very brusque abrupt manner to use the official footpath.

This is private property he informed us. I was very angry. Jan could see I was about to erupt, and steered us away from him. I wanted to lash out at him. How dare he treat us as if we are a couple of stupid little schoolchildren. I had had enough of being spoken to as if I was an idiot. I was being paid for that. I had had 10 years or so of that. I thought I was now away from that sort of environment, but I was wrong.

Jan was so kind and helpful, she could see I was beginning to shake, but managed to defuse the situation before it got out of hand.

When I returned from my walks to Chris's house I always made myself a cup of tea, and tried to towel Shassie down. What a mess I was now bringing her home in. She always thought this was a game, and tried to wonder around the kitchen with me following, but having to give up as a complete total failure.

I never left Shassie on her own. She was beginning to get used to having company all afternoon. What could I do in a strange house until the family came home?

I found the previous weekend's Sunday paper and read that. I noticed in one of the supplements there was an advertisement from an American organisation based in Hawaii, for English ladies to become pen friends to American gentlemen. I took the bull by the horns and wrote off, sending in brief details about my interest's hobbies, and work. I did not know what to expect.

Duncan, I now regarded as my 'ex'. Jan had asked if there was anyone close to me apart from my parents, and I told her of the saga of Duncan. She could not believe his attitude. I said the best thing about him was his dog Lucy the Bearded Collie.

Duncan had managed to put himself out on my behalf. This must have been a first. He had sent me a Christmas card. It was not posted from Glasgow, so he must have returned from there. Last thing I knew, was that was where he was. When he returned home your guess is as good as mine. Was he trying to make me feel guilty because I had not bothered? It would not work. I had had enough.

Officialdom was rearing its ugly head. More bloody forms. The Personnel Department had sent me a claim for Invalidity Benefit as I was going onto half pay in the New Year. I could not handle this. I had to take it to my parents and get them to complete it. There was so much information required, but my immediate reaction was I

151

was going to lose my house, because I could not keep up the payments on the mortgage. Not only had *those bastards* taken away my sanity, but they had taken away my house as well. Would it never end?

I spent Christmas with my parents. They picked me up on the 24th, and I returned on the 28th. We had a very quiet time. I did not add to the jollification, as I could not get in the mood. I felt guilty over this. There was nothing I could do. I felt it was a waste of time, and Christmas for that year should be banned.

Shassie & Tara

Chapter 27

A New Year should herald a new beginning. Will it be for me? Will 1995 be an improvement? It certainly could not be much worse. Could it? I never stay up New Year's Eve, it is just another night. It seems such a waste of time to stay awake till just gone midnight, just to be able to say I've seen the New Year in. A new century is different. This only happens every 100 years, so I may celebrate this turning point. Call me an old stick in the mud if you like, I don't mind, nor care.

My parents came up on New Year's Day. They had been round to their local D.S.S office and obtained yet more forms for me to fill in. Why is this country so obsessed with forms? It seems there are forms for everything except wiping your nose, and going to the loo. Perhaps these two simple tasks will also have to be covered by forms to be completed in quadruplet!

They completed them for me, and I managed to sign. I was still having difficulties in holding a pen steady. Surely there is something wrong with me? Surely it is not normal to shake uncontrollably? Surely I should be able to walk without looking as if I was 3 sheets to the wind? [Drunk]. Surely I should be able to have control of my emotions? I wonder if the latest test will reveal anything. I hope so. The results are still not through yet. I suppose it's been held up by the Christmas and New Year holiday.

On the 4th of January 1995, surprise, surprise, I had a telephone call from *DUNCAN*. I'm surprised he even remembered I existed.

"Hello there" he commences, all bright and breezy.

"Long time, no hear," I reply, continuing "Is this the promised call from the Saturday of the Scottish open, of which I'm still waiting for. It has now been 7 weeks since then. Did you realise that I stayed in the whole of that weekend waiting for your supposed call, I could have gone out, but I said that I was waiting for a call from Duncan, as he promised to call, what's the matter with you, is it impossible for you to ring, do you find the time so pressing that you can't spare five minutes, or is it that picking up shuttles, moving the odd chair, or pressing the odd button more important."

He replies, "You go to bed so early that I don't want to disturb you."

"Is this your way of trying to put the blame on me, you know full well that I'll answer the phone till 21.00 hours" [9 p.m.] "so that excuse won't wash, it's funny that my friends can always contact me, my parents can always manage it, so why can't you?"

He retorts, "You are always out."

"Admittedly I'm out from 08.00 to about 11.00 then from about 14.00 to 17.00, but what about the rest of the time, there are 24 hours in the day you know, you really don't care, I'm not worth anything anymore, am I? I'm just a useless lump now, aren't I?"

"No you're not, and I do care."

"You have a very peculiar way of showing it – you don't ring when you say you are going to, you let me down at the last minute on the one thing that I wanted to do, you treat me as a non-entity, and think you can come and go as you like."

"Well, I've had this pain in my big toe."

"Oh bloody hell, are you now trying to tell me that you use your foot to dial the phone, I know there are some people who have to, but you're not one of them, I've now heard everything."

"No I'm not saying that, its' this arthritis."

"I thought you would come up with an excuse, you don't even know that I've been missing from my home for nearly three weeks, do you?"

"Oh have you been in hospital then?"

"Of course I've been in hospital, I've had the lumbar puncture, and that has no comparison with the little pain in your big toe, I've also been to my parents for Christmas, fat lot you care though."

"Oh have you had the result then, oh by the way I've given the old man his Christmas present and I signed it from both of us."

"No I have not."

I then inquired if there was any further progress on our claim [re the holiday], and was informed there was not as it seemed some of the letters had gone astray in the post.

He was full of apology, and kept repeating he was sorry. Would it have any bearing on him? I wished him well [why, I don't know], and wished him a happy New Year [why, I don't know]. Then put the phone down. As it was coming up for my birthday, I wondered if he would remember, or that it was a special one [my 40th] and whether anything I had said on the phone would 'sink' in. I very much doubt it though.

Chapter 28

Where did I get the strength of character from to speak to Duncan like that? Perhaps its' still there? I've let him walk all over me in the past. Was it, enough is enough? Or, was I still seething as he had let me down in October, on the one thing I so desperately wanted to do? The fact he could not put himself out for me. Also, his insensitive behaviour later on in that month.

Am I now the sort of person who will take so much, then turn, and frighten those nearest to me? On my walks I thought about his behaviour constantly, and about my reactions. I generally came to the same conclusion, that no wonder his wife went off with another man if he treated her in the same lackadaisical contemptuous manner he treated me. Oh, I wish I had the guts to tell him that. Perhaps that might knock some sense into him.

My walks were a great help to me. They enabled me to dissipate my anger. There was a lot stored up inside. It had to come out somehow. All those years of abuse in *that place,* and the insensitive, uncaring, thoughtless behaviour of Duncan. My swimming helped, but of course there is only so much I can do in the pool. I am still unable to swim anything like the amount I could do before all this started.

I wanted to do something special for my birthday. It was my 40th. A turning point in anyone's life. I did not want a party.

I always remembered my 30th. Oh that was hell. I was playing in a badminton match, in a very cold heat free hall. The only place where there was any warmth was in the kitchen, and that was because the home team left the oven door open whilst it was switched on.

Apart from my usual white kit, I also had on two track suits, two pairs of socks, two scarves, a coat, and a pair of sheepskin gloves. I was still frozen. I felt like the 'Michelin' man.

To be official on court, we were supposed to strip down to our whites. Yes, this was a league match, afterall. There was absolutely no way, I was taking off all my layers. I did condescend to remove my coat, scarves and gloves, but that was all.

It was a one court hall, so we were in for a long night. I had to have some semblance of movement. My partner worked 'his socks off'. He played so well, I don't know whether it was the cold, or the fact that I was playing so badly. I could not move, I could not hit this stupid shuttle, and to add insult to injury I got cross. My so called play deteriorated to such a degree, I thought that as I was now 30, I was past it, over the hill. On the downward slope to oblivion.

Therefore with the approaching day, I knew I needed something different.

My parents had booked us all in to the health farm at Henlow Grange. Dad tried to make out he wanted to go, by getting his things together, but really he was only coming to keep us company, and because it was my birthday.

We arrived on the 15th January after having gorged ourselves on pizzas, because Dad was convinced he would not get anything further to eat for a week.

After settling ourselves in, we each had our medical, then the fun started. It was the same package as before, and Dad found that he did enjoy the massages, but Mum was ill at ease with her treatments. She did not feel the benefits that Dad and I both felt.

Dad hates the water, hates swimming, or I should say, hates anything to do with exercise, so we [Mum and I] had to chivvy him up to come in. He could touch the bottom of the pool wherever he went, so he would never be out of his depth. He has this habit, of getting into the pool and gently moving around for about five minutes then gets out. He did however spend quite a lot of time in the whirlpool, he seemed to enjoy this. Mum swam for about 30 minutes and managed at the end of the week about 30 lengths. Me, I was doing the usual. Length, after length, after length. I don't know where I get my love for sport or exercise from, it certainly is not from my parents.

I was spending more and more time in the gym. I wanted to get fit. I wanted to try and stop this excessive feeling of tiredness. I was now battling with the rowing machine. I was having a race with the computer. Could I beat the computerised rower? I set the machine at level 3 for 12 minutes. I had never used one of these machines before, so did not know what to expect. I thrashed him.

The machine informed me to use a higher setting, so I did. Level 6. Again I thrashed him. Am I too strong for the machine? Or is it programmed at a lower level? It was not until the Friday that it beat me. This setting was on Level 15, again for 12 minutes. The time was best for aerobic training. Level 15 was described by the machine as Olympic standard. There must be something wrong, I'm never an Olympic rower. Well, if the machine was to be believed, Mum and Dad now had an Olympic standard rower in the family. The machine had to be programmed at a lower rate. There is no way that a complete novice like me, in my state of health can be that standard.

Dad was pleasantly surprised with the food. Although he could not get his steamed puddings, or apple pie and custard, or spotted Dick, [Mum does not cook these at home, as they are stodgy], but Dad always asks for them when he has meals out. There was ample for everybody, and it was, as one would expect wholesome and nutritious. Dad found he was not hungry at all. This dispelled the myth that all you got to eat was a lettuce leaf and carrot juice.

Mum and Dad found it strange whilst reading the menu, instead of the price list written on the far right hand side, there was the calorie count for each dish. If any guest wanted to follow the diet they could by selecting only those items with the least amount of calories. There was always a choice of two or three dishes for each course.

Mum and Dad both took the opportunity to have a fitness assessment. They were both informed that for their age they were remarkably fit. This came as a complete surprise for Dad because of his abhorrence for any exercise, but I think secretly Mum makes him do some, although he may not realise it.

At the end of the week, I think we all benefited from the rest, relaxation, recuperation, good food, treatments, and exercise. The exercise Instructors, although young, managed to strike a balance with the clientele that were present during the week.

Chapter 29

Chris, Ollie, and Joyce looked after my house, and pussy cat between them. All my post was piled in the lounge, and there was not a thing from Duncan. He had forgotten again. I quite expected him to remember this year, not only having forgotten last year, but also what was said to him over the telephone. Why is he so inconsiderate, and thoughtless? Probably thinks it is not important, at least not to him!

I needed a challenge. I was not working, did not know if I would ever work again, did not know if I could participate in any of my old activities. I needed a purpose to carry on. I still did not feel any better. I had now been off work for over six months, surely there had to be an improvement of some sort, but there was not. Yes, I was swimming four days a week, and yes, I was walking Shassie, but after the life I used to lead, I needed something extra.

The perfect solution. At the pool I noticed there was a *'Swim Fit'* Challenge. It was split into three categories. To swim:-

[a] 22 miles for the Bronze Award.

[b] 44 miles for the Silver Award.

[c] 88 miles for the Gold Award.

This was not as you may be thinking in one go. Nobody in their right mind would swim 88 miles in one go. I may be crazy, but at least, I'm not that crazy. This was an accumulated process to be held during the whole of the year.

I knew it would not be worth my while to tackle the Bronze award, as this would have been completed in about 4 weeks. I needed something substantial. I enrolled for the Gold award. I had 12 months to tackle this, and as I was averaging about 64 lengths [roughly one mile] I thought it would be completed by about mid-June. It was entitled THE CHANNEL CHALLENGES.

The results of my last test were to hand. What would they reveal? Would they indicate there was something wrong with me? Would they prove I was not going insane? Both Mum and I were full of trepidation.

The consultant informed us, as Mum always came in with me, that the test revealed some antibodies. Imagine my relief, there was something wrong with me. What are they? He would not tell me. He just sat there, and said he wanted some more blood tests. I was beginning to get angry. I wanted to know what was wrong. He would not tell me. Was it life threatening? I did not know. All he kept saying was he needed some more blood tests. I was wondering if I would ever know what was wrong. I had to find out. I had every intention of finding out. I felt there had been enough blood taken out of my arm. Where was all this blood going? Surely they had done enough blood tests. He was not helpful, neither was he reassuring. There was something, but he would not tell me. Was it that serious that he could not, or would not tell me?

He wanted to start a course of Acupuncture. I had no idea where the needles would be stuck. I thought it would be in the back, as this is the area to relieve stress and tension, but I still did not know what was wrong. How could he start a course of treatment without the patient knowing what was wrong? I had to find out, and find out I was going to do, I didn't know how, but I was going to succeed.

An appointment was made for four weeks' time for the treatment to start. I did not relish this at all.

My surgery would have to write to me, upon hearing from the Consultant, to arrange the blood tests. I would find out then. Surely he would inform them of the results, and make the diagnosis. My Doctor would need to know what he has to deal with.

Again, another challenge beckoned. The pool were also taking part in the National Swimathon. Having competed in the event before both as an individual and a member of a team, I wondered if the centre was going to enter a team.

Vicky, one of the lifeguards indicated another lady who had expressed an interest. The centre was not as an entity going to enter a team. I spoke to the lady, whilst in the pool, and hoped she did not mind me interrupting her swim. She, like me, swims length after length after length, in the lane section. She told me her name was Jean Fagg, and yes she was interested in taking part.

I informed her of my plight, and said I would not be able to organise anything, but I could swim up to 100 lengths maximum, in one go. I had not achieved this target for some time, but hoped that if required, I could manage it. It was always a regular achievement before I went to work. If I could do it then, why not now?

Jean stated that 2 other ladies had also asked to take part, and yes she was prepared to organise the team. 4 ladies meant it would be 50 lengths each. Easily within each of our capabilities. She introduced me to the other two ladies who were both Margarets.

Chapter 30

Obviously, Duncan's non-relationship with me was now over. I had heard not a thing from him since that telephone call on the 4th January. My comments had as usual fallen upon deaf ears. Stony ground! He was now really showing himself for what he really was.

As I could no longer live life at the pace of life he wanted to lead, and, when he wanted, and, what he wanted, I was of no further use anymore. Egotistical, arrogant, selfish bastard. How does he know if I'll ever be able to lead a full life? Does he know something about my results' that I don't? I don't see how, he has not even bothered to ask if I've had the results' yet.

The National Championships [Badminton] would be played in Norwich during mid-February. How will he explain my absence? Will he tell them the truth? Will he tell them some cock and bull story? He does not know what is wrong with me, he has not been in touch. Oooooooooooh, I wish I could be a fly on the wall, to hear his feeble explanation. I hope I would not get swatted though. Racquet or otherwise.

Of course, after this weekend would be St. Valentine's Day. I had no intention of putting myself out, like I did last year. I was not going to waste my money on a present or a card, when he would be too busy, himself to bother about me.

Mum picked me up after my walk, on the 20th February.

I had met Jan that day, and expressed my misgivings about going to see the specialist. I was to have the first of a series of acupunctures. I hoped he did not want to do this more than on a monthly basis. I didn't think I could go through with it if it needed to be more frequent. Jan was very supportive, but I got the impression she would not relish the idea either.

Upon entering his office, [Mum refused to come in with me, she said she could not bear to see the needles go in], I had to sit facing the couch, and place my head on the pillow. Then it started. All these needles were inserted in the back of the neck. I don't know how many, but it seemed a lot. They hurt. I had to stay in that position for some time, then he pushed them even further in. This time it really hurt. I felt awful. Nauseous again. I thought I had lost that feeling, but it seemed to have come back to haunt me. I seemed to be in that position for ages, at least it seemed a long time. He then extracted them, and still refused to tell me what was wrong.

This treatment is supposed to relax you, I was anything but.

I was staying the night with my parents, and I missed my moggy. Missed the assurance of her on the bed. Missed her purrrrrrrring and snoring in my ear.

I felt very unsure of everything, not able to cope again. I thought I was beginning to get some of my self-assurance back, but I was wrong. I had a lousy night's sleep, and he wanted me to have that weekly. I could not. I would not.

Ohhhhhhhhhh hell I'm going backwards again. I had managed to make the appointment for a month's time as I said Mum could not pick me up each week, she could, but I needed some excuse. I would also miss my swim, and my walks, and I got far more pleasure and satisfaction from those than ever I did seeing the specialist. Was I wrong to put me first? Should I have thought more of the treatment than I did? How could I, I still did not know what was wrong?

The surgery still had not written, requesting my presence for the blood tests. I told the specialist, I had not yet been able to attend for them.

During the week that followed, a package arrives for me. It is in his handwriting. Duncan had actually managed to put something in the post for me. Belated birthday card perhaps, belated Valentine's Day card. Surely not. Upon opening it, it contains several programmes from the National Championships each signed by a number of the umpires, and line judges, wishing me a full and speedy recovery.

They wanted to see me back judging the lines again. He managed to do this for me. I was amazed. Surprised. Also in the parcel was a Valentine's Day card. Well, strike me down with a feather, he has found the time to put himself out for me. How has he managed it? How has he managed to find the time, especially with the pain in his big toe? He has completely forgotten my birthday this time, no feeble excuse will suffice now.

I have to break my commitment and ring him to thank him. I had to leave a message on his blasted answering machine. I contemplated how long it would be before he returns my call. It will be the swimathon soon, I wonder if I can get him to come down for it. Perhaps he can put himself out for me after all. Perhaps he would not let me down this time.

My car insurance was due for renewal, and as I was not happy with the quote, I shopped around for a better premium. I obtained a premium for about £150 less, with a company that dealt direct with the customer. As I had not been informed what was wrong I saw no point in informing them.

All during this difficult time only a handful of my friends bothered to keep in touch. Diana came round to see me at least once a month, she appreciated I was unable to drive, and therefore immobile.

Wendy Smith and Dee Moore from work rang and wrote letters and sent me cuttings of articles to assist.

Muriel Webb visited me at home and telephoned me, but best of all were Don and Peggy Webb. She always managed to ring at the right time. She seemed to have a sixth sense when I was feeling down. She could always tell by the tone of my voice. Although I said I was okay, she knew different, and managed to get out of me what was wrong. I could not do this with Mum as she was too emotionally involved. She was already worried, and I did not want to make matters worse.

The local Vicar had also visited on a couple of occasions. The first one, I disgraced myself. I felt awful. I could not stop crying neither could I stop shaking. It was so childish. During the second visit, however, I was in more control and he seemed pleased there had been an improvement but only slight.

I even summoned up the courage to go to Church again. This was on a Thursday morning, but it took so much out of me, I could not go very often. Even the simplest tasks, were extremely difficult.

When I summoned up enough courage to inform my other friends of my plight, all I received was I'll ring you. I'm still waiting to this day for those calls to be returned. It seems when the chips are down you really do find out who your true friends are. Obviously as I could no longer live life, as I had, and did not know if I ever would, then I was of no use to anyone anymore. I felt even more stupid, useless, and inadequate.

The letter from the surgery had now arrived, requesting my presence for more blood tests. This was my chance to ascertain what was wrong. Did I have the right to do so? It was my body after all. Surely I have every right to know what is wrong.

The patient is the first person to establish if the body was not functioning properly. Mine certainly was not. I had now been off work for some eight months, and I did not seem to be getting any better. I was still very tired, dizzy, clumsy, having to get up in the night several times to go to the loo, and the blurring of the vision. Surely this is more than what occurs in a nervous breakdown.

Whilst the nurse is completing the forms to be attached to the specimens I ask her to explain what is wrong. I told her I had had a diagnosis, but I did not understand it. [I hadn't mind you, so technically I lied, but I had to find out]

She said it was a mild form of Multiple Sclerosis. I did not appear at all flummoxed. This now explained a great deal.

She then went to check the tests required, on the blood sample as they were out of the ordinary. I then managed to have a quick look at the notes, as I have the ability of reading upside down. Years of practice in the Prosecution Department, made me proficient in this, so I suppose I should be thankful for them for something. I noticed the passage had been highlighted, and could see for myself. I felt that a ton weight had been lifted from my shoulders, I now could start sorting my life out. There is no redress on the nurse, I was only finding out for my peace of mind. Surely I had every right in doing so.

Chapter 31

Now I know what is wrong with me. Thank god for that. At least I know now. Perhaps I can at last start sorting my life out. But I still did not have it officially, I had to get the specialist to admit it. And admit it he was going to.

I had to tell Mum. I knew what the reaction would be. She would be even more worried. It was bad enough now, heaven only knows what it would be like after I let them know.

The Swimathon was coming up, so it had to be before then, and the leisure centre had to be informed. I knew all the lifeguards kept an eye on me whilst I was swimming, because they could see I was not well, and I was not attending at my usual hour in the morning. Also my team captain had to be informed.

Duncan still had not returned my call from February, so I had not the slightest idea what his reaction would be. He was uncaring and thoughtless, and all the other derogatory terms already, how on earth would he react?

I summoned up the courage and telephoned Mum. Informing her what the diagnosis was, but not enlightening her how I found out. I just said the surgery told me. On the surface Mum tried to keep her cool, but as I could not see her, I do not know how she reacted to the news. Badly I expect.

I had by now begun to dread the sound of the telephone. I always thought it might be him. Chris did not ring me as she was aware of my plight, but as I saw her most days, the need did not arise, thank goodness.

Late one evening the phone rings. It is Duncan. He never asks whether I've had the results, so I just tell him, in as blunt a fashion as I can think of. There is no help from that quarter. I tell him about the swim and when it is occurring, and he says he will come down. I did not believe him. He had let me down before, so why not again. I did not tell him my parents were coming, let him do some thinking for a change, as to how I'm going to get to and from the pool. He says he would stay in a local hotel overnight, so I would not need to worry.

On the 5th March, I had no idea if Duncan was coming. Or at what time? Did he want a meal? Should I get lunch for him? He just wouldn't tell me anything. I did not bother. If he can't be bothered, then why the hell should I?

At about 16.00 hours a taxi pulls up outside my house, and out steps Duncan. Yes he has come. Yes he has managed to put himself out for me. Better late than never I suppose. He comes in and tries to slobber all over me. I tell him to get off. I'm not interested. He says that he has not seen me for ages.

"Whose fault was that?" I counter

"Mine, I suppose."

"Damn right," I retort.

Still no mention of my birthday, or about my diagnosis. He attempts to enter the kitchen and make a cup of tea.

"I'm quite capable you know, I'm not completely stupid, and it is my kitchen."

He is all jumpy, and will not settle down. Upon drinking his tea he says, "Close your eyes."

"What the hell for?" I ask.

He repeats the question. I find this so childish, but I do as he asks. Whereupon he gives me two teddy bears, which he purchased from Glasgow whilst at the Scottish Open, and a little ornament which was my Christmas present. I hadn't bothered with him for Christmas, I had't known when, or if I would ever see him again. I am completely taken by surprise. How can I be angry? He always gives me presents, but is this to try to placate me. It doesn't work anymore. I will *not* be taken in this way anymore.

"What about my birthday?" I ask.

"Oh lord, have I forgotten?"

"Yes you bloody well have, and you knew that it was a special one, you knew I was 40 in mid-January."

"Oh I thought it was only your 39th."

"Like hell you did."

I left it there. If I hadn't asked him down for this weekend, I wonder when I would have received these items. Would they still be languishing in some cupboard of his?

Mum and Dad arrived, and they got the shock of their lives when they saw Duncan sitting there. I had no time to let them know Duncan was coming. I was unsure if he would turn up anyway.

Mum drives us all to the pool and we meet up with the rest of the team and report in. Jean had called the team 'The Early Birds', as we use the pool at the beginning of the day. The event starts, and Jean completes the first 50 lengths. I was the last one to swim as I was the quickest. We hoped we would complete the distance in under 2 hours 30 minutes. We did it in 2 hours 12 minutes 32 seconds. Very respectable.

I had set my own target of completing my 50 lengths in 25 minutes, equivalent of 30 seconds a length. I had always in the past managed 64 lengths in 35 minutes, but that was when I was fit. 100 lengths in just under 60 minutes, so why not 50 in 25 minutes. I failed, it took me 29 minutes 32 seconds. I had wanted to accelerate after 32 lengths, and asked the lap counter to let me know when I reached that point, but when he informed me there was nothing left in the tank. I could not get any quicker. Blast. I just kept plodding along at the same speed.

At the end of the event, Duncan asked us all out for a Chinese, but Mum and Dad declined stating they had to get home, as it was late. She really thought we should be left alone to try and sort out our differences. It would not work until he became a little more thoughtful.

After the meal he walks me home, then proceeds to walk to the hotel. That was the last I saw of him until I went to Switzerland for the World Badminton Championships on the 15th May, some 10 weeks later.

Chapter 32

I was again due to see the Specialist on 27th March. I would bide my time until then. He was going to admit it, I was going to make him.

I'm glad I let the lifeguards at the centre knew what was wrong, because I needed their help on the 24th March. I was still accumulating my lengths for the Challenge, and had so far completed 2690 out of a total of 5664 lengths.

On this particular day I should not have gone to the pool. I felt lousy. I still did not appreciate what was going wrong with the body. 1 could not co-ordinate properly, neither could I see, my vision was blurring. It took me just over 50 minutes to walk 400 yards. Hell, I can swim quicker than that.

I got in the pool and wished I hadn't. I found I could not swim. I did not know how to. I just about managed 10 lengths, please don't ask me how, but I think it was guts and determination, that saw me through, but when that went I was left with nothing. Oh god, what if I can't swim anymore? What if that really is the end? Vicky [the lifeguard] saw immediately something was wrong.

Jean and another chap [I never did find out his name] helped me out of the pool. I was scared. What if I really can't do it anymore? Have I lost that one small pleasure? The only sporting activity left, that I felt capable of. I was crying, I was shaking, and the more I tried to control myself the worse I became.

Vicky took me to the Jacuzzi where the bubbles helped to settle me down. Another lady then joined me in the bubbles together with her friend. She had asked Vicky if I had got M.S. Vicky confirmed her fears.

The lady introduces herself as Jan [no, not the doggy lady] and her friend as Jo. She tells me she has M.S. and we immediately start comparing our various symptoms. It helped, because here was another sufferer, I was not the freak that I thought I was. The conversation was very stilted, but she told me she tried to swim on Tuesdays and Fridays. She knew what having a bad day was, so did not press any further. Both she and her friend were very supportive, and left her telephone number at reception for me to collect on my way out.

I then tried to finish off my relaxation in the Health Suite, but all the time the same thought kept repeating itself:- *WHAT IF I CAN'T SWIM ANY MORE*? I was petrified over this. It kept going round and around my befuddled brain. To put it in a nutshell I was shit scared.

Next came the walk home. How can I make that? I've got to, I've no other way of getting home. It takes me over an hour. It is only a short trip of as I've said before 400 yards. The normal speed is 3 miles an hour, if

I can't manage 400 yards how am I going to take Shassie out. I was also due to meet Jan and Tara.

Her duties had now been increased with a puppy. A Golden Retriever by the name of Purdey. We always wondered if there would be any jealousy amongst Tara and Shassie, but they all seemed to get on. Purdey just looked a younger, longer haired version of Shassie. Whether she recognised anything in her, I don't know, but she could not keep up with the other two. I did not know where Jan lived, neither did I know her phone number, all we did was meet out on the walks.

Upon my arrival home after my abortive swim, I found resting on the front doormat a presentation of flowers. That's' all I need. I've not heard a word from him since 5th March, it is now the 24th, almost three weeks. I knew they were from Duncan, nobody else ever sent me flowers. Surely it would be cheaper for him to ring once a week, rather than waste his money on flowers. The card is inscribed with 'Just a token of my affection, Love Duncan'. Who does he think he is trying to kid? I did not appreciate them, neither did I want them, today of all days. I was still in a state, I can't swim anymore.

I've got to talk to someone. Who? I telephone Mum. I'm in a state, crying down the phone, stating I can't swim anymore. This is the only thing I manage to say. She says she would come up and join me on my walk. She would also meet Jan, Tara and Purdey for the first time.

Just as I'm leaving to collect Shassie, the phone rings. Oh, it's not Mum saying she can't make it, after all I thought. It is Duncan. Have I yet received the surprise.

"Yes, thank you," was all I managed.

"Oh, by the way I'm coming down tonight to see you."

I have to tell him that I'm not very well.

"Oh, all right then, I won't bother, I'll wait until you're hundred percent."

"Can't you get into your thick head that I never, ever, will be a hundred percent?"

I never gave him a chance to reply as I slammed the phone down. Oh, how can he be so insensitive. I can't swim anymore, and I'm obviously of no use to him anymore. He's only interested if I'm a hundred percent. If I had been mobile, I would have taken these blasted flowers to the local old peoples' hospital.

Jan is surprised to meet Mum, and wonders whatever is wrong. I try to blurt it out, but I can't, all I manage is 'I can't swim anymore'. She asks Mum if she has had to travel far, and realises it is some distance, it is on this day we swap telephone numbers and addresses. At least there is someone local, who will assist.

All through the weekend I'm thinking I can't swim anymore, what if I can't swim anymore, what am I going to do now? There is nothing left to me now. Why carry on? There is no point anymore. Duncan does not want to know. He wants me one hundred percent, not like I am now. I not only feel stupid, useless and inadequate, but now I actually am.

On the Monday morning, should I go to the pool. Should I try it? Should I see if I really can't swim? Should I find out one way or other? I don't know? I can't seem to make any decisions now.

I decide to go. There is only one way of finding out, and that is taking the courage to do so. But what if I can't? I make it to the pool, but whilst I'm changing, I'm still thinking I can't. What gave me the courage to try? I don't know? I was terrified, I was scared, I felt intimidated, and desperate. I got in the water and got out some 50 lengths later. I can still swim. Imagine my relief, I can still do it. It is still there. I felt euphoric. Everybody at the pool was glad of the outcome.

Chapter 33

Jan was surprised to see me on this particular Monday afternoon. She thought I had to see the specialist for my second acupuncture session. I was glad to say it had been cancelled. I did not want to go. It was now the following week. I suppose it's only putting off the inevitable.

She could tell by my demeanour I was better. She asked me how I got on in the pool, and I was as pleased as punch.

"I can still swim, I can still do it. I got in there and swam 50 lengths, why the hell I could not do it on Friday, I really don't know."

Again I apologised for my behaviour on Friday.

The dogs however did not realise they should not have seen each other on this particular day. They carried on as if they had not seen each other for weeks. They were all 'kissy / kissy'. If there was any water or mud, to roll in, it could be guaranteed Shassie and Purdey would find it. I don't know who led who on. They seemed to lead one another on. Tara could not understand this. She was not of the gun dog breed, so did not have a liking for water, or chasing after rabbits, squirrels, or even sticks.

Shassie finds a stick but does not realise it is dead, but tries to shake the life out of it, then demolishes it.

Tara being long haired but with a fine coat, manages to come home in a worse state than the other two. Her undercarriage is congested with bits of twigs and mud. Jan has a difficult time when they get home, in cleaning her off. Purdey on the other hand, although long haired has an oilier coat and the dirt just seems to fall off, but that does not account for the smell sometimes, as she manages to locate the dirtiest and the smelliest water/mud to roll in.

Jan, Shassie, Tara & Purdey

Whilst all this is going on we are continuing our walk, and Jan informs me that her brother's parents in law both have multiple sclerosis. The father who is now in a wheel chair has had the disease for many years but the mother only for a short time. Although they both have it, it has attacked each of them differently. Not one M.S. sufferer is the same. The symptoms may be similar, but the source, of where the nerves have been attacked, can all be different. I was slowly beginning to learn what was going on in the body.

On the Tuesday, I again went to the pool, but not in the same state as the day before, and managed 60 lengths. This is the distance of 1500 metres. Whilst relaxing in the Jacuzzi, Jan and her friend Jo came in. They saw me immediately, and came over and spoke. They could see I was okay, and I explained I could still swim having managed 50 lengths the day before. I apologised for my behaviour on the Friday, but they both understood that I had no control of events, or of my emotions.

I asked Jan who her Specialist was and she told me. It transpired we both had the same. I asked her what she thought of him, and her opinion was the same as mine. 'Not a lot'. I wondered if it was me, and she wondered if it was her, but being of a similar nature, we both came to the conclusion it was him. He never advises you, just sits there doing all the relevant tests and will not communicate. We both feel we are stuck.

I explain that I have to see him the following week, and he will admit I have the disease. So far he will not tell me.

She tells me her brain scans are positive, whilst mine are negative, but she has not had her lumbar puncture. She does not understand why she has to go through with this, as he already has a positive result.

I stated that although he did get a positive result to the lumbar puncture, he refuses to tell what it is, but I obtained the results by devious means.

The day of my dreaded appointment looms. I had a lousy night on the Sunday. I could not sleep. I could not relax. I tried banging the head to knock me out, but this did not work, I then tried pulling my hair out, again this does not work. At 23.00 hours I give up and have a bath, in hot relaxing bubbles, hoping this might restore some sanity. I still can't get the heart rate down. I lay there and toss and turn, and turn and toss. Eventually I drop off. Sheer exhaustion, I suppose.

Mum picks' me up after my shortened walk, and drives to the hospital. I have decided that I am not going through with it. I am not going to have those needles stuck in again. The very thought makes my flesh crawl.

I ask the receptionist to tell him that I will not have it done. I don't have the courage anymore to say anything. I ask Mum to come in with me, as I'm determined to make him admit the diagnosis.

Upon entering his office he is aware that I refuse to go through with it. He says if I'm getting into such a state beforehand then it defeats the objective.

"I've got Multiple Sclerosis, haven't I?"

"The tests are not conclusive."

"But you've got a positive result, all those antibodies in my spine."

Mum realises this is it and states, "That's what Sue's doctor says it is."

His next comment is quite unnerving. "Yes, but it's only in a mild form."

I'm beginning to get angry, "Mild form or not, I've got it, haven't I?"

"Oh, yes, but I see people in a far worse state than you."

"I dare say you probably do, but perhaps they are not first division badminton players or marathon swimmers."

He also told me in his flippant manner, don't exercise.

One thing you don't do is to tell athletes not to exercise.

By this time I was really angry. I could not care about other people, it was my body that was sitting there in front of him not someone else's, but mine. Surely he should have been a little bit more helpful? Surely he could have explained what was going on, or not, as the case maybe?

I was scared, I needed help, but was not getting it from that quarter. I requested counselling. Surely he should have been aware of that? I had to readjust my whole life. I did not know what to do.

The bloody big door had now slammed shut.

The whole of my sporting life had come to an abrupt end. I was trapped, not knowing anything, nor going anywhere.

During the journey home Mum suggested, but it was more than a suggestion, that I should move down to the coast near them. This was something I did not want to do. I knew what would happen. She would completely take over my life, my house. I would lose what vestige of independence I had. Also I would miss Shassie, Jan, Tara and Purdey, as well as all my friends at the Leisure Centre.

I gave the excuse that I could not cope with the stress of moving. She suggested I would not need to worry about that as they would do everything for me. *HELL*, I thought am I really that inept. I did have one thing up my sleeve, I was not sure I would be eligible for a mortgage as I was not working at the present time. I just wanted to stay in my own home where I was best suited. Nothing-more-was-said.

PART 3

MY LIFE AFTER

Chapter 34

Why was the Specialist so off hand with me? Surely he should have had a little more thought as to what he was saying? Here was me totally unsure of what to do, and him so flippant, and frivolous. Was it because, as I was seeing him as a private patient, I did not count? I was under the misapprehension that I should have been treated with a little more thought.

However both Jan and I thought of him in the same manner, and she was a National Health patient, so that was not it. Was it, because I was not serious that I did not count. I still had to readjust my life, so although it was not serious for him it was for me.

The Occupational Health Department of the Civil Service, were beginning to become impatient for a diagnosis. They wanted to know, if to pension me off. Let's hope his reports are better than his on hand care. All he seemed to do was to send me for test after test, after test.

He did say that he wished to see me in July, but I had no intention of ever seeing him again. I hoped he would forget about me. After all, in his eyes I'm a non-entity.

What the hell is Multiple Sclerosis? I had to find out. I did't have any information or guidance from the people who should be in the know. How would I know ifmy Doctor would enlighten me? There were still the outstanding blood test results to come. Perhaps I could wait till they came through. But why the hell should I? I wanted to know now.

Fortunately I'm in possession of a magazine that lists all the charitable organisations. As a member of the Institute of Legal Executives, I was entitled to this brochure, and upon looking through it I ascertained the telephone number and address of the Multiple Sclerosis Society. They were very helpful and sent me a couple of booklets explaining the disease.

Chapter 35

Multiple Sclerosis is not infectious, neither is it a psychiatric nor 'nervous' disorder, nor hereditary disease. It is the most common neurological, condition affecting approximately 80,000 people in the United Kingdom and 250,000 in the U.S.A. It has been recognised for the past 150 years, being known as disseminated sclerosis, the exact cause is as yet unknown, even though considerable research has been carried out.

It is a chronic condition of the central nervous system, which encompasses the brain and the spinal cord. The most common age of diagnosis is late twenties to mid-thirties. Onset is rare before the age of 12 and after the age of 50. It affects more women than men, on a ratio of 3:2. It tends to be a condition of temperate climates and is rare in tropical countries.

The function of the brain is to interpret sensations, and initiate movements, and other responses to these sensations. This activity depends upon a complex communication system of nerves running from the brain to every part of the body via the spinal cord.

Each nerve of this communication system can be compared to an electric cable. The inner part of the nerve, the 'Axon' is made of conductive tissue and carries messages or impulses throughout the body. It is likened to the workings of an electric cable. The 'Axon' is surrounded by a layer of fatty substance, the 'Myelin' sheath, like the insulating cover on an electric cable. [See Figure one over].

The 'Myelin' helps the conduction of messages along the nerves as well as insulating and protecting the nerve.

In Multiple Sclerosis parts of the 'Myelin' sheath are attacked and become inflamed. This inflammation may die down leaving no permanent damage. If the scarring process continues, the 'Myelin' sheath is destroyed at the point of attack leaving fibrous scar tissue known as plaques or sclerosis. [See Figure two over]. This process is known as demyelisation, and as scarring occurs in more than one place, in the brain, and / or spinal cord the condition is known as Multiple Sclerosis.

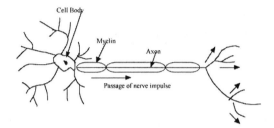

Figure one Healthy Nerve

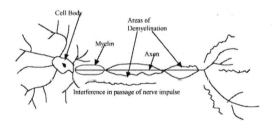

Figure two Damaged Nerve in M.S.

Taken from the booklet entitled 'Diagnosed with M.S.' and issued by the society.

Chapter 36

The All England Badminton Championships, had been held towards the end of March, and I wondered if Duncan had managed to explain my continuing absence. Did he have the guts and fortitude to tell them the truth?

He next contacts me after Easter, some four weeks after my breakdown in the pool. So much for me coming first in his affections. If he thought anything of me surely he would have been in touch quicker than this, knowing full well that I was not very well that particular weekend. He knew I should have been going to the specialist, on the following Monday, but not that it had been cancelled and put back to the following week.

Whenever he does condescend to contact me, I invariably tell him exactly what I think of his behaviour. It is becoming very tiresome.

The only reason I ascertain for this sudden inexplicable communication is not to enquire about my welfare, but to let me know we have received a better offer on that disastrous holiday on the island of Kos, Greece, in October 1993. The offer being in the sum of

£450. I am by now, so fed up with having to sort this problem out I tell him to accept it.

He then tells me he has discussed my problem with the Badminton Association of England. Am I supposed to feel grateful? He makes it sound I should be! 'I've done you a favour', is the feeling that is expressed to me. 'Does that not prove you come first in my affections?', is also the hidden undercurrent, of his attitude. The answer to all my prayers! A panacea!

It has been decided [no thought of what I might think], that I can work from home addressing envelopes and labels. It would give me some extra money.

I nearly exploded. How dare he. I tell him this would make me a prisoner in my own home. I know the job has to be done, but get someone who is fit and able to do it. They can at least escape the boredom and the drudgery of it. I could not. I would be so tired afterwards, I could not possibly go out. At least with the life I lead now, I am getting out and about, I'm swimming, and I'm walking the dog, and I'm meeting people. These pastimes would have to go, if I was to carry out this simple function.

He is not happy with my response. Tough! He does not seem to understand what it is like to have to restrict all my activities. The disease was dictating to me, what I could and could not do with my body.

"Thanks, but no thanks," I manage to reply.

Just because I'm not fit and able anymore, does that mean I have to be kept hidden? 'Don't let her come out, we can't let her be seen by the public, keep her in the corner, away from prying eyes.' This is the feeling which is being portrayed now. Am I that much of a freak? I thought this attitude was long since dead, but it seems to be alive and kicking from a telephone in Kelvedon. Is it he does not understand, or is it, he does not want to understand?

I knew at this stage, that Chris and Ollie and the two children were going on holiday in July. I had summoned up the courage to ask what they were going to do with Shassie, and Chris said she was going to be put in kennels. I said they need not do that, as I would have Shassie whilst they were away.

I did not want to lose my walks every afternoon, and I needed a reason to go out. Shassie was the reason. Chris agreed, but with some reservation, what about my cat? I said she would rule the house, she would spit, and hiss, and growl, just as she had done with Duncan's dog, Lucy. I said I would ask Dad and Duncan to put up a gate at the side of my house, so that Shassie would not get out.

During this particular telephone call I asked Duncan if he could help Dad, with the gate, and the reason why it was being erected. Much to my surprise he agreed, but stated it could not be between 15th May and 29th May, as he would be in Switzerland for the World Badminton Championships. I realised this would be more important, but he said he would ring me when he could make it. How very considerate of him!

I knew about the World Championships, as I had received several letters regarding the tournament. I did not tell him there was a possibility I might be going, let him find out for himself.

I had ignored the first letter, thinking if they did not get a reply, the organisers would think I was unable to volunteer. However they kept communicating. I decided that out of politeness I must reply. I stated I had now been diagnosed with M.S. and was very apologetic but had to let them down. I gave them an opt out, and said that if there was a little job they would like me to do, perhaps they could let me know. Imagine my surprise, I received a positive response.

They wanted my home telephone number so that they could contact me. This was the first positive step to my rehabilitation. They at least were giving me the chance to see for myself that I was not stupid, useless and inadequate. Upon replying, I received a telephone call from Steve Baddelly, who was the Team Coach for the Swiss Badminton Team. He was a former England international.

Yes they did want me, yes they appreciated my problems, and yes accommodation was sorted.

I was being asked to sort out all the food vouchers for all the line judges, and help the Manager of line judges and his deputy to issue volunteers with their uniforms. I was being assigned to the line judges' section, and would be kitted out accordingly. I was going to be accommodated with Jean-Luc's Grandmother.

Jean-Luc was the manager of line judges. Although Jean-Luc was fluent in English, [I had met him in Holland, the previous year] his Grandmother could not speak a word of English. I could not speak a word of French, so it was going to be very interesting. There was also free use of the local swimming pool, for all volunteers.

I asked Steve to give me a little time to think it over. I did not know what to do. Here was a golden opportunity to prove myself. Should I take it? I discussed this proposition with everybody I came into contact with. Mum and Dad, Chris, Joyce, and Jan [the doggy lady], and they were all of the opinion I should go. There was now not much time to organise things, I replied in the affirmative, and booked my flights. At least these could be at my convenience, and not at Duncan's. I had no intention of telling him I was going, let him find out for himself.

Upon completing my Insurance form for the flight, I had to obtain the permission of my doctor I was fit enough to travel. I then realised the diagnosis, although mild was made in January.

So the results were through then, why wait till the beginning of April, and only then because I forced it out of him. On this visit to the surgery I also learnt the blood tests were negative, but I was worried about my weight loss. Was it because of the disease? I had lost over two stone. It was just falling off me. My hips had gone down from 44 inches to 37 1/2 inches. My waist was also much smaller, but nothing off the bust. The one place I would like to lose some and it was not obliging. I was beginning to be top heavy.

The Doctor informed me it was just a change of life style, and diet. This I could understand, it was not the disease that was eating me away, and I had become healthier. This may be hard to believe, with what was going on in my body. I was away from that place; I was eating properly, at the right time of day, and allowing it time to digest properly. It was not that I was doing anymore exercise, because I was not. I was only swimming between 50 to 66 lengths, whereas I always managed before at least 100. Also, then I had played badminton or tennis in the evening depending on the season.

Upon receipt of my letter Jean-Luc telephones me to confirm the details, and that I would be met at the airport and driven to the arena, then onto his Grandmother's apartment. If the Swiss can put themselves out, for a total stranger, and give the first positive help, why can't the English Association, or even Duncan. Steve and Jean-Luc were telephoning me from abroad, in another time zone, albeit only one hour, but managing to find me in, so why couldn't Duncan?

Chapter 37

The only piece of advice I received from the doctor, when I attended to obtain his signature to the insurance form, was not to exercise to exhaustion. Very helpful, I thought. What is exhaustion? I had always pushed my body to the limit, and then found that little bit extra. Was I no longer able to find that little bit extra? Or did it mean I had to stop short of my limit? What the hell was my limit? How far could I go? Perhaps I would find out for myself. Perhaps the body would tell me. I did not know? How could I know? I had no idea what to expect. At least he did not tell me to give up swimming; I invariably found it very therapeutic.

The Doctor also had received from the specialist, advice that I needed counselling. I was told by my doctor, if I needed that, then I had to arrange it. He gave me the telephone number to contact them myself. I was quite taken aback by this attitude. Here was me, needing help, and I had to arrange it. He told me it was a confidential service, and no reports would be sent. This did not allay my fears. Why should I have to organise it? I know I'm the one needing help, but surely someone could put themselves out for me. I had to fight for everything, in the past, got where I was through sheer guts and determination, done everything myself. Now, I was not capable of thinking straight, and, had to organise my own counselling. How the hell would I pay for it? My pay was due to be stopped soon. I did not know whether I was going to have to struggle to get pensioned off from work, how to keep up the payments on my mortgage, and all the other relative bills, and feed myself. Would I still be entitled to the Invalidity Benefit now that the rules had all been changed, and the goal posts moved?

The doctor informed me that the practice put in funds to the counselling service, so I should not worry. But I did. I thought he should have arranged it, not me.

No good speaking to Duncan about this, he only wants me when I'm a hundred percent, but then of course he is not having a relationship. My parents were too emotionally involved, so I could not speak to them. I did not feel I knew either of the two Jans well enough, to trouble them with my problems.

The Jan, who I had met in the pool, was already in receipt of counselling [arranged by her doctor]. I did not feel I could burden her, with me as well. No, this was something I was going to have to come to terms with myself.

The specialist had now reported to the Occupational Health Department of my employers. I have no idea what he said, as I'm not entitled to the reports.

I don't know if he managed to relate to them details of my diagnosis, in the same off hand and frivolous manner as he told me. However, whatever he said worked. The Department were prepared to pension me off, without any argument. Yippeeeee!

I noticed my payslip for April was normal, but within a week of receiving this, I then received one for May. I was flabbergasted. Apparently all money stopped on the 6th May. I was unaware of this; nobody had bothered to tell me this was going to happen. It had only just been agreed to pension me off.

Apparently, when I contacted the Welfare Officer, she was under the impression personnel had informed me, but personnel were of the opinion Welfare had told me. Whoever's fault it was, I did not much care. I was stuck in the middle, with bills to pay, and no way of doing so. *Those miserable cretins* really do want me to lose my house. All was however not yet lost. My pension could be backdated to the 7th May, but it was going to take about six weeks to two months to finalise.

Although that might have suited them, how was I going to make ends meet? Fortunately, I thought something like this might happen, so I had managed to save some money, to see me through. This was yet another example of the Department not caring about its employees. How on earth can they be regarded as having the cares and worries of victims to consider, when they cannot or will not consider the feelings of their employees.

Mum picked me up, early one afternoon, to drive me into Maidstone, to collect my personal belongings from my desk, if it was still in existence. I had not been anywhere near it for nearly a year.

I also needed some new swimming costumes, because of my weight loss nothing fitted anymore. I was now down to a size 12. Whoopeee. I have never been that small. Probably never will be again.

Upon my arrival at the office, all the ordinary members of staff greeted me with open arms. They all knew of the diagnosis, and were amazed it had taken so long to find out. I put it down to the fact that I was fit; or rather the muscles were fit, whereas the body was slowly conking out. My desk was where I had left it, but was not as I had left it. There were papers and files all over it, when I left on that fateful day in June the previous year, but here it was now relatively clear. What had happened to all my work, I did not much care!

I collected all my things, and then proceeded to say goodbye to as many people as I could see. Mum was hoping to see John Hazelden, the lawyer who telephoned her on that day, and whilst we were in the typing pool, in he walks. Mum had a lengthy conversation with him, and she said afterwards that he really is as nice as his voice. She had been quite taken by him. It was the voice, I think.

We then see *her*. *She* is by now aware of the diagnosis. *She* escorts me into her office, and pulls a chair out for me to sit on. *She* then proceeds to treat me as an old friend. I can't believe it.

Mum says after some time, "Do you know, there was this idiot who turned up at Sue's door, one Saturday lunchtime, without any prior notice."

"Yes," *she* replies, "that was me."

Mum was absolutely amazed. She was lost for words. I am by this stage feeling very tired, and so we make our departure. Mum is still amazed, not only by *her* attitude but also by *her* admission. I state it is probably that *she* now realises there is something seriously wrong, and perhaps *she* is now feeling guilty. I was not swinging the lead after all.

Everyone had noticed how well I was looking. Much thinner, but healthier, and I had lost that 'hang dog' expression.

"You know how to remedy that, don't you, get seriously ill, or get M.S., and be off work for about a year, that should do it!" I said.

She was the only one from management I saw, although several of them were in. I could not be bothered with them, if they could not be bothered with me.

Chapter 38

The fact I had Multiple Sclerosis never bothered me. What did bother me was the fact it was now starting to dictate to me how to live my life. I objected to this, I resented this. I could no longer run, jump, play sport, and suffered with loss of confidence and co-ordination. I always thought that when I became too old to participate in any of the sports, then I would at least have my music, but sadly this was lost, too. I could not breathe without feeling dizzy; neither could I stand without looking as if I was 'three sheets to the wind.'

I did have every intention to retire at 50. I thought that I could get by financially. I thought I would be young enough and fit enough to try all the activities I had not had the time to learn. I could quite easily have got hooked on golf if I had had the time. I also wanted to try my hand at white-water canoeing, play lacrosse, and learn archery. I also wanted to try deep sea diving. Everything I had done, and everything I wanted to do in the future, was no longer possible.

During the V.E. Day celebrations, my body really brought it home to me just how much of my life I had lost. I was crying my eyes out at the celebrations from Hyde Park, not because of the sentiment, or the emotion of the occasion, but because I would no longer be able to dance. I could no longer jive. Seeing the boys and girls dressed in their American uniforms jitterbugging to the music of Glen Miller, really brought home to me how inadequate I was. How incomplete I was. I was no longer a whole person. I was only fit for the scrap heap. No one would wish to know me now. I was of no use to anyone. Duncan had certainly made that quite clear.

I was trying to make Dad wait to erect my side gate, until Duncan said he could make it. Dad said he was not prepared to wait any longer. He was going to do it himself. He also said if he ever saw Duncan again he would tell him exactly what he thought of him. Dad very rarely got riled, but when he did, 'whoa hold onto your hats', he could be a heavy disciplinarian.

He and Mum managed the gate between them. Ollie offered his assistance, but Dad declined, thanking him for his thought. I was not much use, though, as I had lost my strength, and I got tired so quickly, but it did not seem to matter.

Duncan still has not rung, not since mid-April. The tournament starts the following weekend, I wonder if he will contact me before he flies out. I hope he is not on the same flight as me. No, he would not do that, would he? Surely it would be at the wrong time of day for him. The flight was booked at my convenience, not his.

On my walks to the pool, I had now met up with another early swimmer. He swims 3 times a week, not like this idiot, who goes 4 times a week. The gentleman is in his late eighties, and through him, I then meet up with other early swimmers. Charles, who also has a black Labrador dog, is very considerate of my plight. He realises there is something seriously wrong, as my walking gait is off balance. I, of course, explain to him what the problem is.

Word gets about, that this demented idiot, with hat, goggles, and nose clips, who ploughs up and down ad nauseam, suffers with M.S. None of the other swimmers can believe it, till they see me get out. I'm like a fish in the water, but on land, nothing better than a wallowing drunk seal! They then give me all the encouragement, they can.

Yes, people do still wish to know me. Some of them even ask advice on how to improve their strokes. Hugh, who does a great impersonation of a sinking stone whilst trying to float, asks how to keep afloat. His wife, Norma, who has given up trying to advise him, asks for my help. I'm completely stumped; I've never had that problem. Hugh then gives up, and continues his impersonation.

After our respective swims, we all meet up in the bar of the Leisure Centre, to drink our tea and coffee and to chat.

On the one morning I do not see Charles, I walk to the pool along the main road. On one occasion, a little Scottish Terrier knocks into me, quite accidentally, but I fall over. My loss of balance is now quite acute. The owner is quite concerned, but is he thinking I'm drunk. However there is no smell of alcohol neither is there the slurred speech, nor the glazed expression in the eyes. I'm extremely apologetic, and recover thanks to the gentleman.

When I see Jan in the pool that morning, we both agree we need to have sweatshirts on with the caption **I'M NOT DRUNK, I JUST SUFFER WITH M.S.**

Although I manage to walk to the pool, I am now finding it increasingly difficult to walk home. My legs do not feel as if they belong to me, neither do I have the energy. I've only got a little more to do on my challenge. Just over a 1000 lengths left. I'm still on target to finish it by mid-June.

Depending on the size of the pool in Switzerland.

My bag is also becoming heavier, and the walk home is now taking on average 45-50 minutes. I wish I could call up the car, by radio to come and pick me up. This is the first time I feel that I want to start driving again. Is it only because I'm now finding it difficult to walk home after my workout? Or, am I now beginning to get some confidence back?

Chapter 39

With the diagnosis, I had to let the authorities know. Notably, the Insurance Company for the car. Being a direct line company, I did not know who they dealt with. I thought it was just the one company.

With this information, they wrote and informed me I was no longer insured, and had 14 days left. Imagine my astonishment, I did not realise I was that much of a risk. However, they were arranging cover with another company, so I should be covered.

I informed Driving and Vehicle Licensing centre in Swansea, of my plight, as advised in the booklet from the M.S. Society.

Just before I was due to leave for Switzerland, I received another recorded delivery letter, stating that my insurance would be terminated in 6 weeks. I could not believe this attitude. I had been driving on a full licence for 22 years; I had no points or endorsements, and had only had 4 accidents in all that time. None of these were even my fault. The last one, was whilst my car was parked under a street light, at about 18.00 hours, outside my badminton partner's, house, facing the correct way, when a woman driver apparently did not like where it was, [the car], so she decided to move it, by attempting to shunt it down the road, and completely demolished my rear end. The car's, not mine. Mind you, the front of her car was a sorry mess. Her excuse was that she did not see it. Surely my vehicle was big enough and ugly enough for her to see it.

This occurred about 6 or 7 years ago. How could I be a bad risk now? I'm only going to be travelling about 200 miles a month, instead of my usual 300 to 400 a week. I would have been more of a risk with that large mileage, than with the paltry mileage I would have been doing.

The company insisted I communicate with D.V.L.C., and wished to know the outcome before continuing, but in any event, it was terminated in 6 weeks, whether I liked it or not. Tough, was their attitude. No thought of how this might affect my fragile confidence, but then why should they have any sentiment. I'm only a has been. I wished I had never told them.

It is no wonder ordinary members of the public are becoming fed up with this attitude. They all wish to be treated as intelligent human beings, not as if they are out to con each and every one. Surely companies could start to take a basic course in politeness. I know there are a lot of people who will try to con anyway, I know I prosecuted a lot of them, but when you try to be honest and up front, you get treated as if you are a criminal. It just is not worth being honest anymore. Why bother?

I decided to wait until my return from Switzerland, before trying to get to grips with this added problem. I was not driving anyway, and would not be in a position to want to for a fortnight, in any event.

I'm beginning to think, it really is not worth trying to live anymore.

Chapter 40

Perhaps life is worth living after all.

The day of my departure for Switzerland dawned. Still no telephone call from Duncan. Obviously, he does not wish to say goodbye before he leaves for Switzerland. I really don't count anymore. So much for me coming first in his so called affections. He is going to be in for a mighty big shock when he finds out I'm not a useless idiot. I'm being given the chance to prove myself. Surprisingly it is foreigners who are giving me this opportunity. I wonder why the English can't do it.

I wonder what reaction I'm going to get from my fellow line judges. The last time they saw me was in Birmingham, at the All England Championships, the previous year, and the European Championships. I do not want pity, or sympathy, I want to be taken for what I am. An intelligent human being. Am I deluding myself? Am I really so useless after all? Am I really not worth bothering with anymore? Duncan obviously does not think so anymore, mind you, did he ever think so beforehand?

I started off the day in the usual manner, with a swim. I was not going anywhere without that. Only just about 1000 lengths to go, on my challenge.

My parents collect me to take me to the airport. My travel agent had arranged with British Airways, for extra special care. Upon checking in, I was met by a motorised, battery operated milk float, without the top, and seats instead of milk. This carried me all the way to the departure lounge, with the driver taking care of passport control, and ensuring my hand luggage went through the X-ray machine. Upon reaching the departure gate, I transferred to a wheelchair and was taken aboard my flight.

I had a quick look around to see if there was anyone I knew, but I failed to recognise anyone. However on the flight Mike Curtis came and spoke to me. He did not shower me with tea or sympathy, and spoke as he had always done in the past. I thanked him, for that, and he said he could not be any other way. We spent the whole of the flight chatting and catching up on old times.

At Geneva airport, after the beautiful approach along the lake, I was met again by a wheelchair, and whisked off through the Arrivals lounge, collected my baggage, and reported to the World Championship's desk.

Mike had completely taken charge, and propelled me to where the Swiss delegate was waiting. We then met up with a contingent from Scotland, and after they got used to seeing me with a walking stick, they spoke and treated me in the same manner. I realised how much fun I would have missed had I not gone.

Everybody spoke English, but the Swiss were having difficulties with the Scottish accent. They were really broad. Even I had difficulty, but then, we all put our own interpretations on what was said. The conversation although clean, I think, got turned round; to suit each and every one's perverse minds. Duncan was not on the flight. Thank goodness, so I did not have to tolerate him going to sleep all the time, as he is unable to make any form of conversation.

I was by now feeling quite tired. I did not know how long it would be before I was taken to Granny's. I think I must have now started on my reserves of energy, which were not much. Certainly nothing like I was in the habit of using.

After the arrival of one of the Official Referees who was from Norway, we were escorted to a mini bus supplied by one of the sponsors, and met one of the volunteer drivers. Mike had taken charge of my luggage, and all I had to do was try to keep up with the others. This I could not do. They unfortunately had to wait for me.

The drive from Geneva to Lausanne took about 30 minutes, and I took the opportunity of going to sleep. I did what Duncan always does, but I think I have a valid excuse, he is just boring.

At the arena we report to the office where we are met by Jean-Luc and Michael [his deputy] and are then kitted out in our uniforms, which consists of a red and white Adidas Track Suit, T-Shirt and training shoes. All supplied by Adidas, one of the sponsors. We were also given our identity badges, and a local road map. It was at this stage I received a shock. Duncan was already there. So there was no way in which I missed his non-existent telephone call. He has waited on purpose to see I'm okay.

Margaret Redfern, who I had met on previous occasions, was convinced Jean-Luc had made a mistake because she was of the opinion I was too ill to attend. She asks to see my letter and after reading it she is convinced I am attending as she recognises my writing. She had got the impression I was too ill from Duncan, but as he had not been in touch how would anybody know how ill I really was?

Duncan is making me feel very nauseous. I ask him why he has not bothered to ring me, to say goodbye, as by the time he returns to England, it will have been about seven weeks without any form of communication. He says he has not had the time [what a fatuous, pathetic remark to make]. He denies it has been that long. Margaret overhears this exchange, but does not say anything at this stage.

Duncan insists on coming with Jean-Luc and I to see I am safely installed with Granny. Who the hell is he trying to kid? Certainly not me anymore. As there are other people around including Yunis Sulleman, he is trying to pretend he cares. It may work with others, but not me. Not now.

Granny is unable to speak a word of English, and I am unable to speak a word of French. Jean-Luc has kindly lent us his Shorter-English / French Dictionary. This book was about four inches thick and the size of A4 paper. If this book was the shorter version, I dread to think what the size of the longer version is. With my phrase book which I purchased at Gatwick before leaving, I hoped we would not run into too many difficulties.

Granny is a lovely sprightly little lady, with her long grey hair kept in a loose bun at the back of her head. After the introductions are made, Duncan and Jean-Luc leave.

After a cup of tea I then retire, pleading extreme tiredness. 'Je suis très fatigué,' I manage in an appalling French accent, however Granny understands. She has been informed of the basic symptoms of the disease, and knows what to expect. I cannot get over how someone can let a complete stranger into her home, and let me treat it as my own.

Jean-Luc gives me his keys, to her apartment. They are so trusting. I must have left some positive mark upon Jean-Luc when I met him in Holland the previous year! I am overcome with the kindness shown, and am unable to express fully how grateful I am, either in English or French.

At breakfast Granny says she is amazed at how much tea I drink, and wonders if all English people are the same. I try to explain no, as my father drinks coffee and mum drinks water. I was unable to explain that Mum does drink tea, but it is so weak, and without milk, that it is almost the colour of beige water only hot. Gnat's pee, I think it is referred to. Although I've never drunk this delightful beverage. I do not know whether she understood, but she seemed to give the right indication. The Dictionary and Phrase Books were already worth their weight in gold.

It had been arranged the previous evening, Granny would take me to the arena on the local bus. Apparently our Identity passes allowed us all free passage on the local public transport, providing we were all wearing them for any inspection that may be made. They were also partly sponsoring the event.

She showed me how to lock her front door, and we set off for the bus stop at the end of her road. It was only a walk of about 50 yards, but towards the end of the tournament it seemed to be miles.

Once on the trolley-bus, she kept gesticulating at me. What on earth is she trying to say? She keeps pointing to all the bus stops, and an electronic sign within the bus. I kept looking to see if I was dressed properly, and that nothing untoward was showing. Yes, all buttons and zips securely fastened. So it was not that. What was it? Towards the end of the journey which lasted about 20 - 25 minutes, I realised what she was saying. The penny had dropped! All the bus stops have names, and the next arrival is shown on the electronic sign. What a brilliant idea. The passenger will always know where he or she is. We change bus route and take the one to the arena.

The arena was situated at the Malley Sports Centre, just outside the city of Lausanne. It is more accustomed to being used as an ice-rink. However, for the duration of the tournament it was a badminton hall. There was not a drop of water or ice to be seen. So it was going to be a very dry event.

There were ten courts laid out. Five on one side of a large heavy-duty navy blue-black curtain, with five the other side.

I was shown my duties, which consisted of date stamping and initialling all the drinks and food vouchers for all the line judges who were on duty in each session.

A session being morning / afternoon / and evening. Usually line judges were on duty for at least two of the three sessions, some, however, were on all three, depending on the numbers.

Each court had assigned between seven to eight line judges, allowing time for breaks. At least that was the theory. Not everyone reported in. There were many absentees. This of course upset the organisation, and it meant some courts were short of bodies, and that placed extra burdens on the judges assigned to those respective courts.

I also had to place in each of the court envelopes a peel-off sticker for all judges assigned to that particular court, and endorse the front of the envelope with the name of the court captain.

The tournament was split, as it was in Birmingham two years previously into a team event and the individual event. This meant there were two official referees. The Sudirman Cup was played first. As the event was starting the following day, this meant I could have the rest of the day to find my bearings, get used to travelling on the buses and most important of all, find the swimming pool.

I knew my pass would allow me free access to the pool. But where was it? Was it difficult to find? Michael shows me on the map, where it is and to which bus stop to alight at. I had no difficulties in finding it, as the bus route was the one past the arena, to the other side of Lausanne. I just had to alight at the correct stop.

Granny had left by this stage, so I was on my own. Having to work it out for myself, in a strange country, where I am unable to communicate. I have enough problems with learning English without the extra problem of a foreign language.

As I'm entering the city I see the sign. 'Piscine'. No, I'm not being rude. I realise, this is what French is, for swimming pool, as the International symbol is under the caption. The symbol is of a person performing the front crawl or freestyle stroke in water and above is a black line at an angle of about 100 degrees. This I knew to be an indoor pool. Thank goodness. I did not relish the idea of swimming outdoors. I know we are in May, but it is still quite cold and wet.

Having gained admittance, I ascertain it is a 25 metre pool, so no different from what I'm accustomed to, with at least four lanes set aside for serious swimmers. There

221

is also a diving pool, and on one occasion there was the synchronised swimming team in training. I was absolutely fascinated. The control needed by those girls is phenomenal. There was also in the complex a children's and a teaching pool. I was not going to be able to use the sauna and steam rooms, mainly because there were not any.

After my swim, I return to the arena to start stamping the tickets for the following day's duties. I wanted to be ahead of myself, in case there was a time when I could not attend.

All the people who were there, who knew me, came and spoke to me, with one notable exception. Duncan. I knew he was there. This was a badminton tournament, he could perform, by moving chairs, and pressing buttons to his heart's delight, and finding any other job which needed doing. He obviously, could not find the time to drag himself away, from whatever he was doing. I was not going to chase around looking for him. If he wanted to speak to me, then he knew where I was. All the others managed it, so why not him? I was not going to move from where I was. Was I now starting to get some inner strength?

I managed to complete the following day's duties, and staggered back to the apartment, feeling absolutely shattered, but pleased with myself. I had managed to find my way around, and used the buses, my French which was non-existent beforehand, was now improving. I had a smattering of the lingo!

I followed the same routine every day. Whilst I was working, it was very boring, several of the line judges, to relieve the drudgery, came in and spoke to me.

It was during one of these occasions Margaret found time to chat. She realised there was something wrong between Duncan and me, and wondered what it was. I told her of his behaviour, how he had let me down in October, regarding the sponsored swim, how little he contacted me, the fact that he was only interested when I was one hundred percent. How he could not, or would not, I didn't know which, ring. Nor could he be bothered to come and visit. He knew I was not mobile.

She said I should not have that to put up with, and I needed someone reliable. I realised what she had said was true, but I did not have the strength of character to tell him to 'sling his hook', I kept hoping he would become, as he had been in the beginning, kind, considerate, thoughtful, and above all, reliable.

I was not allowed to be on my own. They all seemed to take me under their respective wings. I was always accompanied to lunch, and to tea, and helped up all the stairs. They seemed never ending. Wherever I looked, there was the inevitable flight of stairs. I would have hated being confined to a wheelchair, it would have been impossible to get around.

Doug and Ann Morden maintained I should have a seat in the viewing gallery, next to them. If anyone was seated there, then they would move, to make sure I was okay. Yunis was generally concerned, as he had come to the hospital in Holland with me. He was unable to obtain any facts from Duncan, as to my condition, and I enlightened him as to the reasons.

Allen and Marilyn Bray never allowed me to leave the arena in the evening, without being accompanied to the bus stop, and ensuring that I boarded the right one. If Allen was on court, or about to go on court, he made arrangements with one of the others to escort me. A notable absentee in this regard was Duncan. He obviously found it more exciting, and interesting, to be judging lines, moving chairs or pressing buttons. Ha, Ha!

They had all noticed I had lost a great deal of weight, and several wanted to know the secret. I said, it is a bit drastic, but contract M.S. then you will, too, but seriously, it's a change of life style. I'm eating properly, and allowing it time to digest, also I am not under any great stress, or worry.

Mike unfortunately had to lift me up to the seats, as I had managed to trip up the final step.

"Cor blimey, I don't know about the weight loss, but you feel a ton weight," he mutters.

I am, by now, reduced to an uncontrollable state of laughs.

The line judges were not the only ones who were pleased to see me. I had many greetings from the Umpires, not only from the English ones who I know well, but also from the Dutch, Welsh, French and Scottish representatives. It was on this occasion I asked

Richard Atwell, about the qualifications required for the Official Referee.

"Does he need to be an International Umpire," I ask.

"Oh, no. But a general grounding of the knowledge of umpiring is required."

"That's very interesting, but surely there has to be more to it than that?" I ask.

"Oh yes, but all that is needed is to attend and pass the course."

"Is that all?."

"In a nut shell. Yes. He manages the whole tournament, arranges all the matches, when, and at what time, arranges the draw, and oversees all the problems. The disputes as to the speed of the shuttles, and any other problem that may arise. You're not thinking about it are you?"

"Who me, you've got to be kidding. It's a hard enough job just getting up sometimes."

We then continue chatting about other badminton and related issues.

When Duncan actually condescends to manage to find time to talk to me, his concern for my welfare, did not last long, I ask him why he does not do the Official Referee's course.

"Oh, I've not really thought about it," he says.

Now that's, a surprise, I think to myself.

I retort, "I think you should, then you can legitimately have your finger in every pie that's going."

I think he is now shocked that I'm beginning to answer him back.

During the afternoon, I was escorted around the concourse, as I needed to have a little bit of exercise. Again, on one such occasion, Duncan is told to escort me. He would not think to volunteer himself, but when told, he is able and willing. Ohhhhhhhhh, I'm now really beginning to get very short with him. I'm finding it hard to stay polite.

I ask whether we have had our money through from that disastrous holiday yet. He was supposed to have accepted the offer in April [mid] and here we were over a month later, and not heard anything. I don't believe he's even replied, I think to myself. I reckon he's been too busy. He says he has not received any communication, so I suggest he chases it up. He agrees that when he arrives home, he will write again. I wonder when, it could be 2 months later, he will still be home then.

There are some very funny people about. I do not mean in the literal sense. I mean with one certain man [I think] who was swimming at the same time as me, one morning. I was doing my usual. Just ploughing up and down length after length with my favourite stroke the front crawl or freestyle. As I reached the end of one of my lengths, there was this person standing with his back to the wall exposing himself. I was quite taken aback. I ignored it, and turned and carried on. Should I have been distracted by this turn of events? I wondered if I was seeing things. On my return, he had not moved, and was still in the same position, as before. I was not seeing things. Its' a good job I don't manage the tumble turns as I might have knocked it off. Accidentally, on purpose, of course.

I wondered if this was normal behaviour for the Swiss, and did not say anything, until I returned to the arena. Both Beverly and Yvette wanted to know where the pool was so they could see for themselves. I said there was not much to get excited about anyway. Once you've seen one, you've seen them all I tell the two girls. I think there is no uglier sight than a naked man, unless its two naked men!

On one of my jaunts to the pool, Kai, who is a Dutch/Chinese gentleman, had befriended me and spoken to me as an intelligent human being, joined me. I had met him originally in Holland, and as he is in the medical profession he understands my disease. He is amazed at the way I can swim. Afterwards, we have tea together, and I ascertain he can speak four languages fluently. Dutch, his own Arubenese dialect which is Papiamentu, French and of course English. He also had a command for German. It really does make us English look so uneducated. But with everyone speaking English, why bother to learn another language.

When a contingent from Sweden arrived, Michael was on hand to greet them, and I wondered what language was going to be used. Michael can speak,

227

German, Swiss German, French, and English. The language used, was, yes, English.

On the one day off for the whole tournament, it rained. It absolutely threw it down. I wanted to try and make my way to the Olympic Museum, which was situated on the shore of Lake Geneva. I now realised that I was doing too much. The body was beginning to rebel. I was determined to go, and nothing was going to stop me. I was on my own, but met up with several friends in the museum. It was amazing.

The comparison of the old and new forms of equipment especially in the winter sports department was astounding. There was no form of protection on the bob sleigh, being made almost entirely of wood. The clothing for the skiers, bore no resemblance to the types and styles worn in the 1990s. During the twenties the clothing consisted of heavy duty sweaters and coats, and leather boots. These just appeared to be similar to the walking boots of today. Obviously not made for fast times, or giving the appearance of being elegant.

Some of the exhibits had been donated by the sports stars themselves.

One such item was a badminton racket owned and used by World Champion and number 1 seed Susi Susanti of Indonesia.

Upon my return to the apartment, I noticed that my legs, especially my right leg, were becoming more and more objectionable. They were not operating as they should. Obviously the messages were becoming increasingly distorted. Blast it! I'm going to get back, whether it takes me three or four hours. At every opportunity I took a rest, but as it was still raining, this caused me to get rather wet.

Granny has now by this stage returned to her other apartment, and I was therefore left on my own. I did not mind this, as I therefore did not feel obliged to try and make conversation. As I was absolutely knackered, I retired straight after a hot relaxing bath.

I was not, however, allowed to sleep. My body was still rebelling. It kept requiring me to use the loo. I lost count after my seventh trip in 30 minutes. Each time was worth it, though. I don't know where all the water was coming from, I had not drunk that much during the day. Perhaps it was in answer to all the rain that I had walked through. Perhaps it was trying to keep up.

At the arena during the afternoon, I managed to watch some of the matches being played, but the body was still rebelling. My vision was blurring at the end of the afternoon.

Margaret had to keep me informed of the score on one of the far courts because the match being played was a men's doubles involving an English pairing of Chris Hunt & Simon Archer who were seeded 5/8.

My right leg thigh muscle seemed to become very weak, it felt like a sponge. Ann had a poke, and said it must be very disconcerting. I was now becoming accustomed to all the oddities that were going on, but when they first appeared I was naturally concerned.

At lunch one afternoon, Allen was complaining that he only had five line judges on his court. Some of the Swiss contingent had not reported in. This meant there was only one spare, making it very difficult to have a break, and find time to use the loo. It was virtually non-stop judging. This makes it very tough to maintain the high levels of concentration required. I kept thinking, could I? Should I? What if I make a mistake? Have I got the ability anymore? I can't, can I? I took the bull by the horns.

"Allen, if you're that short, would it help you if I did a line? It may give someone the time to have some lunch."

Allen was pleased with my offer, and accepted it. Oh, shit, what have I done. Gone and put both feet in it. I can't back out now. In the hall, Allen clears my suggestion with Jean-Luc and suggests a ladies' singles match between Norway and Czech Republic.

They allow me to walk to the court before the match is announced, and suggest I cover the base line. There's no getting out of it now. Me and my big mouth! The match is announced, and I fall into step with the other 3 judges, Allen and the 2 from Scotland. I knew I was in good company.

The match progresses, and I make all my calls in my old familiar confident manner. I can still do it. I'm glad it was not a long game, as I was, towards the end having difficulty, not only with concentrating, but with my vision. When I came off court, I was euphoric. Yes, I could still do it, but only in a very limited capacity.

I said to Allen, who was very grateful, that I did not feel I could do any more. But, I did a line. So I'm not stupid or useless or inadequate. 'Yaaa booooo sucks, to you, you lanky moustached twit!' I'll let you consider as to whom I'm referring to!

The final of the team competition [the Sudirman Cup] was between Korea and Indonesia, and the respective supporters take their badminton very seriously, and are very vociferous. It did not last long, with Korea being the eventual winners.

This was not at the same standard as the final between these two countries in 1993. With Korea managing to attain the win in three straight games, the supporters decided to have a 'punch up'. I did not think this sort of thing happened in badminton.

The Indonesian players were very angry, especially as missiles were being thrown at them, and it was decided by the official referee, and the organising committee that the final two games need not be played.

On the final Saturday, play was not due to start until the afternoon, so I decided to take the opportunity and make my way to the Cathedral. It was also market day, and when I alighted from the bus, and followed the signs, I came upon a flight of steps. Oh, hell, not again. I'm fed up with all these. I managed to walk up them, but they seemed never ending.

231

When I reached the main road, I then saw there was another flight of stairs. Oh, shit. I'm not going to be able to get there. I was at this stage near to tears. I decided to walk round to see if there was a path I could follow. I was determined to get there. I came across a very steep single track road. I took it.

Found the Cathedral, and went inside. I was very disappointed. Have I struggled to get here, just for this, I thought to myself. Was it really worth it? I asked myself. All it was inside was a small empty shell with seats for pews. I've seen far better stained glass windows on our own village Parish Churches. I expected something superior, after all this was the Cathedral. The Organ was also very tiny compared with the rest of the building.

Having struggled to get there, I had to struggle to get to the arena. I was not going down the same way that I came. I refused to go up or down any more stairs. To hell with them. I've had enough. I knew by now the route of the bus and boarded it as soon as I came to the relevant stop.

Before reaching it, however, I had to cross a high level bridge. Not only did I feel very nauseous, but I was also extremely dizzy. Was this a reaction, to my disappointment, or was it another form of the similar symptoms already experienced?

Upon reaching the arena, I broke down. Fortunately, Marilyn and Allen were already there and took control of the situation. They realised I was having a rough time, and explained I could not possibly perform my duties for that day, but they did manage to get me my lunch voucher. I rested for the rest of the day, either stretched out on the benches in the changing rooms, or watching the semi-finals, and a couple of the finals.

The finals, the next day, were rather disappointing, and did not live up to my expectations of the play which I had experienced in 1993, or at the All England in 1994.

At the end of the play we all said our goodbyes, and exchanged addresses.

Kai wanted mine. Imagine my surprise, here was someone who regarded me as an intelligent human being, and worth knowing. I did not feel I was stupid useless or inadequate anymore. Everybody, [except you know who] treated me in the same way they had treated me before. Once they got used to me using a stick, it did not seem to affect any of them. I had a wonderful time, although I was absolutely knackered, I knew I was a somebody.

As I was leaving the arena I accidentally bumped into Duncan. What bloody useless timing that was. Our conversation, if you can call it that, was very one-sided, but I did manage to ascertain, in a very cynical fashion, Duncan would not be on my flight, he would be on the first flight home as usual.

Mike was on the same flight home as me, and therefore we arranged our transport with Jean-Luc, who took us both to the airport. Mike behaved, as he had done on the way out, and took complete charge of my baggage, and checked us both in. I again received the special treatment with wheelchair assistance, as before.

At Gatwick, Mike and I said goodbye, and I was met by my parents and driven home.

Chapter 41

Although I was absolutely knackered, I felt satisfied. There were still some things I could do, although not many. I was not, as **SIR** had made me feel, useless or stupid or inadequate. He was the only one who did not want to know me. I bet if the boot was on the other foot, though, and it was him who had contracted this disease, he would be wallowing in self-pity, and thinking he should just give up and feel everybody should jump to his tune. Mind you, would this have been any different anyway? He expected me to do what he wanted, when he wanted, and how he wanted. He would probably just stay at home and vegetate. Some men are bad enough if they just have a little cold, or a pain in their big toe, they think they are dying.

I had very little time to get my head back in shape, if I ever could get it back in shape, as at the weekend my parents were taking me to the health farm again. All three of us were going again. This time Dad did not need to be chivvied as he was quite looking forward to it, as he knew what to expect.

I did not swim on the Tuesday, as I was still feeling the effects of the previous fortnight.

My moggy sulked. She was not happy, that she had had her routine messed about, but Shassie on the other hand, was happy to see me. She greeted me with a bone, and the customary wagging of the tail and the shaking of her whole body. It meant she was going to be taken for her walks again, and she would be meeting her two friends, Tara and Purdey and they would be all 'kissy/kissy' as well as front paws cuddling each other.

Chris had kindly piled up my post, by the telephone, out of sight of preying eyes, and upon opening it, there was a letter from the States. It was my first response to the advert, which I replied to before Christmas. It was from a Gentleman, from the Reno, Nevada area, and he was 50 years of age, and described his job as Deputy State Fire Marshal/Inspector. He did not know that I had contracted M.S., and being an open sort of character I informed him straight away. I gave him an opt out clause, if he did not want to continue communicating with me.

Also there was the customary form to complete for the Driving and Vehicle Licensing Centre, Swansea. This was very difficult, as the questions did not seem to relate to me. On a good day, when of course you would drive, there would appear to be nothing wrong, but on a bad day the responsible driver would not even venture out. Also, if you knew you were going to be busy whilst out, other arrangements would have to be made. However, I completed it as best I could and returned it.

Surely they have come across this disease before. I cannot possibly be unique.

I had to start ringing around again to see about my car insurance. Although some companies were prepared to insure me, I was being quoted very silly premiums. Anything between £300 - £600. I was not prepared to pay these ridiculous prices. I was only going to be travelling about 200 miles a month at the most. In desperation, I wrote to the M.S. Society asking if this was normal.

I then tried the final number. Again an 0800 number. Before the girl could give me the customary sales spiel, which I had heard on numerous occasions before.

"Cut the crap, will you insure someone with M.S." I said.

"Providing there are no restrictions on the licence, yes."

"Not as yet."

"Would you like a quote."

"Yes please."

I then gave her all the details, when the diagnosis was made, how long I'd been driving, no convictions or points, full no claims bonus, the fact that I was retired and the amount of mileage contemplated. I gave her details of the vehicle, and explained I would be changing it for an automatic/power steering baby car as soon as I could. I waited with some trepidation as to the premium cost. It was, £137.93. I could have been knocked down by a feather. This was not only the cheapest quote I received, but was even cheaper than before I was ill. I accepted it immediately, and felt that a great weight had been taken from my shoulders. This was based on small user, and I was allowed 5000 miles in a year. At least now, I could seriously think about becoming mobile again. I think that after my sojourn in Switzerland I was beginning to think positively. 'Geronimo' I thought, I'm beginning to get somewhere.

I also requested a quote for my contents insurance, as this was due within the next week or so, and found that this was a lot cheaper, than my present company. I flippantly said, does the premium become loaded because of the disease. The reply was no. I do not think she appreciated my cynical sense of humour. I accepted it immediately again, and was informed that there would be a cheque from them, as a discount for taking out both policies at the same time.

Just before I went to Switzerland, my local Vicar called upon me again. He commented on, how improved I was, compared to the last visit. It seemed to him that each time he saw me, I was beginning to get stronger. He asked if I would like to meet a lady called Barbara. She suffers with M.S., but is in a wheel chair. As my specialist so pointedly stated, 'I see people in a far worse state than you'. I agreed, and about 30 minutes after he had left the telephone rings, and it is Barbara.

"Blimey," I said. "He doesn't waste much time, does he."

"Well, you know, David and I also don't like to let the grass grow beneath my feet."

I knew she had a dry sense of humour, something akin to my own. I arranged to meet her, and we chatted and laughed, just like old friends.

Upon my return, I called upon her again, and by this time she had received my postcard. I did not send sensible ones, but they were all pictures of cartoon type cats, carrying out various tasks. I put a caption under each card I sent, 'Line judges at play', 'Line judges in the canteen', or 'Line judges on duty'. She knew, I also had a mischievous sense of humour. Why be sensible, in this day and age.

She was very interested in everything that went on, and could not comprehend the behaviour of Duncan. We chatted and laughed, and it seemed to be good for both of us. The saga of my on / off relationship, more off than on, seemed like something out of 'Peyton Place'. Now that really dates me. Her parents live with her and her husband Clive, and their daughter Lynne. She explains to me about the allowances she receives, and thinks I could apply for the Mobility, part of the Disability Living Allowance. More bloody forms, I think to myself. Would I be eligible, as I can still get about, in a fashion? She explains further that there are two rates, and I should qualify for the lower one. Had I also applied for the Orange Badge parking permit? I had to admit I had not, as at this stage I did not regard myself as disabled.

Barbara contracted the disease when she was 28/29 years of age some 17 years ago. She was already married but had not had Lynne at this stage.

She is of the opinion it started because she had chicken pox, as an adult. She knew there was something seriously wrong when she could not lift or move her left leg from the bed. She was also unable to use the loo for 17 hours. The complete reverse to me in Switzerland. She was taken to the Brook Hospital in London, and was so relieved when they inserted a catheter. She then had to undergo all the tests. Lumbar puncture and an E.E.G. Both Clive and Barbara were informed at this stage she had polyneuritis [which is a collective name for anything that goes wrong with the nerves]. She was still carrying on in ignorance, and still working. After about seven months she returned to see her consultant for a check-up.

Unbeknown to him, Barbara had watched a programme on the television about the disease Multiple Sclerosis. In it, the victim was describing all her symptoms, and the tests with which she had to undergo. Hey, thinks Barbara, that's me. She is describing everything that has occurred to me!

Upon being ushered into his office, Barbara asks, "Have I got M.S.?"

His immediate response was, "Yes you have."

"Thanks a million, but aren't you supposed to prevaricate before telling me!"

Both Barbara and Clive are very pleased to hear of the diagnosis, as she was of the opinion she had a brain tumour, especially after all the tests. Clive now proved to be a tower of strength. She felt a great weight was now off her shoulders.

All through his formative years, he had helped his granny cope with her mobility problems, so helping Barbara just came naturally. It seems to me, he was a kind, considerate, and thoughtful man, not like someone who I have been unfortunate to know.

Clive however had always wanted a family. Could, or should Barbara become pregnant? Would she pass on the disease to any offspring? Is it hereditary? She had kept herself informed of the disease, and managed to obtain and digest all the information that was currently published. She came to the conclusion quite unselfishly she could have a family, it was not hereditary, and gladly fell pregnant, and nine months later was blessed with Lynne. Clive at this stage was over the moon. Barbara received 70 cards welcoming her new addition.

When she was four months pregnant, Barbara succumbed to a wheelchair. Her only regret was she was unable to push Lynne around in the pram, or buggy, but Clive had constructed a 'dead man's' brake handle to the pram, so she could attempt at least, to be like other mums.

Lynne has not known her Mum in any other way, and treats her as any other normal teenager would.

Although Barbara is unable to undertake either full or part time work, she helps out on a voluntary basis for two hours a week only at the local school's library.

Barbara states she may be ill but at least she's cute!

The only way to combat this disease or any other form of disability is to be positive and 'not let the bastards grind you down'.

Chapter 42

At Henlow Grange Health Farm we followed the same routine as before. I knew I was going to improve.

The fortnight in Switzerland had really taken it out of me. I realised this, as on the Friday I had only managed 14 lengths in the pool. This was my worst time in the pool since the 24th March when I broke down and thought I could not swim anymore. As I had managed to realise then, my feeling of extreme failure was only temporary, I knew after the Traditional week I would almost be back to normal. Normality for me was never one hundred percent. I knew I would never attain this state, as Duncan had wanted me to.

Being the summer, but wet, we walked in the grounds, between all the showers. My parents were able to feel the full picture of the beautiful and peaceful grounds, with plenty of walks in the neighbouring countryside.

The only problem this time; there was a 'gremlin' in the fire alarm. It chose the most inhospitable time to set off. The first occasion was on the Wednesday at about

06.30 hours. It transpired one of the sensors in the conservatory was faulty.

The next occasion was on the following morning at 05.30 hours. Now this is early, even for me. Each time, the building had to be evacuated, as it was uncertain whether it was a false alarm. When it went off the second time, I was just in the process of waking up. I swore incessantly, and tried to ignore it. However the bell is so piercing this reaction is impossible. Most of the guests were asleep, and did not appreciate the early morning call. Mum was one of those. Although we opened our windows, and patio doors, we did not venture out. Dad made a cup of tea, and as we were drinking it, Graham, the Assistant Manager knocks on the door, and in walks four burly fire officers. If I had felt in a better state, I might have misbehaved myself. They were men. I mean real men. 'Corrrrrr.' It is a pity that it was at that hour in the morning, when I am at my worst.

Apparently the gremlin had now moved to the sensor in my parents' room. It seemed to move around at will!

When a reservation is made the guests choose as to whether they wish to smoke in their room, or not. Depending on the reply, the allocations are then made. Smoking is only allowed in certain areas. They are outside, in the smoking room, or your own room, providing your room is reserved for that purpose.

I happened to state at breakfast in a jovial manner to some people who we had met, and knew we were avid non-smokers, that the reason why it had gone off, Dad was having a quiet puff on his pipe. Someone overheard this and thought I was being serious. Hence the rumour the alarm was started because someone was caught having a surreptitious smoke in their room. In reality, the sensor was at fault, and replaced. The alarm did not trouble us again.

At the end of the week I had completed 5384 lengths out of a total of 5664, on my challenge. Only 280 left. If I had been fit and able, I could have done that in two sessions.

On the 10th June we returned home feeling relaxed and at peace.

Chapter 43

My money worries were beginning to dissipate. My pension had been back dated, so perhaps those idiots can do something after all. Also my lump sum was through. This I was going to have to use to purchase a new car. Although I was presently using, although not driving at this stage, a Rover 216, and prior to this a Rover 213S, and immediately before that a Ford Escort 1.6GL, I was accustomed to a certain amount of comfort and luxury and performance. I saw no reason why, because of my disease I should lower my standards. I had every intention to purchase a British car, but which one?

I had made a list of all the requirements which were essential that my new acquisition was to have. These included:-

[a] Automatic Transmission

[b] Power Steering

[c] Stereo Radio Cassette

[d] Dipping rear view mirror

[e] Rear wash wipe

[f] Central Locking

[g] Clock

[h] Rev. Counter

[I] Trip mileage Recorder

To ascertain which vehicle included all the above items as standard, I purchased 'What Car' magazine. I then researched the section which sets out all the new makes and models currently on the market. With this in mind a short list is made, and I telephoned all the 0800 numbers to obtain the literature.

I am amazed that if you wish to spend about £30,000 for a new Mercedes, most of the items that I require are all optional extras. I would have thought, that if you are spending this amount of money, all these items should have been standard. But obviously I'm thinking logically, which is something the ordinary purchaser is not supposed to be able to do.

In my price bracket I am amazed there are only two makes of vehicle which have all the above requirements as standard, and they are a Vauxhall Corsa or a Renault Cleo. I was not impressed with the shape of the Vauxhall, so I settled for the Cleo. This also came with electric windows as standard. I wondered how it would be for comfort, or performance. I was surprised and very disappointed that I was going to have to purchase a foreign car.

I now knew how much I was going to have coming in each and every month. I was still in receipt of my invalidity benefit, and now, also my small pension. I was going to have to curtail my standards. If I wanted to continue to save, although this is frowned upon if on any form of benefit, I realised my mortgage was going to be difficult to maintain at the current monthly payment.

The Building Societies' all maintain if you let them know of any problems before they become out of hand, then other arrangements can be made. I was seriously going to put this to the test. How would they react? I did not seek to get M.S., neither did I wish to be pensioned off from any form of work permanently, nor did I wish to lose my home. I was not suffering from negative equity, and in comparison to most people my mortgage was quite small.

My parents started the ball rolling, and it was the Building Society's suggestion I may be able to get Income Support, because if this was possible then the interest would be paid. I was penalised, from this, because I had too much in the way of savings. As I do not drink, or smoke, or have a riotous living I was always able to have some money behind me. I felt that if you try to make something of your life then the Government penalise people for being or trying to be independent.

At first the Society were most unhelpful, and suggested a reduction of only £30 per month. If I could make those payments, then surely I could struggle with the whole amount. There were no dependents. When I die the property will have be sold, so they will get their money anyway.

I struggled to maintain the payments, and finally wrote again towards the end of June, demanding assistance. I did not hear anything. I felt I had been ignored. When I telephoned the Branch Manager, I was told it had been passed on to Head Office. Why the hell could they not tell me that? Why do we always feel we need a crystal ball? Is it impossible for companies to have any form of common courtesy? Why leave us in the dark?

I was extremely worried at this stage. I was trying to make ends meet, trying to save at the same time. I did not know if my Invalidity Benefit would continue, or for how long. With this disease, the victim is not supposed to be under any form of stress, the Building Society were making matters worse by not keeping me informed of the current situation.

There is nothing worse than losing one's home through someone else's incompetence. This was how I was thinking. Obviously not clear headed, or able to think straight. All I was able to contemplate was, I was going to lose my home.

Finally after much prevarication and soul searching they let me pay the interest only. I requested that if I had managed to save up enough money would I able to reduce my capital. With what seemed an age, they agreed stating it must be a minimum of £500 and this must be stated to come off the capital.

249

All through this time I also wrote to the union. They were supposed to be there to help members with their problems irrespective of whether they are work related or financial. After several denials of receiving any form of communication, either verbal or written, they sent me an application form for a Benevolent Grant. After completing this and returning it, they refused me. I do not know why? Obviously they have their reasons.

I complained incessantly that if the C.P.S. did not change their working practises then the union would have an epidemic of sufferers with M.S. I always maintained I contracted this disease because of the excessive stress levels required to maintain some modicum of job satisfaction, and to cope with the inefficiency of the Management, who were, it seemed only concerned with form filling. The only response the union could give me was to write to the M.S. society. They had written to the society on my behalf to warn them I maybe communicating with them.

Had I paid my union fees for all those years, for that useless piece of time wasting and their impersonation of assistance? I demanded all my fees to be returned with interest. I am still awaiting their response. I had, of course, already been in touch with the society. Did the union really think I was that stupid not to have communicated with the society in the first place?

Chapter 44

My walk to the pool was now becoming even harder. I have a small slope to negotiate, at the end of the road, and this really took its toll out of me. By the time I reached the pool I was knackered, and I still had my swim to accomplish, and the walk home. I really must now start to get mobile, and drive again, but it is still not a year since my last blackout.

If it was not for Shassie, pulling me up the hill for our walks in the afternoon, I would never make it. I wish I had her with me for the morning walk, though, but I dread to think what she would be like at the pool. There would be no finesse, but straight in. Would she beat me, or would I beat her. How would the other swimmers react if they saw this golden-haired demented idiot lane swimming?

My driving licence has been returned and although there are no restrictions, it is now for a duration of 3 years only.

When I change at the pool, it has to be whilst I am sitting on the benches, as I am unable to stand or balance on one leg. More and more people are requesting my assistance as to how to improve their strokes, and whether to use goggles and / or nose clips.

With all these requests I wonder if I could possibly attain my swimming instructors' certificate. I specifically wanted it to enable me to instruct disabled people. I felt that if they could see the way I was in the water and the confidence I had, it may give them some form of encouragement. They may think 'Well look at her, and she can't walk very well, but to see her in the water, you'd think there was nothing wrong'. This was what I wanted to try and get over to any prospective student.

Barbara's comment about being disabled kept ringing in my brain. As I am now unable to carry out my normal functions, and live life at the pace I wanted, instead of being dictated to by my 'god forsaken right leg', I must be disabled.

I telephoned the Disabled hot line which is shown in the 'Phone Book' and they gave me the telephone number and person to whom to contact. I spoke to Jackie Farr [nee Hails], the Kent Sports Development Officer. I explained the situation to her, and she gave me details of a course that was currently running at Valence School near Sevenoaks Kent, and invited me to attend one of the sessions.

Mum drove me there on the Saturday in question, and I introduced myself to the Course Instructor. It was an ideal opportunity for me, as they were working in the pool. I did so long to get in.

Whenever I see a pool, no matter how big I just want to swim.

The students who were all able bodied had two handicapped adults to take through their paces. The students worked on a rota basis, of one to each swimmer, and therefore the two swimmers were in the water the whole time. The class lasted for over 1 1/2 hours.

I realised straight away that I would be unable to pass the course. Part of the qualification was to be able to lead the disabled swimmer into the water. Anybody leans on me, and I fall over. So I would take them down with me, we would end up in the water, providing I fell that way but not in the conventional manner. There would be a mighty big splash, and I think the water in the pool would get out.

The swimmers were shown how to blow a table-tennis ball across the water, how to bounce in the water using aids, how to put their head under water and how to make a splash using their legs. This did not take much teaching as they seemed to adapt very quickly and the bigger the splash, the better.

The students were also shown how to use the hoist, and I again realised I could not pass the certificate as I would not have the strength or the co-ordination to get anyone in it.

Although I was disappointed that I would not be able to pass the certificate, I realised there may be a future for me in the pool. The Course Instructor suggested I may be interested in taking my main stream Instructors

Certificate. This would unfortunately have to involve teaching children. I neither had the patience, nor the understanding, nor the interest to teach children. I specifically wanted to be with adults.

Upon leaving the school, Mum who had been fascinated with the whole procedure, drove us back to Tenterden, where we went to the 'Lace Fair' being held at the Leisure Centre.

We met up with Jan [the two dogs] and Mum was interested in seeing how lace was made. She is very practical, being an excellent knitter, and seamstress. None of these attributes ever landed on me. All I ever wanted to do was play sport, even now. I was always intrigued as to how Jan found the time to pursue her interests in craft work, with all her duties at the house.

After this demonstration, Mum and I then went to see Barbara.

I thought it may help Mum, to come to terms with my problem if she could chat to another Mother of a similar age to herself, with a daughter who had had the disease far longer than me, and in a more serious condition. As my Specialist had so pointedly stated 'I see people in a far worse state than you'.

Both Barbara and I were trying to listen in, but this is difficult when there are two doors and a hallway between you. We tried, but the ears would not stretch that far. Barbara and I then realised this was a futile exercise, so we just did the usual and ended up in a fit of giggles at the funny stories we told. Neither of us found

out what was said. Neither of the Mums was
forthcoming.

Chapter 45

It was now half way through June and I had not quite finished my challenge. I had hoped when I started on the 15th January 1995, it would only take me 6 months, but here was I, on the 16th June having only completed 5636 lengths out of 5664. It would need another session to swim the 88 miles for the Gold Channel Challenge. As there was only another 28 lengths to do, this was achieved on the 19th. I have now done it! I did actually complete 60 lengths on this date, so I had gone over.

What do I do now? I've done it! I need a challenge of some sort. But what? I can only swim. It comes to something when my swimming is quicker than my walking. If I could have an indoor pool instead of the pavement to use, I would not need to think about getting mobile. I could swim everywhere. There would of course be locks to install, so that I would not need to negotiate hills or steps. I think this may be a little impractical. How on earth would I do my shopping? It would be terribly soggy when I got home. Especially with bits of 'All Bran' floating in the water. UGH.

I still could not pace myself. I was still pushing the body to the extreme. This is what I had always done. It was something I could not get used to. I objected to my body, and especially my right leg telling me what I could and could not do. In my dictionary there has never been that word 'can't'. I always went by the maxim 'where there's a will there's a way'.

I noticed on one occasion when I crawled out of the pool, fortunately there are no steps to use, and swimmers can walk in and out at will, I was having difficulty in putting one leg in front of the other.

Although I was severely talking to it, I think people around who overheard me must have thought I was going mad. I was telling it, in forcible English that it could move, and it was going to, whether it liked it or not. My two legs just seemed stuck in the same position. The messages from my brain [yes I do have one] were just not getting through. I was telling my right leg to move, at least six inches forward. It would not. It was being stubborn. Well, if it was going to be stubborn, then so was I! It was going to move, and eventually it did after what seemed an age.

I had hoped after my time in the Steam room and Sauna, all my 'bits' would be placed back in order. Obviously at this point there were some which were in the wrong place, where they were I have no idea but I think they were in the body somewhere. However, my hot treatment did not seem to work. I still could not walk, at least not very well. I realised if I did not do something about it then I would be unable to take

Shassie out, or more correctly Shassie take me. As I was meeting up with Jan and her two, I did not wish to miss out.

I remembered how more mobile I became after I had had a massage at the Health Farm. On seeing one of the therapists at the Centre, I asked if it was possible to have a leg massage. She saw the state I was in, and knew I was a regular customer, she managed to fit me in, in between appointments. It worked wonders. I could now walk. I still had the long trek home, which took just about 1 hour. This is only a walk of some 400 yards, and at this stage I could swim 400 metres [which are longer] in just under 10 minutes. I can swim 50 lengths which is 1250 metres in just over 28 minutes.

After my arrival home, I rested. I had to. There was no other option.

After lunch I met up with Shassie and we started off. She hates being on the lead, and pulls. This helps, especially when I have the hills to negotiate, but she still thinks I have long legs and can keep up with her. I cannot. Eventually we reach the recreation ground and she comes off the lead. She will not leave my side. She must know I'm not feeling very well. We trudge round to where I meet up with Jan, and she sees me sitting on the ground, not being able to move. After about 1/2 hour with the dogs becoming impatient, they want to run, and get wet, we set off. Jan takes me back to her house and after a cup of tea she drives me home.

The garden is now beginning to grow. I am unable to manage the housework and mowing of the lawns. How best to work it? The only solution is, that one day a week I mow the lawns, but the following week I dust and vacuum. Fortunately the mower is an automatic electric contraption. It has auto drive, but my problem is keeping up with it. I switch it on, and it pulls me along. There is only one speed, fast or fast. I do not care how the lawns look, or where the grass clippings are, but at least it is cut. Providing I only work for about 45 minutes I am generally okay. Also I need a lot of rest. This is not me being lazy, I am just unable to complete any task in the efficient and speedy manner I was accustomed to.

I was now realising there was something amiss with my left foot. I was cutting my toenails in the normal fashion with nail clippers, when I saw my foot was covered with blood. Where the hell did all that lot come from? A little spot really does make a tremendous mess, especially when you do not think you have cut yourself. I did not feel anything. Apparently I had cut my toe next to the little toe rather deeply. I had not felt a thing. Obviously the nerves are damaged in my left foot. Damn it, that maxim of 'no sense no feeling' really is true. I am now going to have to be careful when carrying out simple tasks, or at least they were simple tasks a few months ago.

About this time, I realised if I became ill with something ordinary and mundane I could not fight it. The 'flu was now upon me. Although I ached normally, all the time, having the 'flu with all its ordinary symptoms drains every little bit of energy out of the victim. I found on waking one Saturday morning I could not move. I was going to be unable to make the very short trip to the paper shop to collect my paper. Knowing that Ollie takes the children to school, I crawled to the telephone on all fours, and rang and asked if he could get my paper for me. I must have given the appearance of a sick snuffly crab whilst on the floor. Ollie agrees, and returns with it.

Through the post came yet more forms. Bloody hell, will they never stop. This is I think bureaucracy gone mad. I had requested some assistance from the Benefits Agency, as I was unsure of any further entitlements. I was also worried about the changes to the Invalidity Benefit and was concerned if I was going to need to take the work test. They now knew what the diagnosis was, and stated as it was a recognisable disease, I should not worry. This is easier said than done. The forms that were sent were for the Disability Living Allowance. It was like a book to complete about 1/2 inch thick.

My parents came up that weekend to help me complete them. My writing is now virtually illegible, as I find it difficult to hold a pen for any length of time. Mum completed it for me. I only needed the mobility part of the Allowance, as I was still capable of caring for myself.

Dad also lent me a battery charger, as it was coming up for a year since my last blackout, so I was going to attempt to get the car to work. It needed taxing but before that, it needed an M.O.T.

On inserting the key in the ignition, [I still know where it is and how to do it] the engine did not even flicker. It was as dead as a door nail. The battery was completely flat. It was not even 1/4 inch thick. No spark, no whirr, completely and utterly dead. The radio did not work neither did any of the lights on the dashboard. The battery charger stayed on for some 48 hours until the garage came to collect it, and got it going.

Chapter 46

It was now a month since I returned from Switzerland and I had not heard a word from Duncan. It was also two and a half months since he was supposed to have written and accepted the offer of £450 for the abysmal holiday. Still I had not heard a thing. I suppose I am going to have to leave another message on his blasted machine. Why on earth is he unable to treat me with any concern? Why is it always me that has to do the chasing? I am fed up with being treated as a non-entity. I am someone, I'm not a doormat, so surely I should command some form of consideration.

Two days after my message, a cheque arrives in the post for the full amount. No letter, just the cheque. Oh bloody hell, he's sent me the whole lot. I only wanted half. That was all I was expecting. That was all of my contribution. Just half. Is he unable to do anything right?

In the evening the telephone rings.

"Hello," I say very guardedly.

"Hello there." Oh god it's him.

"Long time no hear, to what do I owe this honour?"

"Have you received the cheque?"

"Yes, but you've sent me the whole amount, I was only expecting half."

"Yes I did that on purpose, I thought that your need was greater than mine."

"Why, thank you, but there was no need, I only wanted half."

"How are you," he asks as a backhander.

"I'm fine, not that you care, though."

"I do care," he tries to maintain.

"No you don't, if you did you would communicate more."

"Well I've been in hospital."

"Oh, have you?" Was I supposed to feel any sympathy, because if I was, I didn't. I could not have cared less.

"What was the problem?"

"I broke a rib."

"Oh, really, how the hell did you manage that? In too much of a hurry I expect."

"I fell down an escalator in the shopping centre."

"Oh, really. I expect you were running and tripped up, weren't you?"

"Yes."

Finally, I've got an admission. I carry on, "Well if you're looking for any sympathy from me forget it."

"I was unable to do anything for weeks."

"Well, now you know what it's like for me, don't you." I was hoping with this experience he might change his attitude towards me. Fat chance. It is impossible to teach a dog new tricks, or for the cat to change its spots.

"Yes," he replies.

"Is it impossible for you to communicate, find five precious minutes in your valuable time a week to pick up the phone and ring me?"

Out comes the usual boring excuse,

"You are always out."

I am fed up of hearing this platitude; I've heard it so many times now that it is totally unconvincing.

"Don't give me such crap, there are 24 hours in the day, I'm in bed for 10 hours that leaves you 14 hours, I'm out for five hours on four days a week that leaves you nine hours in which to ring. On two days a week, I don't go out at all, so that gives you 14 hours, in which to ring, and on the other day I'm only out for 3 hours, so that leaves you 11 hours in which to ring, if you could be bothered. I have told you this so many times before that I'm fed up of having to repeat myself. It is obvious to me that all you require out of a woman is for a walking doormat. Someone who you can wipe your feet over as and when it suits you. Someone who will be at your beck and call as and when you want. To be able to do what you want, when you want, and how you want. With no thought for the feelings for the person in question. I am not, neither will I, be that person. How many times have you put yourself out to come and see me, just twice. You let me down; you are totally unreliable, inconsiderate, insensitive, and thoughtless. I thought that your behaviour towards me in Switzerland was appalling."

"Why? I didn't do anything."

"That's just it. You treated me as if I was a complete non-entity. Did you bother to ask me what I was doing on the one day off, *NO,* all you asked me was if I wanted to take part in any of the tours, and that was at the beginning of the tournament. I said that I could not as I would not be able to keep up, and I did not want to become a burden to anyone. On my arrival, you were all over me, with this great pretence of caring, I don't know who it fooled, but it did not fool me. At the museum, you knew that I was in there, as Doug and Anne had told you, but did you bother to come to find me? You did not. You knew full well that I was unable to run around looking for you. If you had wanted to you would have put yourself out. When I left the arena did you bother to escort me to the bus stop, *NO,* it was left to others. Allen always made sure that I was escorted, and the person who came with me waited with me until I got on the bus. You could not even be bothered to come swimming on one morning when you were not on duty. I know that you were prepared, as you insisted on taking a number of swimming hats when you came to the Swimathon. Kai managed it, so why couldn't you? Not fit in with your on-the-go routine obviously, because you only want someone who is one hundred percent. You wait until you're like this."

"I'm sorry," is all he manages to say.

"I'm fed up of hearing your apologies, that's all you ever say to me. You haven't even got the guts to tell me it is all over." There follows a long pause.

"Well it is, isn't it? As far as you're concerned it never got going in the first place, as you were not having a relationship." Again another long silence. I am by this stage becoming very angry.

"Well for god's sake say something."

All I ever received was, "M M M m m m m m m m m," down to nothingness.

I carry on, "If you treated your wife in the same lackadaisical contemptuous manner that you treat me, then no wonder she went off with another man."

I've said it. I've told him exactly what I think of him. I've done it.

"Don't you want the side gate erected?"

"It now fits in with your routine does it. Well don't bother; Dad could not wait any longer for when it was convenient for you to come and help, so he did it himself. I'm surprised that you even remembered that it needed to be done?"

"That goes to show that I do care."

"Crap. Goodbye."

And good riddance, I think to myself as I slam the telephone down. I've done it. At long last, I've said what has been going through my brain often enough on my walks. Where did I get the strength of character from? I hope I shook him.

This was the first time I was able to pour out all my pent up emotions to him. I was really in the mood. Perhaps I'm not the insignificant stupid, useless, inadequate twit I thought I was because of his behaviour.

Chapter 47

I've done it. I've actually had the guts to tell him. Even that thought about his wife. I wonder if he actually thought of her in the same way as he thought of me. It is no wonder she never had a meal cooked for him when he returned from work. If he never told her the time of his arrival home, how could she? He always told me he had to do the shopping, I can understand that now. If he never communicated with her, how would she know what or how many to cater for.

At least I will no longer be worried when the telephone rings. Wondering if he has nothing better to do, so will scrounge off me for a weekend. At least I shall know the food I purchase will not be wasted, as I shall not be let down at the last minute. I also know I will not need to do any emergency shopping on the Friday, because he has telephoned me on the Thursday evening saying he is coming down for the weekend or for part of the weekend as it suits him.

I now find it very difficult to carry any heavy bags even though it is only a short distance. I notice this with the purchase of my milk, as I refuse to pay the price of

40p a pint from the doorstep milkman, when I can purchase two pints for 53p. and freeze the container not being used.

If I was always out, how did Duncan manage to contact me when he wanted something, or when it suited him, or when he could be bothered to find five minutes, or when I had to leave a message on that blasted answering machine of his? He invariably found the time then, but always left it, at least seven to eight weeks between telephone calls.

I never did ascertain the real reason why he could not be bothered to communicate. I think it was easier to talk to a stuffed dummy than it was to him. At least I would not expect a reply, yet alone get one. I had more communication with my cat with her long drawn out miaoooooooooow than ever I did from him. Was it he was just too busy, or did I not feature in any of his thoughts?

I will not now be walked on, or taken for granted, especially by him. I've got my freedom back again, or as much as my body will allow me to have. At least I will not need to chase him over the refund of the holiday. It is now finalised, and paid. I do not need to ring at all now. It is all over. Thank goodness. What a relief!

The car was sick! Having explained my problem to the garage, they then collected it and took it to pass its M.O.T. They had the vehicle for a few days, as I was in no hurry, but it cost me a small fortune. It is not surprising having been left for a year. Still the battery would not hold any form of charge. It was still dead. Needless to say I needed to purchase a new battery. Having collected the certificate, I then had to purchase the tax disc. This required me to walk the short distance to the Post Office, but I was in great difficulty. Having had my swim, I now find it extremely hard to carry out my normal functions, and it took me about half an hour to collect it. I only really had to cross the road.

I drove home on the 30th June 1995, this being the first time behind the wheel for just over a year. I wondered how I would react. A stupid woman decided to put my reactions to the test immediately, and stepped out in front of me. I came to an abrupt halt, and called her all the names I could think of. As I was in the car, all she could see was my mouth moving. I hoped she could not lip read, as I was not very polite. She mouthed back that she had not seen me. Not looked, more likely. I did not feel I had not driven for a year, it all seemed so natural. Like riding a bicycle I think.

At the weekend, to reassure me I was not being deceived, I asked Ollie to come for a drive. He did not feel in any way threatened, and thought I had kept my road sense. It was an odd occurrence for him to be driven, as he does all the driving for the family. Although Chris has her own vehicle, and drives Ollie's car, it is always she who is in the passenger seat.

The problem I noticed immediately was that I had lost the strength in my arms and legs. I could not manoeuvre the car. It felt like a ton weight. My arms felt the strain, every time I moved the steering wheel.

Whenever I parked my vehicle when I was fit and healthy I always reversed into any space. Where the hell is reverse! I'm sure it should be in the same position in the gear box as and when I last had to find it and use it. It is there, it is still in the same place, but I cannot press down hard enough on the clutch to put it in, as the 'actress said to the Bishop.' I also have not got the strength to press down on the gear lever to move it. I now have to use 2 hands.

I could virtually turn that vehicle on a sixpence. I could not now. It took too much energy in turning the wheel. If I needed to park, I had to have a large space in which to do so. Whenever other drivers saw me struggling I expect they thought ' there's another woman driver who can't reverse, should not be allowed out on the roads!' Just spare a thought, that person may be disabled, and may be waiting for a vehicle with power steering.

I had to struggle with the garage door. I did not think it was that heavy. Oh, this is ridiculous I am now unable to lift the door with one hand. Am I really that weak now, or is it I'm out of practice. Anyone seeing me in the pool would not think I could be like this on dry land. It is only an up and over door, quite simple really, but not to me. Having struggled with the car, I now have to struggle with the garage door, fortunately as it is the summer, I can leave the car on the driveway until I get my new vehicle.

I was hoping that the mobility allowance would come through at the full rate, and then I could transfer to the Motability Charity, and obtain a new car. I also hoped the allowance would not be too long in coming through if they thought me worthy of it. I could not keep driving this car, it wears me out.

I was now mobile again, although in a limited capacity. I did not need to worry about the walk home from the Leisure Centre, as I could now drive. I was now able to do my own shopping once a month, and not have to rely on Mum to take me.

Chapter 48

It was now time for Shassie's holiday. How would the cat react? Would she feel offended there was now a large golden demented dog in the house? Would she sulk? Or would she behave, as she had at the time I had Duncan's pets' over in Christmas 1993, in complete control and lauding over everything? Shassie is the female equivalent of the 'Peter Pan' of the dog world.

Ollie brought over all her food for the two and a half weeks, together with her bedding, and toys on the evening before their departure. He also gave me the dog's harness to use in the car, as well as her lead. Now I was mobile [of sorts] I had every intention of travelling to my parents on a Thursday, so she could play in the sea, and hopefully wear herself out that way.

This also meant I was going to have to take her for a walk before I had my swim. Would I manage to cope with this? I'm glad I have now finished with my challenge.

I had explained I would be unable to take her for a walk during the afternoons of both Saturday and Sunday, as on these two days I attempt just to look after the house and garden, and rest as much as possible. She would, though, have a short walk in the evening before I went to bed. Neither Chris nor Ollie minded about this problem. They seemed to understand my energy levels were greatly reduced with the onset of the disease.

My bedroom was going to be off limits to Shassie. I wanted at least one room where the cat felt at ease, knowing she was the only animal allowed in there [apart from me]. I placed another dirt box in the corner and moved her food bowls towards the front window. As she is on a special dry diet, I had no worries as to smell or flies.

When Shassie arrived she was as usual shaking every part of her. She saw the cat and started to chase her, but Calam was having none of it. She just turned and faced Shassie, ears down, fur up, and teeth and claws out, and hisssssssed and spat, her way round the house. Shassie did not know what to do; she looked at me with her great big brown eyes questioning the behaviour of the cat. Shassie was not accustomed to this sort of reaction; she chases them, but does not expect them to turn on her.

Shassie followed me everywhere in the house, even into the loo. She understood though, the meaning of the word NO. She knew she was not allowed in the bedroom. Anywhere else, she could and did go, but not into my room. Shassie has this habit of eating everything in sight, even if it is inedible, so I wanted to maintain she could not eat the cat's food, which is the main reason why I was so disciplined in this regard.

I placed the dog's basket under the kitchen table, but she did not seem to feel comfortable there as there did not appear to be much room. I had not bargained on her being so big. It is not until she was in the house I realised just how large she was. Where else to put it? The only place where there was any room was behind the settee. As this item is situated in the middle of the room, it seemed to me to be the only logical conclusion. I expect Mr. Spock ['Star Trek'] would have been surprised I could be so logical!

During the afternoon of the Saturday, the cat slipped out of the open patio doors, and did the proverbial runner. She would not come back in, and disregarded all forms of coaching. She had suddenly gone deaf!

She was still out, about 8 hours later. I was at this stage becoming rather worried. I took Shassie for her walk around the field, and hoped the cat would be waiting on the doorstep for me to come home. She was not. She was nowhere to be seen. Although I kept calling her, even though it was now quite late and I wanted to go to bed, but I needed to get the cat inside somehow. This was, of course, easier said than done.

I managed to spot her at the bottom of the garden, due mainly to the light shining in her eyes, and, I could determine her colours. Would she come in? No. She just sat there and glared. I even went down the garden to try and get her in, but she scampered off. Blast her! If she wants to stay out all night, then she bloody well can!

It was very difficult for me to maintain that hard attitude. I could not. At various times during the night I got up to see if she was about, but she was not. I think Shassie must have thought I had gone mental. She may, of course have been right. However at 03.00 hours I spotted the cat in her little house which is situated just outside the patio doors. I grabbed her before she could run off again. Shassie just stayed put and looked at me with her big brown eyes asking if she was ever going to be allowed to have an uninterrupted night's sleep.

This was the only time I had any problems, after this experience I think the cat must have realised the dog was here to stay, and therefore she was going to have to 'like it or lump it'.

I wondered how Shassie was going to react to being put to bed so early. She is accustomed to a lively busy household, not to someone living on her own and retiring so early in the evening. She did not seem to mind, she adapted very quickly. She may be demented and stupid, but she is really very intelligent.

Feeding time was fun. It seemed I was catering for the 5000; Calam let me know that she was hungry. Out poured a long drawn out incessant miaoooooooooooow. Shassie just looked at me expectantly.

However Chris manages with 2 cats and Shassie, I really don't know. I fed Calam first. I just could not tolerate that row for very long. After placing her bowls in the bedroom, I then mixed up Shassie's meal. As soon as I have put the bowl on the floor then the cat makes a quick bee line for it and starts eating it. Shassie just looks at me, knowing what would happen if she nosed the cat out of the way.

I pick her up and move her back to the bedroom, and get hissed at, and spat at for my trouble. Before Calam can return to Shassie's bowl all the contents have been quickly and efficiently devoured down her throat in what seemed one gulp.

At one point, Calam went to eat out of Shassie's bowl, so Shassie thought I'll go and eat out of hers, with this Calam just gave Shassie a right royal four penny one round the chops! Shassie then realised who was boss!

During the latter part of one morning, Shassie was stretched out between the kitchen door and the front door. Calam wanted to get to the front room. She could quite easily have jumped over Shassie, or walked behind her, but NO, she did neither of these things. She just spat and hissed, whereupon Shassie just backpedalled into the kitchen, and Calam just strutted into the front room without a backward glance. When Shassie realised she was past she then plonked herself back where she had started from.

As Shassie followed me everywhere, I had to be very careful when I was baking or cooking. She is so quiet, I would not hear her creep up behind me. As my sense of balance is off and I am clumsy, I cannot risk having a dog in the kitchen in case I fall over her after I have got a dish out of the oven. Upon opening the door I have to place the dish on the floor so that I can get a better hold of it before reaching to place it on the table. Therefore I did not want to risk throwing a steaming hot casserole either over the dog or over the walls of the kitchen. This would have created rather a mess to clear up, but I think I may have had some form of assistance in the form of licking, if it was to the taste of the cats' delicate pernickety taste buds. I therefore insisted Shassie stayed out of the kitchen at all times. She understood, also the meaning of the word OUT. She backpedalled out and sat on the floor by the door looking at me, questioningly.

On the mornings of my swims I took her home, and left her in the kitchen, as this was her usual environment. I also knew Joyce would be over during the morning as she was looking after their cats, George and Sooty.

As promised, on the Thursday morning, I drove to my parents, who live by the seaside. This was no easy task. First, I had to place the harness on Shassie. She was so excited at seeing it because it meant that she was going in the car. For me, to try to get hold of a dog that is jumping around like a demented chicken meant that I was going to need great control over my balance. I could not stand up, so I had to resort to chasing her around the house on all fours, until I got hold of her collar. Then I proceeded to sit on her.

The harness is about three inches wide and is black webbing. It has various clips on it, and has to be placed around her front legs, up her chest and is secured between her shoulder blades. There is a handle which the car's safety belt goes through. When it is secured and the safety belt is in place the dog is unable to suddenly dive into the front seat. This makes the journey much safer.

Upon our arrival at my parents' she is thoroughly spoilt. We go into the back garden and play, then the short walk to the beach. It is impossible to tell a dog she is not supposed to drink the sea water. She dives straight in, and carries on until eventually we leave for home and lunch.

During the afternoon we return to the beach and the tide is now coming in. Mum finds some sticks and all we do is sit on the stones and throw them in to the surf. Shassie swims out retrieves them and swims back, insisting upon shaking herself over us. If I was quick enough, I could throw the second stick, before she had time to recover. I wondered who would get worn out first, her or me. I'm also not sure who was wetter, Shassie, Mum or me.

Upon our arrival home Dad decided he was going to clean Shassie off. He did not want her traipsing wet English Channel salt through the house.

This meant somehow we were going to have to give her a bath of some sort. Again, easier said than done. Shassie seemed to know what Dad was up to, and followed him to the shed where he got out the hose. If Shassie had been excited beforehand she was now totally stupid. She was trying to bite the end off, and this was before it was attached to the tap, and turned on! Shassie just jumped up at the hose's spout as the water came out and tried to bite it. The higher we put the hose, the higher she jumped. Her head and snout was rinsed, but not the rest of her. Wherever the hose was pointed she just jumped at it, and bit it.

She should of course have been tired. I have no idea where she got her energy from. Dad asked me to hold her, but I did not want a cold shower. I would have been just as wet as her, but her back, chest, underbelly, and legs would have still been covered in salt. Wherever the hose was aimed Shassie was biting the water. Dad was quite unsure of what to make of it. He had never seen anything like it. We had to give up. Ollie had warned me what happens with hoses and water, but even this passed my expectations.

When I took her for her early morning stroll, I knew what the weather was going to be for that day. It was getting hotter and hotter. More and more humid. This was beginning to play havoc with my constitution. I could not cope with it. All the energy I had, which was not much, was being drained away. I was now finding it extremely difficult even to have my swim, but I persevered. The weather just seemed to exacerbate all the symptoms that I had.

Both Shassie and I, still managed to meet up with Jan, Tara and Purdey, and the 3 of them did not seem to mind the hot weather, as they still ran everywhere chasing all the invisible squirrels and rabbits. The streams were not as full as they had been, but of course this did not stop them. They still managed to find enough water to jump into.

Upon the second Thursday of her holiday, I travelled again to my parents following the same procedure as before. As I felt even more tired than before, I could not take her to the beach. All we could do was play in the garden. Dad did though take her for a walk in the afternoon, although I think it a more accurate description would be that Shassie took him!

Dad does not like having a dirty car on the front driveway. My car is always dirty and especially now as it had not been used a great deal for a year, it was even more caked in mud. Dad thought he might try and clean the car.

He had of course reckoned without the assistance of Shassie. She followed him outside, as if being psychic, and gave all her help to Dad as he got the hose out of the shed. She again was biting the end off. As he attached the hose onto the tap, Shassie knew she was going to have a fun time. Dad failed abysmally in his attempts to clean the car. She just would not let him direct the water onto the car. In the end he had to give up, and just hose the dog. If she had been to the beach this would have been a reasonable excuse to rinse her off.

Towards the end of the holiday, I realised the toll that was being taken out of me, as I took her for her walks, both morning and night. I knew I could not keep this up. Shassie therefore had to be content with just one walk during the day, and the use of the garden.

Kirsty and Steven came to pick her up upon their return from their holiday and she was glad to see them. I think, though, she enjoyed her holiday with me, and gave me a lick for my troubles. Calam was glad to see the back of her!

Chapter 49

Now that I was mobile, I no longer needed to rely on Mum to take me shopping once a month. I could do it myself. I think. It is a job I have always detested. I cannot think of anything more boring than wandering around a supermarket filling up a trolley which always seems have a mind of its own. I do not know if it is just me, but they always seem to move when they want to, and go in the direction they want to. They never seem to operate as they should.

This operation took more out of me than I thought. Battling with the trolley, and my unusual gait, and with screaming children, all seemed to exacerbate my delicate constitution. I am surprised parents are unable to discipline their children, so as not to cause irritation to others. I feel because they have children, their obnoxious behaviour has to be suffered by everyone, whether or not they have children of their own.

Whilst I was at the checkout, wobbling from side to side, dressed I must admit, in white Tennis kit, the lady behind me in the queue said "If you will play these

283

dangerous games then you have to take the consequences of any injuries!"

I was absolutely dumbfounded.

I retorted, "This is not, I repeat not, a sports' injury. It happens to be a permanent disability that I got from working too hard but if it had been a sports' injury then I could have accepted it far quicker than I am able to at the moment."

I turned to the cashier and said, "I still have all my P.E. equipment to wear and see no reason why I should not."

I paid my bill and tottered out. I hoped the lady who said it felt two inches tall or that the earth would open up and swallow her. Perhaps she was trying to lighten the atmosphere by being funny. If this was supposed to be a pun then it fell on deaf ears.

This was the first time I had admitted I was disabled. Barbara had said I was, but I could not accept it. The only way to improve one's situation is to admit there is a problem. Once this has been achieved then the victim's quality of life can be improved. Either with help, or by themselves, but they have to admit to themselves there is a problem. It is similar to an alcoholic or a drug addict, if they are unable to admit there is a problem then their situation will never improve.

I had now admitted I was disabled, perhaps my life would soon improve, and I could find something constructive to do. I was unable to work at least full time or even part time, as I would be so unreliable. I could not guarantee I could last a day, or even a few hours. The extreme fatigue one feels is so frustrating, and debilitating. With the tiredness comes the blurred vision. Who wants to employ someone who cannot stand up on their own two feet, without the appearance of being drunk or see straight? I would be unable to drive very far, and even if I managed it, I would have to either sit or preferably lie down for at least 30 minutes. What employer is going to tolerate that sort of behaviour? Also, when it was time to leave, I would need to lie down before making my return journey. What employer is going to tolerate that? Further, what employer is going to tolerate absenteeism, probably on a grand scale, and not on a regular basis?

Surely I would be entitled to some social life. If I worked, for any time during the day, no matter for how long, I would be unable to carry out any social functions. Any sport I now manage, although on a very limited basis would disappear completely. Would, or should I expect some quality of life? Perhaps I am after all the insignificant useless inadequate twit Duncan made me feel.

With this admission I was now disabled, I applied for the Orange Disabled Parking permit. With this, if granted, would enable me to park within reason almost where it suited me. I would no longer have to carry bags of shopping home although it only contained my milk, I could park nearer to the shops, nearer to the entrances of Official Buildings, walking would be simpler. I would no longer need to worry about access.

Again with this admission of being disabled, I reread some sports newsletters Jackie Farr [nee Hails] the Kent Sports Development Officer had sent to me some couple of months earlier.

In the December 1994 issue there was an advert entitled 'Are you disabled'; with the caption 'Would you like to swim competitively'. I pondered over this, for some time. I had been competitive all my life, first with hockey, and athletics, and then badminton, tennis and squash. Swimming [if it could be called that, being a mixture of the doggy paddle and something unmentionable!] had never been on the agenda. I just did it for fitness and to help my breathing. I had only been swimming [so called] since August 1990, some five years previously, so would I be good enough? I had no idea of the standard required, or the distance to swim. As I was regularly achieving between 50 and 60 lengths in a time of 30 - 35 minutes, I wondered if I would be good enough.

I wrote to Jackie and set out in as much detail as I could, the standard I had reached, the distance covered, and asked whether it would be worth my while to start being competitive, even though I was now over 40 years of age, and swimming is a young persons' sport, not for old codgers' like me. I needed a goal. I needed something to aim for. I wanted to have a reason for carrying on.

Ken, my American pen friend had continued to write, and he had given me a 12 month gift membership of National Geographic Magazine. I have received more care and consideration from someone whom I have never met than ever I received from Duncan. Ken seemed to treat me as an intelligent human being.

I was also waiting to hear from the Building Society. Surely they would not insist I make the full payments. I had done what they had asked for, and kept them informed of my situation, but were they keeping me informed of any decisions. It seemed to me you have to push all the time to get anywhere.

Although I looked out for the postman every morning, I dreaded receiving any mail. In case it was bad news. My hands were perpetually shaking, I could not control them. The more I tried the worse it became. As soon as I recognised the writing, or opening it, I found the shaking subsided. If it was bad news, then the whole of me took on the shakes. It was totally uncontrollable.

It had been several weeks, since my application had been received for the Mobility Allowance, surely I should hear soon. I also wondered if Duncan might have the nerve to write. He had never written in the past, but I thought my conversation last month might have struck a chord. I wondered if there was any conscience behind his lackadaisical exterior. As Sir Heneage Ogilvie stated, 'The really idle man gets nowhere. The perpetually busy man does not get much further'.

Chapter 50

During the second week of Shassie's holiday, my body was rebelling. It was telling me it did not appreciate the early morning walks neither did it approve of the trek around the field at night. I chose to ignore this feeling, and put it down to being lazy. It was ignored, of course, at my peril.

On the Monday, I took Shassie home as is my usual manner, and then walked to the pool. Although I was mobile, I did not see the necessity in driving my car only some 400 yards. It seemed such a waste of petrol and, of course a waste of money.

I managed the usual distance in the pool, more by guts and determination than finesse.

Whilst I was having a conversation with the Manager, my right leg decided, without asking my permission first, to collapse under me. This had never happened to me in public, and I worked myself into a state. I was crying, and shaking both at the same time. I felt a complete imbecile. Fortunately, as I was leaning against the reception desk, I grabbed hold of it with both arms and hung on. I did not land on the floor. Vicky, the life guard saw what was happening and sat me down on the nearest chair. There I had to stay for about 30 minutes. Hence my conversation came to an abrupt halt.

I was now faced with the walk home. Oh shit! I should have brought the car after all. I wished I could radio it up to come and collect me. Joyce had said on a previous occasion when I was in difficulties to ring her, and she would come and collect me, but I was still trying to maintain my independence, and therefore I would attempt to get home myself. I did not want to cause her any inconvenience. I was still unable to admit I could no longer live the way **I** wanted to live.

The walk home was everlasting. It seemed interminable. It was, though, only 400 yards. The sprinters can run this distance in under 50 seconds. Here was me, trudging along for what seemed hours. The little green man on the pedestrian crossing was going out before I even managed to get half way across. I'm sure it must be timed for the Linford Christie's of this world, or perhaps I should put myself on the end of Steve Backley's javelin. I would manage to cross in time then. It actually took me about 1 hour and 15 minutes, to walk home. Surely this was not normal.

It was now close on being lunchtime. I would therefore not have much time to get my act together and meet Jan. I managed it though, but I do not know how. My guts and determination must be working overtime; I hope they do not 'conk' out, like the rest of me.

Jan could always tell the sort of day I was having, by the way I was walking. Although I tried to hide it as best I could, I did not succeed. We trudged back to her house, as I was incapable of going any further, had a cup of tea and then proceeded to throw tennis balls in the garden so the dogs would get some exercise.

All Jan and I did was sit in the gazebo, and let them do the work. Tara thought this was totally stupid. She was of the opinion I think, to chase a ball and return it, in one's mouth was below her intelligence. Instead, she chased after them and hid them! Shassie and Purdey then found other items to chase, even invisible ones.

It ensured I had some rest, and at the end of the afternoon Jan drove me home.

On the Tuesday, I did not even attempt to have a swim; neither did I manage to take Shassie for a walk. She had to be content with the garden, and me, throwing tennis balls down the bottom of the garden. She just looked at me with her great big brown eyes pleading ' please, Auntie Sue, aren't we going out'. I managed to keep my resolve and not give in.

The Wednesday dawned, and again I did not feel like a swim. Things were serious; this made it two sessions missed. Something unheard of. Would I ever have the courage to get back in the pool? I am not sure whether the weather had turned cooler, but I was shivering. I had to put the central heating back on, and did not get dressed until I had to meet Jan. I was determined to go, mainly because Shassie enjoys her run with Tara and

Purdey, but also because she had not been out since Monday. Also we were due at my parents on the Thursday.

In the second post an important letter arrived. It was from the Disability Living Allowance Agency. I recognised it immediately, as I had had several like it in the past. I was shaking. I could not hold it to open it. I demolished the envelope in my clumsiness. I screamed, upon reading the contents. THEY HAVE REFUSED ME. Shit! Shit! And Shit! How could they? I can't move. I can't even get to the pool even with the use of the car. Am I supposed to be a prisoner in my own home? I was crying with disbelief. What am I supposed to do?

Shassie just looked at me, knowing there was something seriously wrong, but unable to help.

I screamed, "Oh God, take me, I hate this life, and I don't want to live anymore, take me, now."

There was a telephone number to ring, and I blindly rang the number. I was laying on the floor, my only comfortable position, and crying my eyes out. I asked why had I been refused, I can't even get to the Post Office, or to the newsagent. All the switchboard operator said was that if I was dissatisfied with the decision write in and appeal against the decision. Surely this stupid girl could hear the state I was in? Surely she could, and should have been more sympathetic?

I did not know what to do? I kept thumping the floor, tears streaming down my face praying for God to take me. I no longer wanted to live anymore. I saw no reason in carrying on. It is just as well that I do not wear any makeup, as my face would have been streaked with black smudges! If I was to live the rest of my life like this, then.

I screamed again "GOD, PLEASE TAKE ME, THERE IS NO POINT IN CARRYING ON".

HE was ignoring me! How could HE?

I got myself together, I don't know how, got dressed, again I don't know how, had a bite to eat which I did not want, and went to meet Jan. I was already seated on the ground. As I was feeling the cold I had on a coat, and Jan knew immediately something serious was wrong.

I burst out crying and said I had been refused the allowance. She was dumbfounded. She tried to console me as best she could, but it was a hopeless task. She managed to get me up, and helped me back to her house, for the second time this week. By the end of the afternoon, I was feeling better, after several cups of tea. Shassie was very worried. She is a very sensitive dog. Purdey did not know what to make of it. Tara though had seen me in a state before, notably on the first occasion we met, so she ignored me.

Jan asked me if I was going to appeal, and I said I would. She asked me if I was going to tell Mum, I said I was not, as Mum was already worried about Dad, as one of his knee replacement's was causing problems, and I did not want to add to her anxiety. She had her plate full as it was. Mum is a natural born worrier, and makes a mountain out of a mole hill, and I could not cope with her smothering me to any great extent. I was going to have to hide my problem, until I had heard about my appeal. As I was unable to walk, Jan took me home in the car.

On the Friday, I drove to the pool. I was not going to be caught out this time. In the lane part, was a stranger. He had a very peculiar breast stroke. It seemed that he had a fifteen foot wing span, with a leg kick just as big. I was, needless to say much quicker than him and always overtaking him, on or about my every two lengths. I kept bumping into him, accidentally. I could not help it. I swam down the middle of the lane, so as to avoid other swimmers. It was a very rare occurrence if there was anyone quicker than me.

As I swim using the front crawl, [or freestyle] I am unable to see what is in front of me. I have to allow for swimmers in the opposite direction, and am unable to see them coming towards me, so I cannot, out of politeness to others stray too far over. I was just making my turn to start my sixteenth length, when my right ankle is grabbed by this stranger, and my first thought was that someone was trying to drown me, I realised it was him and he immediately gave me an harangue. I could not believe it. He kept complaining that I was not giving him enough room. He did realise, though, that I was quicker than him. I do not know how much room he thought he needed. I could not give him anymore.

This episode had a completely demoralising effect on me. When I reached the other end, I was crying my eyes out – this is very difficult when wearing goggles and nose clips! – saying to myself, I'm not even being allowed to swim anymore. Joan and Ray, who I have met regularly were very helpful. As was Vicky, who was on poolside duty. Joan helped me out of the pool, and Vicky then took charge, and came running in to get me. She made me sit down, and drink a cup of tea.

I explained, or tried to explain what had happened and suggested that maybe perhaps I should swim in the disabled sessions, once a week. She thought I might not like that. I had no intention of getting back into the pool that morning. Vicky suggested I carry on as normal and go into the Health Suite and relax in the steam room and the sauna, and try to ignore him. She said I was to continue swimming as it bought me so much pleasure.

However, I heard later the man had received a thorough ticking off by another swimmer. He was told, not too politely, if he could not handle swimming in the lane part, then he should get out and swim in the general part of the pool, and was he aware I had got M.S. He tried to justify his actions by saying he had had a triple heart by-pass operation. Tosh! I still kept thinking I was not being allowed to swim anymore. The only thing left, and he is trying to stop me from doing it.

Joan and Ray, together with Charles, Norma Hugh and Audrey were all worried as to my demeanour. They made me join them for tea, although I did not feel like being sociable Peter offered to drive me home, but I declined stating for once I had the car. I saw that man in the cafe and wondered if he would have the guts to apologise. He did not. I saw him again on other occasions in the pool, but he never had the guts to say sorry.

Upon my arrival home I wrote out my Appeal. It was not very legible as my writing has deteriorated. I used lined A4 paper and it was two pages long. I set out in graphic detail what happened to my leg on Monday, stating it took me over an hour to walk home, a distance of only 400 yards. I asked if this was normal? Again I asked if it was normal for the leg to collapse under me? I stated I could no longer get to the post office or to the newsagent. I pleaded with them to assess me physically, as it is impossible to see how mobile I was just by reading a form. I also pleaded with them to contact my doctor, who would support any further inquiries. I asked if it was normal to be a prisoner in my own home? I asked if I was entitled to any form of quality of life or independence as at the moment I had neither of these? I also stated I felt I was being penalised because I was endeavouring to keep myself going and I was not sitting at home vegetating.

Come the afternoon, I meet up with Jan again. Oh! She is such a pillar of strength. I told her what had happened that morning in the pool, and she was astonished at the behaviour of him. Nothing surprises me anymore, I have met all sorts of characters whilst I was prosecuting. I also said I had entered my appeal.

It was now becoming a regular occurrence to go back to Jan's house, and on this occasion I met Bob, her husband. He is a tall white haired gentleman who is looking forward to his retirement next year. He could also see immediately that something was wrong, so did not say a great deal, and kept his distance.

Bob decided to clean the car. He of course, had reckoned without the assistance of Shassie. She must have thought it was her birthday. Two days running she was going to get hosed. I tried to warn Bob, that he would not succeed, but he tried anyway. Neither Jan nor Bob had seen anything quite like it.

Shassie behaved exactly the same as she did with Dad, both yesterday, and the previous Thursday. Purdey looked on in complete astonishment, and when the hose was turned on her she ran off. Tara was nowhere to be seen. She was not going to get wet. This seemed to lighten the atmosphere and I was laughing again. Again Jan drove me home. Now we had the customary bark from Shassie, as we drove out the gate, then the whimper. She was obviously saying goodbye to her friends. I told her she would be seeing them again.

My week was still not over. Whilst I was using the vacuum cleaner on the Saturday morning, my right hand twitched, and the plug hit an internal window and broke it. My language was not very clean. It has stayed broken, just to remind me to be more careful, and try to have more control.

What a bloody awful week! Surely, life can only improve, it cannot get much worse, can it?

Chapter 51

Several years ago Dad had undergone two knee replacement operations. Not both at the same time. That would be asking too much of anybody, but in consecutive years. Neither had been a great success. He was, though, up until this time without pain, although one knee cap wobbled from side to side. I put it down to lack of exercise, but Dad would argue against it. The one which did not wobble, he always classed it, as his good knee and it was this one that was swelling up, and causing pain.

It came to a head, when he could not move, and was therefore admitted to hospital. It had gone septic. It needed to be drained, and he would be kept in until it was clear. This meant many blood tests, and an operation.

I knew how worried Mum would get, and therefore asked Jan if she could drive me to Hastings to visit him. I left Shassie with Tara and Purdey, having driven to her house with the dog. Again, having the fight with the harness. She becomes so excitable when she sees it. I did not relish the drive to Hastings, especially in that 10 ton weight, I unfortunately called a car. Jan did not mind.

Before going into the hospital, I asked Jan not to mention anything about the allowance being refused, as I still had not said anything to my parents.

I do not know if Dad remembers seeing Jan on that day, but he says he does. This may of course have been a misconception. Mum asked me whether I had heard anything about the mobility allowance, and I said I had not, and she suggested I write to them informing them of the problem with my right leg, when it collapsed. Jan said she thought it was a good idea. I was not going to admit I already had done so in my Appeal letter. I just muttered a very non-committal answer, and changed the subject.

Dad was all prepared for his operation, having already had his 'pre-med'. All he had on was a hospital night shirt, and he seemed to be worried about showing all. I do not know if this was supposed to be for my benefit or Jan's. It could not possibly be for Mum, they have been married for over 45 years, and surely in all that time she must have seen all. The nurses all seem to refer to this part of a man's anatomy as his 'crown jewels'.

After the visit Mum thanks Jan for bringing me, and I was by this time absolutely shattered. I am glad I did not drive, as I do not think I would have made it, not in one piece, though. Dad is in hospital for a long period, as his knee just will not seem to clear. All his blood test results are negative, and he spends his birthday in there. The specialist is rather baffled. That is par for the course; it seems to run in the family.

The hospital caterer makes him a cake, but I do not think it had seventy four candles on it. Imagine the breath needed to blow out that lot and the mess. I do not think Dad's lung capacity could cope.

I actually managed to make the drive to Hastings, in my own car on two occasions. After the operation Dad felt a fraud, as in himself he felt a lot better, it was just his knee would not drain clear. He was not allowed to move, but this would have been difficult with all the tubes and bottles dangling down by the side of the bed. I think he rather enjoyed all the attention, and the 'molly coddling'. I am yet to find a man who does not enjoy being smothered and petted. He knew all the nurses by their Christian names and I think he really rather enjoyed himself.

Chapter 52

After that bloody awful week in July, when I pleaded with God to take me away, I was now beginning to get a response to all the letters I had written over that period. I suppose HE must have had his reasons for keeping me on this earth. I could not see it though.

I was still in a state every time the postman called. Shaking every time. Wondering if I was ever going to receive any good news. Although I wanted him to call, I also did not. Both at the same time.

I have now received an acknowledgement from the Disability Living Allowance regarding my Appeal. Well, at least they can read the address and the name, so at least that part is legible, let's hope they can read the rest of it.

The Building Society with whom I have my mortgage, finally agreed to allow me to pay the interest only, and pay at least £500 off capital, in one instalment as and when I could. This meant a reduction of nearly £100 per month. This I agreed to, as it was a much better solution than previously put forward. It just goes to show, that if you push, and push hard enough they will assist, but the onus is on you, all the time. They will not bend unless they have to.

Also, at the beginning of the month of August I received my Orange Disabled Parking Permit. This does not give me the entitlement to park just anywhere, but allows me to park on double and single yellow lines, providing I am not causing an obstruction or am in a dangerous position, for up to a three hour limit. This is, of course, referring to the position of the vehicle and not to me personally! I do not think I could get into a dangerous position because I am unable to move quickly enough. I have to use the pedestrian crossings even though the green man goes out long before I am able to finish crossing. I suppose this could be construed as getting into a dangerous position.

The biggest surprise was yet to come! Jackie Farr [nee Hails] the Kent Sports Development Officer for Disabled People had replied in the affirmative. They did want me competitive. Imagine, me at my age, swimming competitively. THEY DID WANT ME! She stated in her letter and I quote, 'I think it would be a super idea if you considered swimming competitively and we have a County squad for talent identification and training. We meet bi-monthly and swimmers complete a log-book in between so we know the kind of work being done on their own. Through the squad, if, your times improve, you would be eligible to qualify for Regional and National events so I'd definitely encourage you to 'give it a go'!

She also sent me an information pack together with the log-book which I could start using straight away. I was informed that all the swimmers currently in the squad were under 20 but it was not their intention to restrict the age and therefore, I would be most welcome. She also suggested I would need to swim 50 metres freestyle in around 1 minute 05 seconds in order to compete at National Level. This was given as a guideline only, because without actually seeing me in the water, or knowing my level of disability it would be very difficult to gauge the time required for the distances.

I was now given a lot of reading to do. The information pack was 60 pages long, setting out the various times required for the various strokes and distances. A vast amount of information was given as to the profiling system. For the various degrees of disability the swimmers are placed into categories. There are over 50 different ranges of disability.

Jackie is going to have a very difficult task in fitting me into a category, because, as usual, I am not normal. I have all my bits! I am just unable to use them all, or co-ordinate them. I could not possibly race with someone who has no legs as it would be unfair on them. It would also be unfair on me, to have me up against people who can dive in. They would be half way down the pool before I even got started. I am unable to dive in because I am unable to get on the starting blocks. Even if I could get on them, I could not stand still long enough, without falling in, before the gun went off. After two attempts at this I would be disqualified. This of course, would defeat the purpose of trying to be competitive. I would over balance, have one of my customary dizzy spells and fall in with a big splash, either head or bum first. As I went in, the water would get out! In protest I think. The different categories are then placed into 10 functional disability groups, three visual disability groups, and one learning disability group.

My biggest disappointment was the longest distance available is only 400 metres. The equivalent of 16 lengths of a 25 metre pool or 8 lengths of a championship size pool [i.e. 50 metres]. It seems hardly worth my while in just getting in and swimming 16 lengths. I know this would be in a race, but I would hardly have got going before I had to get out. I had hoped I would be able to compete at 800 metres, to start with. I am not a sprinter, unlike my competition at Athletics when all I could do was a quick dash for 100 metres or in hockey when my position was right wing, again a speedy position.

I now have something to aim for. My life has a purpose again. I have a reason to swim, and am not ploughing up and down the pool aimlessly. In chatting to the various friends at the pool, I learnt that Len had been in the past, Chairman of Gillingham Swimming Club. I hoped he would not mind if I asked how I could speed up. I knew I needed to get quicker, but how? He suggested I should not change my stroke, but straighten my arms upon entering the water, and push through the water harder.

I also knew I needed to learn the tumble turns. But how? I know of no coaches in the area, and I could not afford to pay for one. Having watched swimming events on the television, I knew that upon coming up to the wall, you execute a front somersault. But how far away, from the wall? If too close, you bash into the wall, and that hurts, as I learned to my cost when I clobbered the wall with my left ankle. If too far away, then you are disqualified for not having touched the wall. You need to kick off the wall to get the momentum going again. It is a very fine balance. In the execution of the somersault there has to be a twist, so you come up face down in the water, ready to continue with the stroke.

If I was to concentrate on the breaststroke then I would not need to worry about the tumble turns, as you have to touch the wall with both hands, if you have them. I do not feel comfortable with the breaststroke as my right leg will not behave itself as it does its own thing. I wanted to swim the front crawl [or freestyle] and learn these blasted turns, and I was going to succeed.

In the execution of the front somersault I was unable to control my legs. They would not stay together, and kick off the wall as is required. My arms were all over the place, and it seemed I could not control them either. I discovered, after many futile attempts the twist is put in as you kick off the wall. This is all very well, providing you are near enough to kick off the wall! Len was unable to show me, as having had a heart by-pass operation, his movement was restricted, and therefore I did not want to put any pressure upon him. Len's wife, Olive, also swam, but she had not been a competitor.

I had requested assistance from the lifeguards with my times. On 23rd August, Keith agreed to time me over the distance of 400 metres. It was in a time of 9 minutes 06 seconds. The first two lengths were in under 60 seconds. If only I could keep that up. I was rather disappointed, but at least it was something to work on. If I could average 30 seconds a length, then I could complete the distance in 8 minutes. This was my aim.

I now attempted all the other strokes. Backstroke, and Butterfly, as well as my normal ones. I wanted to be invited to attend my first training session, so therefore I needed as broad a range as possible in the hope they would accept me.

I happened to overhear a comment from one of the regulars, "I don't know, she is now buggering about with other strokes and is STILL beating us!"

As the butterfly is such an antisocial stroke, at least it is when I do it; I had to make sure the lane part was relatively clear of swimmers. Hugh, who swims in the general part, stated he would not need to ask for the wave machine to be switched on, as I was creating enough turbulence to satisfy the whole of the pool. I could now swim two lengths of butterfly but not in one go. I needed a rest after the first 25 metres.

Although I had now increased my training I still managed several sessions when I swam a casual long distance. This meant I was now including endurance training together with speed work. Just because I had the disease, I was not going to let it dictate to me how, and when I could swim. I wanted to be accepted in the squad. I wanted to prove I was not a useless, inadequate, and stupid twit! On some occasions the swim was extremely difficult, and in the log book it requested my personal reactions. If it wanted to know my personal feelings it was going to be told. If I felt pissed off and knackered then I entered this in the book.

Towards the beginning of September I informed Jackie, as to how I was progressing, and hoped I would be invited along. I knew the next training session was on the 30th September at Coombe Bank School. Wherever that is!

I had heard that Ashford have a Disabled Session early on a Sunday evening. I decided to attend, and spoke to one of the coaches. I said I was having difficulty with the tumble turns, as I could not control my arms and legs. She suggested, as I come into the wall, just dip the right shoulder. This movement automatically twists the body and therefore the legs are able to kick off the wall. I tried it. It worked. It actually worked. Just a simple movement, why the hell could I not think of that? It also did not seem to matter if I was virtually on top of the wall, although it would be quicker if I could be the correct distance away.

I was unable to maintain the same stroke rate with each length, and therefore some of my turns were still a bit 'naff'. Although I felt that I had improved. For the first time in my life I felt I was actually beginning to swim properly. No more of a cross between the doggy paddle and something unmentionable!

Jackie invited me to attend the Official Opening of the Whitstable Swimming Pool on the 30th September. This should have been my first training session. Karen Pickering who represented Great Britain in swimming at the 1992 Olympics and won medals at the 1993 European and World Championships, and the 1994 Commonwealth Games, together with Marc Woods a swimming medallist in 2 Paralympic Games were going to be in attendance.

Demonstrations were going to be made by the Herne Bay Lifeguard and Swimming Club, Kent County Disabled Swimming Squad, and the Canterbury Sub Aqua Club.

I was unsure if I was going to be allowed to swim. They had not seen me in the water, and only had my correspondence to go on. I could have been exaggerating my capabilities. I saw no point in attending if I could not swim. Jackie reassured me that I was to swim.

Mum took me to the pool, as I would be unable to drive the distance, swim in an alien environment, be put through my paces by the coaches, who can be very hard, at least they are in other sports, and I see no reason why these should be any different, and then be in a fit state to drive home again.

Upon arrival at the pool, I was surprised to learn half of it was open for general use and the 3 groups who were invited to give demonstrations were sharing the lanes in the other half.

A new group were also giving a demonstration. I had always wanted to learn synchronised swimming, but this was now going to be impossible. They had not been formed long, but already some of the girls, displayed strong control. They showed the basic movements and strokes. This was the only group who had half of the pool to themselves.

Jackie had hoped they could show how they initiate a new recruit, and wanted to let everyone know it was for all ages and not just for youngsters. This was going to be impossible . I was introduced to Mike Geer, the Chief Coach, and upon getting into the water he told me to swim at least 20 lengths as fast as possible. This I did, and then Alan Cook, another Coach, suggested I do it again. How many lengths do they want, I asked myself? I was happy to oblige. If they want me to swim, then swim I bloody well shall!

Karen Pickering and Marc Woods were solely there to run a form of master class. Both Mum and I were hoping that they would dive in and show us how it should be done. Marc is classed as a below knee amputee.

After having swum for nearly an hour I was absolutely knackered. Would I be accepted? Would I be good enough? Was I too old? Did I feel there was anything there for the coaches to work with? Yes they did want me. Yes I was good enough. Being so knackered it did not sink in at the time. Alan had to help me out of the pool, and escort me back to collect my stick and towel.

Alan and Jackie on poolside with Sue and Sarah Photograph by Graham Bool Reproduced by permission of Kent Sport [Formerly Kent Sports Development Unit]

In the café part of the centre Jackie formally invited me to join, and gave me the T-shirt. There must be something in my size, as she insisted that I needed 'Extra Large'. Was this due to the amount of water I had displaced? She also gave me a float. This is a blue and white striped polystyrene mould in the shape of a figure of 8. I had no idea what to do with it, and was informed by Jackie you stick it between the legs!

I was good enough! They did want me! I was not too old!

Chapter 53

All through this period of intensive increased training, I was seeing less of Jan. This was not due to the swimming, but because her daughter, Bec, was getting married at the beginning of September. Jan's craft talents were stretched to the extreme.

She was baking and decorating, a three-tier wedding cake, making two bridesmaids' dresses, and hand crafting a garter in lace. Is there no end to the talents, of this girl? With all this going on, she still had the large house and gardens to look after, and the meals to cook, as and when her employers were in residence. She managed to get out at least once a week, and give the dogs a run. Where did she find all the energy from? Certainly not from me!

I was amazed at the standard and the quality of the decoration. This was Jan's first attempt at icing; such a large undertaking. The surface was smooth, with not a wrinkle in sight, and she decorated the sides with iced frills. I did not realise that through the pillars to hold the weight of the first and second tiers are placed metal rods. I suppose if I had thought about it, it would seem logical, so as to prevent the tops from collapsing under the weight. She did not put any lace on the cake, as she was making this for the garter. She created a posy to decorate the top and sides of the cakes, made out of silk flowers in the colours of the dresses. After the wedding, I was given a piece of the cake, and it was the best cake I have ever tasted. Absolutely delicious. I came back for second helpings!

I left my stick in her house, quite accidentally on one Friday, and being the weekend Bob delivered it on the Saturday morning. I was still at this stage feeling fairly useless. I did not know what to do. Bob spoke to me in a manner that depicted I was not useless. He was impressed with my swimming, and suggested I try something in that line. I stated I already had, and realised fairly quickly, I would be unable to get any form of instructor's certificate. I was not artistic, or crafty in any shape or form, neither was I a good cook. I was a sportswoman, but I could no longer do it. Bob certainly gave me food for thought! Not in the edible sense though!

On one Friday, though, I had the pleasure of meeting Jan's brother Jeff, and his family. His parents-in-law are both stricken with the disease M.S. Jeff spent much of the time chatting to me, about my feelings, and how I had adjusted, also to the fact that I was still determined to be competitive in some form of activity. We spent a great deal of the time just comparing notes between all of the victims. I felt, although the disease is not hereditary, Carolyn would and should wish to live life to

312

the full, bearing in mind both her parents have the disease. She must, I feel, stand a greater risk of contracting it, as it is so indelibly in the family.

I took the bull by the horns, and started to go back to church. The first service I attended was the V.J. Day commemoration. Apart from Don and Peggy Webb, and Muriel Webb, together with the vicar, no one else had been in touch. They knew where I lived, and could quite easily have contacted me by the telephone even though I am ex-directory. They could have ascertained my number if they could be bothered to. They did not. However, after the service, I was surprised how many were inquiring as to my well-being. If they showed this much concern in church, why could they not bother to communicate with me out side church. I was totally cheesed off with the double standards of so many people!

My specialist had not forgotten me. More's the pity. He sent me an appointment for a date in September. I was supposed to visit him in July, but had not, on purpose. If he thinks I am going to waste my time in seeing him, only to be dismissed in a flippant and inconsiderate attitude, then he has another think coming. *I will not see him.* On the day before my appointment, I telephoned the hospital, stating the appointment given was inconvenient.

I was asked if I wanted to make another, and I stated "Any appointment with that man would be inconvenient," said goodbye and broke the connection.

I still had in mind, my conversation with Bob. I wondered if I could help out on a voluntary basis in the adult swimming lessons. I knew they were held on a Wednesday morning after the schools. I also knew they were mainly ladies ranging from the age of about 35 upwards. There seemed no upper age limit. I decided to write and ask, if it would be possible to help out on a voluntary basis. I did not want to be employed because I knew I could not guarantee my attendance every week.

I was asked to meet Penny Fowler, who then introduced me to Irene, who actually takes the lessons. They agreed to me helping them. I was amazed. They both knew I swam, and disabled, and I wanted all the students to know of my disability, as I felt it might give them encouragement in learning to swim.

Some of them had a fear of the water. Me, I'm like a fish in the water. I think in one of my previous lives' I must have been a fish, or maybe a dolphin.

I was asked to assist at two lessons on the Wednesday morning, the first being beginners, and the second, not quite so beginners. They were for 30 minutes duration each. The lessons were due to start in mid-September, and it was not until Irene saw her ladies, as to whether I could be of any help. If they were unable to get in to the water I would have to wait until the second class to assist.

It had now been a month since I had submitted my Appeal to the Mobility Allowance, and all through this time I still had not told Mum I had been refused. I was keeping it from her for as long as I could.

My car was now really irritating me. I could not manage it any longer. I had to part exchange it. I now decided to purchase a second hand Renault Cleo, with little mileage, and under 2 years old. I found the perfect vehicle in a Renault garage in Bexhill-on-Sea, and after a little haggling I got a reasonable price for my vehicle.

On my test drive, I found it was much easier to drive as it had power steering, but it was not as comfortable as my old one, but this is only to be expected as it is a smaller vehicle. Although it has a smaller engine, I did not notice the performance was any less restricting, compared to my old 1600 Rover. I checked the back shelf would dismantle, so there would be enough room for Shassie.

I needed a few days to get a cheque from my savings building society and it was arranged I could collect the vehicle the following weekend. The cheque arrived on the day before I was collecting the car. They are cutting it a bit fine, I think to myself. They were perfectly well aware of the situation, but they kept me on tenterhooks as to whether it would arrive on time.

The garage were unable to accept the cheque even if I endorsed it over. I therefore had to give a personal cheque for the whole amount. On the next working day I paid the cheque into my account, and as it was one of their own cheques' I did not appreciate there would be a problem. Towards the end of the week, I received a letter from them stating there was not enough funds in my account, and they had charged me £25 for the privilege of going overdrawn.

Imagine my amazement, I knew I had paid the cheque in; it was one of theirs' from my closed savings account. I was flabbergasted. How dare they? They even had the audacity to remove £25 of my hard earned cash. How dare they? I was furious. I knew the garage could commandeer the vehicle. It was my only means of getting about. What was I to do? I did not want to lose the car. I went to see the manageress, but got nowhere. My right leg decided to collapse under me, and I was in a state. Oh God! Am I going backwards again? I thought I was improving. It seems every time I'm under stress, or in a situation when I'm not in control, I quiver and shake, and the right leg will not behave itself. Due to the misbehaviour of my right leg, and the fact I could not control it, I burst out crying. Oh, bugger this!

She said she had tried to telephone me, but as I was ex-directory she was unable to confirm the situation. I was furious. Even if she did have my number there was no guarantee I could have been reached, as I swim in the mornings. She said she would telephone the garage as the cheque had now been cleared, and I now had sufficient funds to meet it, and inform the garage to represent. I told her to ring, and to at least try and earn the extortionate amount taken from my account. I was still furious and in a state, as according to their rules they were unable to refund me the £25. I was still concerned about losing the car. It was my only form of transport. I would be a prisoner in my own home without it. Perhaps I should be a prisoner, perhaps I should stay at home and vegetate, and then I would not be a problem to anyone. Perhaps I should give up trying to be independent.

I'm not like that though. It is not in my nature. Why the hell should it be???

I did not let the matter rest there. I wrote to the chief executive of the building society, complaining about the treatment handed out to someone who is disabled with M.S. Also about their intransigence, and demanded the return of the £25. I also wanted confirmation I had not lost any interest on my account neither had I been black listed as to my credit rating.

My correspondence was passed to the area manager, and a full refund of the £25 was made, and confirmation there had been no loss of interest. I should think so too. They informed me they did not register credit ratings. They still insisted the fault was mine because I am ex-directory, with regard to the telephone. I was not going to argue any more. I had had enough.

I was still very worried about this, and felt I had been treated shabbily. I had never been overdrawn ever since I took out my account, and they should have inspected my account to see I had operated it correctly. I did not want to lose the car. Again, it shows if you complain, and push hard enough then these large institutions will take account of customers' feelings, but, we should never be put into that situation in the first place.

317

All during this period I was having problems with my ears. They kept popping, and I had a great difficulty in hearing. I forget the number of times I had to keep saying pardon, or can you repeat that. I was forever sticking a finger in both the left and the right, not at the same time though, that would have looked ridiculous, but the right was worse, to try to unblock them, and soothe the pain. Not very pleasant especially if in company. On attending the doctor, he had a look in them, only to state there was not much wax, so it must be the M.S. Am I going to have to tolerate this sort of attitude from now on?

I was not happy with this response, so I purchased an Ear Wax remover solution and the problem cleared up within a few days.

If this is the attitude of the medical profession, I am rather concerned that if I should have a more fundamental problem is it going to be dismissed in the same flippant manner? It is just the M.S. Stop making a fuss and get on with life. That's how it seems to be portrayed. I am not one to make a fuss. I am trying to make the best of it. Surely he should see that.

I stated it would seem the Specialist wished to see me but on no account was I going to be bothered with him. I explained the reasons, and the only response I got was 'point taken'. He was then going to refer me to see someone at the local hospital. It seemed to me that the 'old boy network' ruled, 'sod your feelings', was the impression I got.

It all happens during mid-September. My lessons start. Imagine, me, assisting others to swim. All the ladies are amazed I am disabled, but soon start to ask me questions on how to do things. I am now learning the basics. I never knew how to stand up in the water, I just did it, or to glide, or to float. The first thing to learn is to put your head in the water and breath out. This was automatic for me. But I never knew the reason until now. There are only 3 elements to swimming.

[1] Breathing,

[2] Arms, and

[3] Legs.

Once all these are mastered then swimming is one of the most pleasurable relaxing of pastimes.

In one of the classes one of the more elderly ladies called me a bully. She was trying to kick off the wall and glide on her front.

I was guiding her, holding onto her hands, but she kept saying "I can't do it."

"Yes you can, there's no such word as can't."

In the end she succeeded, so it was worth me being called a bully!

In the second class I was mainly demonstrating the various strokes. They frequently got cross because I

319

made the front crawl look so easy. Irene said it is easy, when done properly. I got annoyed with myself, because I am unable to perform the leg kick in the breast stroke. My right leg, again, has a habit of doing its own thing. I do not seem to have the control over my rear end! Oh, sod that right leg of mine! As Irene is teaching the ladies properly they can all manage the kick. Me, I fail abysmally.

A letter arrives. Oh, God! It's from the Mobility Allowance. I was shaking. This was it. This letter is different though, the address is hand written, not typed as in the past. Upon demolishing the envelope, I read the contents with trepidation.

They have accepted me. I've been granted it, at the full rate for life. I cannot believe it. They have granted it. I read, and re read the contents over and over again. They have completely changed their minds. They have even backdated it to the date of my Application. Back in June. Some three months ago.

How on earth can they go from complete rejection, to granting it at the full rate for life, in a period of three months? They must have managed to read my illegible writing. What made them change their minds? This is bureaucracy gone mad! Do they have a habit of rejecting everyone irrespective of disability, on the first application, then wait for the appeals to arrive? Hoping, that rejection means less work? Upon receipt of the appeals do they then look at the applications properly?

On this day, I was in a state of euphoria. I would have run the London marathon, if I could only walk properly! I immediately telephoned Mum to let her know I had at long last been accepted, and I had been refused in the first instance. She was not cross for not knowing, neither did she voice any surprise, at my admission. Had she somehow guessed? All she wanted to know was what had I put in my appeal.

As I was meeting Jan on this afternoon, I did not telephone her, but waited to see her, with my exceptional news.

On my way, Shassie decides to do a 'dollop' on the grass verge outside someone's house. Before I have time to even get the plastic bag out of my pocket, and before Shassie has even finished, this householder gives me a very abusive harangue. I am completely taken by surprise. I tell him in a very short manner he wants to be sure of his facts first, before being abusive. He questions me as to what facts he needs to be sure of.

As I'm pulling out the bag, I ask him "What's this, Scotch mist?"

He still tries to justify his manner, and because I was not going to succumb to his diatribe, he turned round and said "I was one of them."

What he meant by this, I do not know. I have not got a clue. He could see I was not too secure on my pins, as I use a walking stick. I finished clearing it up, and perhaps should have dumped it on his lawn!

I retorted as I walked off, "He was no gentleman, in fact he was not even a man, and he was in fact an arrogant, conceited, male chauvinistic pig!"

As I continued on my way, I started to shake. Oh, sod it, is that blasted right leg going to give out on me again? I was also near to tears. Upon meeting Jan, she immediately notices there is something wrong. Sits me down, and I tell her what happened.

"Oh, why are men so obnoxious?" I ask.

She informs me they are not all like that. No, I think, but why do I only ever attract morons. What is there about me? What the hell is wrong with me? She just tells me I have not met the right one yet. How will I know if it is the right one? When will Mr. Right appear? I now inform her I have been granted my allowance, and it is being backdated.

The dogs are totally oblivious to all of my problems. They are rushing everywhere, in all the dirty water, and finding the smelliest, odious concoctions to swim in.

I had invited Jan and Bob to lunch on the Saturday following this. It would also give Dad the opportunity to meet Jan, in a more favourable situation, and for both of them to meet Bob.

Knowing Jan is such a good cook, and, me so lousy, I needed to try something impressive. I started the meal with smoked salmon, and a little side salad together with small triangles of bread. The main meal was a meat fondue. Knowing how fond Jan is of cooking, I thought she should not get away with a weekend where she did not cook. She and Bob were going to have to cook it themselves! At least I cannot be blamed if they burn their steak! Or it drops off their forks! A fondue is one of the easiest meals to prepare, as it is all done before hand, and the table looks quite impressive with all the sauces and the salads. Jan and Bob had never had a fondue before and thoroughly enjoyed the experience.

At least they can joke, and say how Sue invited them to lunch, and made them cook their own meal! I must admit to cheating with the dessert, though, as this came out of a packet. It was a trifle, with an added can of fruit. Dad then made everyone a cup of tea or coffee.

Chapter 54

My life started to settle down. I had hoped all my problems had now been eradicated. It had taken a long time. It was now about 20 months since I started to feel really ill. Surely, there is now, only one way to go, and that is up.

I kept to my routine of swimming 4 mornings a week, using the Sauna and Steam room, basically to put all my bits back in order, if it is possible, looking after Shassie every day, and my lessons. I found, though, after them on the Wednesday, I was not fit for anything. I was absolutely knackered. Shassie had unfortunately to forego her walk. I was unable to put one foot in front of the other. The legs did not seem to know what they were supposed to do! There they were, attached at the hip.

I think, just looking at me, saying, if they could speak, "If you want to walk, forget it! We have had enough! We are both going on strike! So there!"

If they thought they were going to get the better of me, they had another think coming. I put Shassie in the back of the car and drove to Jan's. So there! Once there, she managed to meet up with Tara and Purdey, and have a run in the large gardens, and so wear herself out that way. The only problem was, there was no water in which she and Purdey could get into. I suppose this was a blessing in disguise as at least I took her home clean. This should be chalked down as a first.

The car was an absolute godsend. I was not in the least bit tired driving it. It was so easy on the arms and the legs. My only problem was the garage door. It seemed to be getting heavier and heavier, or I was getting weaker and weaker, I'm not sure which.

Some of the regulars were rather confused. Why was I having lessons? They were under the impression I could already swim. I explained, although I could not get my Instructors Certificate to teach disabled swimmers, less fortunate than me, I was assisting Irene in her adults' classes. I went on to state I did not have lessons, but coaching, when I was with the squad.

Having now been accepted by the Kent Squad, I was working towards the next training session on 11th November. I needed to get quicker. I needed to work harder. I therefore had to reduce the amount of lengths I was doing, and put it into speed sessions. At least this was the theory. I was roughly covering 100 metres in just over two minutes. I was unable, though, to maintain this speed for the whole of the 400 metres. I wanted to endeavour to achieve the 400 metres in about eight minutes. This meant I would have to cover the whole distance in 30 seconds a length. An impossible task. At least at the moment. I had to lose just over a minute. The coaches had not asked me to do this, but it was my decision. Mad fool me! I will do it, I don't know how, but I will.

I was now looking to take part in competitions. I wanted to show that idiotic, uncaring, thoughtless, dispassionate, unreliable cretin, I was not a useless idiot. I was neither, useless, stupid or inadequate. I knew the Paralympics were taking place in Atlanta, United States of America, in 1996. After the ordinary Olympics. Could I possibly have aspirations to be selected. Swimming is a young person's sport, though. Here was me, in my early 40s thinking I might be good enough.

My first competition, if I qualify, would be the National Championships to be held at the beginning of June 1996, in Sheffield. In a 50 metre pool! I have never swum in a 50 metre. I wonder what it is like?

I had asked one of the coaches for her opinion whilst I was at Whitstable.

"It is terrifying, you look down your lane, and it seems to go on for ever." She said.

Oh, shit, what have I let myself in for?

I considered my tactics very carefully, after having another try at the 400 metres flat out. This time it was just under nine minutes. I managed some lengths in 32 - 33 seconds. Still not good enough though. I needed to build up slowly. I thought I would swim flat out for two lengths, then have a rest, then flat out for another two lengths. Then on another session put the two and the two together to make four. Then do another four, and hopefully in the next session eight. This is all very well in theory, but practice is another thing.

I could manage the two lengths in just under a minute, then I managed the next two, in just under a minute. At my next speed session I attempted four lengths in two minutes. This occurred 10 days later, but I failed. I did it in two minutes three seconds. I am obviously going to have to concentrate even more. It is going to take some time. Towards the end of October I tried another time trial, this time it worked, I managed the four lengths in 1 minute 58 seconds. I was really pleased with myself.

Thumping the wall with my fist shouting "I've done it, I've done it."

It was impossible for me to attempt another four lengths flat out. I was knackered. Everyone wondered what I had done, until I explained.

In between my speed sessions I still managed to complete long distances. Doing anything between 40 and 50 lengths. Is this girl mad, or what? I referred to these sessions as endurance training. How I wish the longest distance was 800 metres. My pace is so even over the longer distance. After all these lengths, I generally still manage to speed up and swim the last four in roughly two minutes.

A week before the next training session with the squad, I tried six lengths timed. I wanted it in a time of three minutes, but I actually did it in three minutes six seconds. This is really going to be difficult. On the days

I chose for speed work, I had to make sure the body was operating on all cylinders, or at least as many cylinders that wanted to operate. It would and could go phutt phutt at any time it wanted. The problem I am faced with is I am not going to be able to guarantee, that when I have a competition the body will function properly.

I was still noticing problems with my legs. Not standing this time, but in the water. They felt that they were kicking in mid-air. I had first noticed this in March, but now it was a regular occurrence. It feels as if they are in a vacuum. There is no feeling around them. As I am still in a straight line, and going forward, I ignore it. I know they are kicking, but quite what, I have no idea.

As I was experiencing problems with my legs, Dad was still having a problem with what he classed as his good knee. It was still swelling up and becoming very hot. It transpired he needed another operation on it. The x ray revealed the false knee cap was cracked, and needed to be removed. Mum, was by this stage resigned to Dad having another spell in hospital. It transpired it was not as long as before, and all the nurses on his ward remembered him. Who could forget him! I managed to visit on a couple of occasions, actually driving myself.

Jan's mother was also in hospital. She was undergoing her second hip replacement operation. As Bob had the car, Jan was unable to visit her mother during the day, so I drove her into Tunbridge Wells, for a visit. Jan had always driven me, up to this point, so it must have been very peculiar for her to be driven. Still, she did not seem to mind her experience on the road with me.

Dad was due to leave hospital on the day of the training session, and therefore Mum had arranged for Dad to remain, until she collected him late in the afternoon.

She picked me up, as I am unable to attend a two hour session, having driven there and back. My vision, concentration, and co-ordination, would be failing me. Upon our arrival we met up with the other members of the squad, and Jessica takes us for a warm up on poolside. She has represented England at the European Championships. She is only 15 or 16 years of age. My warm-up exercises take place in the pool, as I am unable to stand. The swimming starts.

Mike asks me to swim as many lengths as I can, as quickly as I can. After about 30, he stops me. He and Alan Cook [Jessica's Father, and another coach] have been watching me.

My stroke is too relaxed. It is too casual. They then proceed to change it. I have got to straighten my arms, and push harder through the water. This is easier said than done. I do not have much strength especially in my right side. It is then noticed I am not only have a problem with one leg [which I knew about] but with the left as well. Although not nearly so bad.

I am so wrapped up in what I am trying to do that I forget about all the others. There are several who use wheelchairs, several with limbs missing, and some with learning difficulties. We all swim our hearts out. Me, I'm the eldest by about 22 years. It seems strange to have the lane to myself. I am so accustomed to overtaking other swimmers.

Mike is aware of what I hope to achieve. But I must get quicker. Therefore I am going to have to get used to this new stroke.

I then place the float [pull buoy] which Jackie had given me at Whitstable, between my legs, so I can concentrate on the arms. It seems strange I'm almost as fast with the float, as without it. This means, there is not much speed from the legs, and it is all upper body strength.

After many lengths, and about one and a half hours in the water, I'm beginning to feel knackered. I then cool down by swimming using the breast stroke. This is the easiest, and slowest. Mike immediately notices I've changed, and proceeds to remind me to push harder. I ask him if he is trying to kill me off!

"You wait till you've seen the butterfly," I call to him!

"We'll have that next time," he states.

Me and my big mouth! I then explain there is not much strength, especially in my right side, and he is surprised I am as quick as I am. He then has a short conversation with Mum, to find out what is wrong. As in the water, I give the appearance of being one hundred percent. Perhaps that ignorant cretin will want to know me now! To give me something to aim for, Mike says if

I can get the 400 metres down to eight minutes then I can be entered in the Nationals.

After the session has finished, Jackie then asks for assistance at a forth coming junior event, to be held later in the week. I wonder if I could possibly assist. She says they really need someone on the P.A. system. To announce the next event and competitors. As I have been accustomed to stage work, although singing, I am used to speaking in a clear distinct manner, so I offer my services.

Chapter 55

After a training session I am fit for absolutely nothing! It completely wears me out. I knew I would be unable to do, or go anywhere on the Sunday. Mike's words kept repeating themselves round and around my brain. It was still functioning. Of sorts. I think. I've got till March to achieve the time. This may sound a long way off, but it is only three full months. All the applications have to be submitted by then, for the Nationals. Before that, I've got to have my profile worked out. Jackie is going to have a very difficult task, as I do not fit into any convenient category. It is like trying to fit a square peg into a round hole. Rather like work, I suppose! Then, I've got to achieve the qualifying times, somehow.

When I next attended at the pool on the Monday morning, I tried out the new stroke. Not only have I to straighten my arms, and push through the water harder, but when I start the next stroke, to move them much quicker in the air, as they are not creating any propulsion between strokes. I am not to waste time. This obviously puts more pressure on the arms, but hopefully I can achieve it eventually. It wears me out much quicker though. I only manage about 20 - 30 lengths, but these were not all in one go. Ohhhhhhh this is knackering. I can regularly do four lengths in about two minutes and two lengths in less than a minute. I am going to have to build up slowly again. This is really going to take some time. Blast it; I thought that I was getting along nicely. Still, for competition I must not be casual or relaxed. I found I could only manage it, in bouts of 4 lengths.

On the Wednesday I completed 10 lengths between five to six minutes, and now I was slowly becoming quicker, I am having to readjust my tumble turns, as I am on top of the wall. Figuratively speaking, not literally! I wanted the new stroke to be natural, rather like riding a bicycle, or jumping off a log. If only! If only!

On Thursday I drove to Sevenoaks to assist at the BT Regional Swimming Championships in a 25 metre pool. It was sponsored by BT and organised on behalf of the British Sports Association for the Disabled [B.S.A.D.] by the Kent County Council's Sports' Development Unit. In other words, Jackie. It was officiated by the Kent Amateur Swimming Association.

There were 12 Schools, Clubs, and Organisations taking part, with all ranges of disability catered for. All the South East Regional Counties were represented. The largest contingent was from Angmering School, West Sussex with 19 competitors, and the smallest were Ashford Dolphins, Kent, and Woking Dolphins, Surrey, with one competitor each.

There were two age groups. Group A were competitors who were 10 years of age on or before 3rd

March 1996 and under 14 years of age on that date. Group B were competitors aged 14 years of age on or before 3 March 1996 and under 18 years of age on that date. Under B.S.A.D. rules, swimmers under the age of 10 are not normally eligible for Regional or National competitions, although exceptions at regional level can be made.

Alan Cook was present, but not coaching. I expect I wore him out on the previous Saturday. At least I hope I did. It seemed rather amusing to see him smart, in a suit, as I'm only accustomed to seeing him in casuals, with the Kent Swimming Squad sweat shirt, and jeans. It was rather like the old cliché, 'I did not recognise you, with your clothes on'.

He was present in his capacity as Chairman of the B.S.A.D. [South East]; his wife was also attending and working, as she is the Secretary. Their daughter Jessica was entered to swim but had to withdraw because of the 'flu. There were many other dignitaries present, including the Mayor and Mayoress of Sevenoaks who were presenting the medals.

I was seated at the front desk where all the participants arrived, and had to greet them with their respective information packs, T-shirts, and hats, which were given to the team managers. After all the arrivals had checked in, I then had to remain for the dignitaries. Mike Geer arrived and was surprised to see me, as jokingly, he thought he had given me a hard enough time on Saturday, but then, I had also given him a hard time. The feelings were very mutual, and on a jovial basis.

The competition started, with all the swimmers allowed in the pool for a short warm up session. I reported to the tournament desk, and took over the microphone. I'm glad I was seated, as I was very unstable on my legs.

I had to announce each race in turn, and then call for the swimmers in the following race to report in. If some of those taking part were juniors, then they were rather large. Some of the lads were very tall and strapping. Coooooooooooor, if only I was younger, a lot younger. Some of the times which were being accomplished were, I thought rather quick. In fact, I was terrified. Some of these, I could be racing against, as seniors are 12 years of age or over on or before 31st August / 1st September, providing they comply with the National Standard times.

All the strokes that is freestyle [front crawl], backstroke, breast stroke, and butterfly, were accomplished. One young lad was rather confused, as he was entered for the breast stroke, but did the butterfly instead. Another young lad was attempting the breast stroke, but his arms insisted on doing the front crawl and the breast stroke in an alternate fashion, with the kick to match.

I was highly confused, thinking I may have made a mix up in the announcing. There were variable distances, ranging from 25 metres to 100 metres, depending on levels of disability, ability, age, and time. There were in all 44 races.

I was becoming rather dry, with all the announcing, but all that could be given for a drink was orangeade, lemonade, or coke. Nothing stronger. More's the pity! But then I'm tee-total. Ahhhhhh boring! I could have murdered a burger as well. Totally unhealthy, but I did not care.

Whilst I was announcing the races, one young girl, who was mentally handicapped, came and stood by my side. She knew all the names of the boys in her team, and was screaming encouragement to all of them.

She then kept turning towards me saying "It's not my race yet, it's not my race yet."

I knew, but I wished her event would occur quickly.

I had to very careful about using the microphone, as this had to activated when she was drawing breath, so therefore for a short period of time she was quiet. I did not want her voice echoing all around the swimming pool. However, I made sure it was switched off when each of the races were in progress I did not want to impinge on their concentration.

There was only one time when I used it to encourage one girl competitor. She was the sole representative from Ashford Dolphins, and entered in the 100 metres backstroke [mixed]. Unfortunately, her profile had not been calculated, neither had her time been submitted, so the organisers had to enter her in the fastest and strongest group. She was only racing against one other large strapping lad. Having been born on the 9th February 1985, she was totally outclassed. She finished the race, did not give up and touched the wall with a round of applause from all the spectators and her fellow competitors. I think she will remember it for the rest of her life.

On looking at the names, I had to be careful as to pronunciation I hoped I did not make any large clangers especially with the foreign sounding names. They can sometimes make you feel you are speaking a foreign language. This is of course extremely hard for me, as I am too thick to cope with anything foreign.

At about 16.00 hours I had had enough. I had been working for about three hours, and knew I had the drive home. The body was beginning to rebel. I was, by now, just becoming accustomed to being dictated to by my body. I handed the microphone to another helper, and sought out Jackie to make my goodbyes. She thanked me for the effort made, and gave me a car sticker, badge and a pin to remind me of the gala.

Chapter 56

The temperature had now turned cold. There was now, something amiss with my circulation. My feet and hands were cold. They were like blocks of ice. I'm glad I sleep on my own, as my partner would leave just because of my ice cold extremities. I do not think he would appreciate my cold feet and hands on his back or front, just to get them warm. My bed, although I had an electric blanket, was not warm enough. Ohhhhhhh sod this bloody awful disease. The blood supply must be going somewhere. It was not coming out, so why was it not keeping my 'bits' warm? Perhaps, it had now turned to water. I don't know! There is no point in going to the doctor about this, as all I would receive in the way of advice; it would seem to me, would be, 'It's just the M.S., get on with life and stop whingeing'.

Obviously my quilt of tog value 13.5 was not thick enough. But they only manufacture them up to tog 15. How would I know if that would be enough? Probably not, knowing me. I then resurrect my old one of tog value 10.5. They are gradually going up in thickness, over the years. Perhaps if I had one which was a ton weight I would be warm enough. I do like a lot on top of me!

I now had the task of putting the two together, and hoped my quilt cover was large enough. It now meant the value of my quilts were 24. Surely, this would be enough. Making the bed had now become a feat by itself. It really wears me out just to change the sheets. I feel as if I have played in a badminton match against County opposition all night, and not just changed the sheets. Oh, shiiiit, I'm knackered!

I was shortly due to see the specialist. How would he react? Would he be the same as the other one, flippant and dismissive? Just because I'm not serious enough, and not in a wheelchair, am I not worth bothering with. Will I, at long last receive some advice? I've been trying to carry on with life up the proverbial blind alley. I still do not know if I'm carrying on in the correct manner for this disease.

Before seeing him, I wear myself out. This is not difficult. I had timed to carry out my shopping before my appointment. As the Superstore is virtually next door to the hospital, it saved me making two trips. I was knackered, but at least I was relatively warm, as the heating system in the car is good. My right leg did the usual. It gave out on me. If it had not been for the trolley, actually behaving itself this time, surprise, surprise, and the immediate assistance of the staff, I would have completely toppled over. Oh bugger this, I feel so stupid. I would then have had the embarrassing task of trying to explain I am not drunk. This is 09.00

hours after all. I think I was stone cold sober, as I'm tee-total, I must have been, so obviously I'm not drunk.

At the hospital I provide my sample as requested, and as I heard nothing further, I assumed it was clear. Why the hell can't they tell you? Are the workings' of our bodies that much of a trade secret. Surely we can cope with being informed of the result, good or bad.

I had also provided my brain scans, so there would not be the necessity in having to go through them again. I did not wish to repeat any of the tests. Especially the lumbar puncture. I had to explain why I changed specialists. It was like the 'old boy network', all over again. 'We must stick together, for appearances sake.' They do not seem to be able to treat us as intelligent human beings, why, I don't know. Is it because I'm a woman, so therefore I don't count, and, being a woman am I not supposed to have a brain?

He again stipulated that the tests were not conclusive. Just sticking together, I suppose. Although the lumbar puncture was positive, with all the antibodies. I could not be bothered to argue with him. I knew my body was not functioning properly. Why bother to try to explain all over again? They do not seem to listen, or even care. Just like the government, and any politician!

However, he did take the time and trouble to carry out some mobility and strength tests, especially on the right side. Comparing them with the left. He put my right leg, into a position that it did not want to go.

"Ohhhhh shit that hurt!" I exclaimed.

He then asked where, and did the same position all over again. Was not the first time satisfactory? He then took hold of my right ankle and foot, and told me to push against him. I was, but I do not think he believed me.

"Push harder," he again requested.

I was pushing, or at least I thought I was. The brain was telling me that I was pushing, but obviously the messages were not getting through. There is no strength in that blasted leg. This procedure was then carried out on all 4 limbs, and it transpired that the right side is far weaker than the left. Ohhhhhh hell! I am of course, right handed.

He then checked my walking, and manoeuvrability out of a chair. He then finally recommended I have physiotherapy. At long last, I am now getting some advice, and help. Why could not the other one have done that? He must have seen the problems I was having, and with his experience, [I presume he has some], he must have realised my mobility would deteriorate

Surely it would be better to keep the muscles and limbs working correctly as soon as there was a problem, and not let them work incorrectly. At least he did not tell me I would have to give up swimming. If he had said that, I would have told him to get lost, or 'on yer bike, pal'. I have no intention of giving up the only form of exercise and social recreation that I can do, and do well.

I went swimming again, on the following day, but this session was extremely difficult. I was still feeling the effects of being pulled about by the specialist, so I broke the number of lengths down.

I was not able to complete a long distance, so, I therefore completed three lots of 10 lengths of my favourite stroke, the front crawl. Suffering with cramp, pain in the right leg, and the feeling of kicking in mid-air. After this, I then managed four lengths of breast stroke, then four more of crawl, and finally two of butterfly, then to finish off, and also to completely finish me off as well, I ended the session with two lengths of casual front crawl, and I mean casual. I suppose to most people the amount I achieved on this particular morning would seem a lot, but not to me. I was still thinking I should be able to swim my normal distance of 100 lengths. This was now totally impossible, but I found it very hard to accept, that never again would I manage to swim marathons. Ohhhhhh, sod this feeling of inadequacy.

The next official training session was approaching, and I therefore did not swim on the Friday immediately preceding it. However, Jackie telephoned me to state the session had to be cancelled, because there would only be a few who would be fit, because of the 'flu epidemic. Oh, blast. I wanted to see how I was progressing. I needed help on how to become quicker. I seemed to have come to a full stop. My speed was not increasing.

The weather had now really deteriorated. We had just received our first fall of snow. If it thought that it was going to keep me in, it had another think coming. I had never let the weather dictate to me before, so I saw no reason why it should start to dictate to me now.

As the lane was empty, I tried a time trial, for the 400 metres. 16 lengths flat out. Oh, why do I do this? Is it stupidity, or what? I must be mad! It was between 8 minutes 20 - 25 seconds. Oh hell, I've still got a lot to lose. I've still got to shave off 25 - 30 seconds. I have now got it down by over 30 seconds since September, not bad I suppose, but not good enough. I do not trust my stop watch, as it seemed to have a mind of its own, takes after the body I think and the owner, as when I attempted it before, it showed I completed the distance in 45 seconds. If only! That must be impossible, even for the Mark Fosters of this world. I do not think even Mark Spitz [USA], in his heyday could have achieved that!

My life has now started to change. I had been invited by my Church to take tea with the Archbishop of Canterbury. As Tenterden is in his Diocese, he likes to visit the various Parishes as and when his commitments allowed him.

I could not understand why me. I'm a nobody. I'm nothing special. Why me? Why did they want me there? With only a few members of the congregation bothering to communicate with me outside of the Church walls, I thought this might be yet another hypocritical action. When I received the invite, I asked in my reply if I could keep my attendance open, as I would be unable to state how I would be feeling.

Don and Peggy took me to Church one evening for the Advent Carol Service and the Church Warden agreed I could keep my attendance open. I stated I had no intention of giving up my normal pursuits on the Friday before, just to make sure I could make tea. My swimming, and my walks with Jan and the three dogs, Shassie, Tara and Purdey, are more important and enjoyable. Peggy had said she was attending, so I therefore knew there would be at least one person who would talk to me. I would be unable to circulate; neither could I help in any way. I started to feel vulnerable again. Oh, hell, why am I like this? Why me???? I hate this feeling of inadequacy.

Before I attended, I needed to purchase a decent pair of shoes. I could hardly have a dress on, with black tights, and a pair of training shoes on my feet. Most unladylike. Especially with the state of my training shoes. Although at least I would be comfortable. The shoes needed to be flat, with no heel, sturdy, and with a good grip. These, I thought were only to be found in the form of 'Granny type' shoes. I did not wish to look old before my time. I managed to purchase a pair in Maidstone, and they did not give the appearance of 'Granny', neither did I look old.

Peggy rang me on the Saturday, to confirm I would be attending and she would save me a seat. Upon my entering the room, I was escorted to where Peggy was and made to sit down. Tea was taken and the Archbishop came in and gave us a short talk on the meaning of life. At least I think that that was what it was about. I was struggling not to drop my piece of cake and cup of tea on the floor, so I was unable to concentrate on what was being said. I just could not seem to co-ordinate my movements. I was also trying hard not to laugh at my own inadequacy.

The session then turned into a question and answer debate. I started the ball rolling. As usual, me and my big mouth.

I have a grave problem with the Creation. It did not happen as stated in the Bible in Genesis. Charles Darwin showed this was untrue with the theory of evolution. Therefore, taking this line of thought further, the story of Adam and Eve, is also untrue. I am unable to accept in any form Woman came from a rib of Adam. I am not a feminist! I have never burned my bra, and neither will I, it would be too uncomfortable not to wear one. All that uncontrollable flab bouncing up and down!

The perfect answer, I thought, was standing in front of me. If anyone could put my mind at rest, it would be the Archbishop. Surely he has been faced with this problem before. I cannot be the first to have grave misgivings about this. He told me to treat the Adam and Eve story as a parable between good and evil. This I could understand, but I still did not have an answer to my question. Perhaps I was expecting too much. Perhaps I thought I was going to hear the magical explanation. I was still left in mid-air, hanging by my fingernails.

The questions then turned to other matters, about the feelings of the Church to the behaviour of Prince

Charles, and how to explain the meaning of atrocities to small children who keep asking, 'WHY?'. 'IS THERE A GOD'. To the last question he related a funny story. A mother is in the kitchen with her young son.

"Is God in this house, Mummy?" asks the child.

"Yes, dear," replies the mother.

"Is God in this kitchen, Mummy?"

"Yes, dear."

"Is God on this table, Mummy?"

"Yes, dear."

"Is God in this cup, Mummy?"

"Yes, dear."

The child then slams his hand across the top of the cup and screams, "GOTCHA!"

We all then burst out laughing. After a while it broke up and, I was then approached by several people asking me how I was. As soon as possible I left, and drove the short distance home. I was on my knees. Absolutely worn out.

Although I did not do anything on the Sunday, I thought I would be okay for a swim first thing Monday morning. I should have known better. I only managed 34 lengths. This was not all in one go; it had to be broken down into sets of eight and four. I knew a walk on this afternoon was also out of the question, as I was going out in the Evening. My first night out. How would the body react? Would it behave itself? Would I twitch uncontrollably?

The office had invited me to the Christmas party. This invite did not come from the 'Management', as I do not think there is any, or at least any who think about their staff instead of driving them into the ground. It was from my former colleagues. They had not forgotten about me. Once seen, never forgotten I suppose. When I received the invite, I again replied requesting to leave my attendance open. Again it was accepted I may or may not attend.

As I was a little early, I drove to the office, and waited in the reception area until it was time to leave.

The Boss saw me sitting there, and all he said was "Hello, Sue."

That was it, nothing further. I have by now reached the point of no return with them. I do not care what I say, or how I say it.

As he was still in ear shot, I had a one way conversation, with myself.

"Hello, Sue, it is nice to see you, how are you doing, are you managing okay, have you managed to come to terms with it? I'm managing very well thank you, and yes, I think I'm managing to come to terms with it, although it is difficult. I'm hoping to qualify for the National Championships next year."

All these phrases were said with me moving my head from side to side. Whether it had any effect on him, I rather doubt, as he managed to ignore me all evening. Various people who were in the reception area who overheard this one way conversation could not control themselves through laughing so much. They all understood what was going on, or not going on as the case may be.

Ali and Malc Hingston, who sent out the invitations, were glad I had arrived, and after changing I drove them to the pub. The party was a joint affair with the staff of the Crown Court. I wondered if any of the barristers would remember me, or whether they would treat me as the so called "Management" did. With complete indifference and ignorance.

The party was in two parts. There was food, music and drinks upstairs, and downstairs, just the bar. I could not manage the stairs. These are now a no go area for me. Ali therefore filled a plate for me of food and brought it down to me. I sat in the same position all night.

All the barristers who saw me, and remembered me, even many of the younger ones, who were just beginning to be briefed by us, all spoke to me as a long lost friend. They all wanted to know how I was getting on. Police officers and crown court staff all remembered me. If they could all talk to me, why couldn't the Management?'

She then came bounding in. *She* saw me sitting there, and immediately came over and spoke. Saying, that *she* was just going upstairs for a bite to eat and a drink and would be down for a chat. I did not make a hasty escape, but waited for the audience with some trepidation.

I was still waiting one and a half hours later and still no materialisation, so I said my goodbyes and left. As the time was approaching 21.00 hours, way past my bedtime, I could not wait any longer. I had to drive over 20 miles to get home.

It was a long drink, and a lot to eat as far as *she* was concerned. *She* was the only one from 'Management' who bothered to say anything. If *she* could not put herself out, then why the hell should I? Surely *she* did not expect me to negotiate the stairs, and find *her*. Surely *she* should realise I cannot cope with stairs, especially when they are winding and twisty.

I quite thought *she* would bother to speak to me, as, during the summer ***she*** drove Dee down and we went out for tea in one of the many tea shops in Tenterden. If then, why not now?

I heard from many of my former colleagues that morale was now non-existent, and there was no job satisfaction. It was like being on a treadmill. Many of them were hoping for early retirement, and it seemed 'Management' did not want any experienced staff.

Their attitude was, it seemed, "If you don't like it, then get out, there are plenty out there who could do your job."

However, they would not have the experience, and this does not happen overnight, in the legal profession. The Defence Lawyers would run rings round them, then where would the victims be? These are just people who have been in the wrong place at the wrong time, and are therefore only a statistic. They do not count; they are not worth bothering about. This is the impression I am left with.

It certainly has deteriorated even since I was forced to finish. I feel I'm now better off, even though I'm disabled, due to their incompetence [The 'Management' that is]. If only the Bosses, and 'Management' would treat their staff with respect, trust, honesty, and having a little intelligence then they would get more out of them. They would feel they were contributing to the smooth running of the prosecutions, and therefore morale and job satisfaction would increase. There is of course the old adage, 'If you pay peanuts, then you get monkeys'. Perhaps, that is what they want.

I realised during my drive home I had done too much. As I was nearing my home, my vision started to blur. I was able to compensate for it, and as I only had a few more yards to go, I knew I would make it. So, therefore it was just as well I did not wait for the 'audience'. I wondered if *she* would write to me.

I had already come to the conclusion a swim was out of the question on the Tuesday, as I would be too tired, so therefore the next time in the pool was the Wednesday. I took the session very casually, and managed a total of 54 lengths. Not bad I thought! I expect some people would think far from casual.

The pool management, were requesting in a survey as to our attendance during the week after Christmas. They wished to know if they needed to open at 06.30 hours. I responded I would be swimming on all my regular days whenever they opened. However, I was not prepared for the response, as I learnt the pool was closing for essential maintenance the week preceding Christmas. Ahhhhhh, I would not be able to swim, what the hell was I going to do. I know once in a while the pool has to be emptied and cleaned, but why now? I selfishly think. I'm so near my goal. I can't afford to miss any sessions.

Margaret, one of our team members for the Swimathon, was especially annoyed, as she would be unable to swim for a fortnight, as she has to be at work by the time the pool would reopen after Christmas. They were not opening until 09.00 hours, and through her annoyance the local reporter for the 'Kentish Express' learnt of my plight.

I was asked to contact her, whereupon I was interviewed, and pictures taken, for the next publication. The fact I was in training for the National Championships was in her eyes exceptional, especially with my disability and age.

Joan and Ray, two of the many regulars I have befriended over the months, were also unhappy the pool was closing, and offered to take me to Maidstone on a couple of occasions to swim in the larger pool. They both helped me in, as there are steps to negotiate, and we started our swim.

Maidstone's pool is 33 1/3 metres. Therefore 8 1/3 metres longer than Tenterden. Why, they did not build a 50 metre to start with, or even extend it to 50 metres when a large extension was built is beyond my compression.

I wondered how the longer pool would feel. Would I notice it was longer? Would it take more out of me? Would I feel I should be turning more? I was using this experience to help me, when I'm faced with Sheffield. If I make it. I managed 30 lengths straight off, then another 4 of breast stroke, and it was not until I was on the back I noticed it was a bloody long way. Oh, shit this is a long way! I had by now swum approximately 1265.4 metres, roughly 50.6 lengths in my pool. I'm glad I did not notice too much discomfort. Yipeeeeeee I've done it. I've managed a longer pool, and not noticed it, well not really.

We next arranged to travel to Maidstone on the Wednesday of that week. Unfortunately I had now gone down with the 'flu. I had finally succumbed, after having successfully fought it off, for so long. A swim was totally out of the question. I suppose it could be considered a blessing in disguise Tenterden was closed, because I would have forced myself to swim although the body would be screaming against it.

As the body is not operating at full capacity, any form of infection, no matter how mild it is, is serious. It takes much longer to fight off its effects than normal. As Christmas would soon be upon us, I hoped I would be reasonably fit by then.

Mum rang me, about a week before Christmas. This was not normal. It was at the wrong time of day. This was in the evening; she normally telephones me in the morning after my swim. It is a warning. Duncan has rung her.

"What the hell did he want?" I ask.

"He wanted to know how you were."

"He what! Oh shit, after all this time, when he has not had the guts to be in touch. What's the matter with the boy?"

"I know," she says, and carries on, "I knew it was him, because of the 'hello there', with which he always starts. He rang me to ask how you were, I told him to ring you, as you were at home, and he said 'Oh I daren't do that, she blows hot and cold'. With that I launched. I told him exactly what I thought of him, which wasn't much. What did he expect? Where were you when she needed help and support nowhere to be seen? Where were you when she needed guidance, again nowhere to be seen? She has now started to get her life back together again, and she does *not* want you messing up the fine balance. Have you any idea what it's like to be treated in the way you treated her. He did admit that it was his fault though."

I reply, "Shit, shit, and double shit. How could he not admit he's at fault, what the hell was he after, a free weekend away, holiday over Christmas, company at Christmas, what's the matter with his old man? Surely he should be thinking of him now, perhaps he's' died now, and is feeling lonely, why wait six months before communicating? What the hell's the matter with him, what's he after?"

"I really don't know," Mum says, "I can't remember everything I said to him, but we agonised over whether to tell you, Dad felt that I should."

"I'm glad you did, at least I will be forewarned, and does he know I've made the squad?"

"No."

"Does he know I'm mobile again?"

"No."

"Does he know about the report in the paper?"

"No."

"I'm glad you've told me. Thank you, and sorry for being inconvenienced."

I put the telephone down, thinking am I now going to be plagued with him again after all this time. If he wanted to know how I was, why wait six months? The last conversation I had with him was way back in June, about, two to three weeks after Switzerland. Surely he hasn't been summoning up the courage to ring since then, and why my parents for God's sake? Surely he has the guts to ring me. I'm surprised he still has their phone number, and can find it.

At about 19.45 hours one evening, the telephone rings. Oh, Christ, it's not him is it? I am by now a nervous wreck, and pick up the instrument as if it is going to explode in my hand.

I very cautiously say hello, and get this female voice at the other end.

"What the hell is the matter with you, it's Sandra here, and you sound as if you're shit- scared."

"You could put it like that, Mum has just rung to tell *SIR* has rung her to find out how I was, and I thought it was him phoning again."

All she wanted to know was if I was going to Church on the Sunday, as she wanted to give me, my Christmas card. She was astounded he even remembered I existed. What a relief, it was only Sandra, but am I now going to be in trepidation every time that blasted bloody object rings?

Christmas comes and goes. I again, could not be bothered with it. It seems to be a load of hype, and nothing more. Mum and Dad wanted me to stay, but I did not want to be away from the pool.

The day after Boxing Day, the pool reopened, at 09.00 hours, after its major clean-up operation. I waddled into the water, only to find it was cold.

"Bleeding hell it's cold" I exclaim.

Normally, I find the water too warm, as I do, what ninety-nine percent of the people do not do, and that is swim. For me to notice it was cold, it really must have been cold. Unfortunately the centre had had a problem with one of their boilers and the water was not up to temperature. The fact it was so cold did not put me off. I had not swum for nine days and I needed my fix. It is like a drug to me, I'm an addict. At least this is a healthy addiction. I managed a total of 32 lengths, and realised I was still suffering from the effects of the 'flu. Blast it, I'm never satisfied.

During the school holidays the pool is open for general use on a Thursday morning. I took the opportunity and had another session. I was really having my fill of fixes' this week. Must be making up for lost time. Although the water had warmed up, to many people, it was still **too** cold, but not to me, it was perfect. The ideal temperature. I later discovered it was at competition standard, so therefore, no wonder I found it ideal. At least I knew what to expect, if and when I got to Sheffield. There were still many complaints the water was too cold, but not from me! The effects of the 'flu had still not worn off, and again I only managed 32 lengths, but I felt that my first 20 were quicker than yesterday. I'm still not satisfied!

The Friday, dawned and again I had my fix. The water was too warm, but for all the other patrons it was still too cold, even for the regulars. I managed a long distance casual swim, of 50 lengths. At first, I thought I would not make it. The first 30 were sheer hell. Purgatory! It was a complete struggle, my arms and legs did not know what to do. The only part that was functioning was my brain. I'm surprised it had not come out on strike in sympathy.

I was suffering with pain in the right leg, and felt I was kicking in mid-air. This is a constant feeling, as I am unable to feel the water round my legs. The left side equally affected as the right. After this agonising period, I then found my rhythm, [I'm referring to the swimming, in case you are thinking of something else] and timing, and the next 20 were really easy. I wish I could always be like that. I found, though, I had done too much, I was knackered, the body had now given up, completely and I was reduced to a quivering wreck.

The year was at an end, thank goodness. I had completely changed my way of living, and my eating habits, I had no other option. Although I am now disabled I feel I am healthier. This is probably an anachronism. If I was to survive I had to be occupied, or at least as occupied as the body would allow me. I had to keep the brain, such as it is, in some semblance of working order. Which meant of course developing the swimming, and if possible develop my connections with the Sports Development Unit for Disabled People, through Jackie. I don't know how, or what, but perhaps something will come up. As you only get out of life what you put in. If nothing goes in, then life is a complete and utter waste of time. A bore. First things first, though, I've got to qualify for the BT National Open Swimming Championships. *THAT IS A MUST.*

Chapter 57

The New Year dawned. Surely it could not be any worse than the last. There must be an improvement, surely.

I knew I had to qualify for the National Championships before March. The closing date for entries was at the end of the month. I further knew there would be another training session. As the one in December was cancelled, I hoped, beyond hope there would be one in January, then again in February, and also in March. I'm not wishful thinking; at least I do not think I am. More in hope than in judgment.

I speak to Jackie, many times on the telephone, I now, do not worry if that blasted instrument rings, as I've not heard a word from *SIR,* not even a Christmas Card, so I assume he does not wish to follow up his so called concern about me. Also, *she* [who must be obeyed], has also not bothered to write. Obviously, the fact I left the 'Christmas bash' before *she* was able to communicate with me, had no bearing upon *her.*

Jackie has sent me the entry forms, together with the qualifying times, and a Video of last year's Championships. It enables me to get a feel of the Gala, and also to try and compare myself with the 'professionals'. I had always been concerned that Mike, the Chief Coach, would, after having seen me swim the butterfly, although it is a terribly anti-social stroke, try to enter me for the 200 metres Individual Medley. [Hugh had always said there was no need for the centre to switch on the wave machine, when I was attempting the butterfly, as I created enough turbulence for the whole pool]

This would mean, 50 metres each of butterfly, back stroke, breast stroke, and finally freestyle. After having watched last year's finalists, I knew this option would be completely and utterly out of the question. I would fight him all the way on this subject, and he would not get the better of me, no matter how hard he tried. When my mind is made up that it will *not* do something, there is no force on earth, that will change its opinion. Even a bribe would fail. My brain was still able to say *NO*. I was determined to compete in the freestyle.

I knew I would not be classified in the three blind groups, or the group for learning difficulties. I had no idea, how, or what the profile would be, so I had to work on the times given. Group 10 is the least disabled, whilst Group 1 is the most disabled. I had worked on the assumption, as I could still get around, of sorts, without a wheelchair, although, I would be unable to stand, or dive in, this would preclude me from Group 10, and perhaps Group 9, so therefore, I looked at the qualifying times for Group 8.

Group 8 includes profile 18 which is 'able to walk, but one leg severally impaired, other leg less impaired'. This, I thought would be me. Also in this group are [1] profile 15A - unilateral arm/leg amputee, with stumps longer than 2/3 [i.e. below elbow/knee], [2] profile 16 - one upper arm has little or no use, or maybe absent, [3] profile 20B - bilateral lower limbs amputee, stumps greater than 1/2 thigh and less 1/3 half lower leg.

Group 9, includes [1] profile 19 - able to walk, one leg impaired, or totally absent e.g. above knee amputee, [2] profile 20A - two lower limbs moderately affected, able to kick both legs in the water, this, I also thought this may also be me, and, other less severe amputees.

I was completely at a loss to where I fitted in. As per normal. My heart was set on the 400 metres. There was no possibility of swimming the 800 metres, which is more my distance, as this does not apply for disabled people. I was going to compete at whatever distance I could qualify at. Trust me to be awkward!

For Group 8, the time was 8 minutes 56 seconds for the 400 metres. I knew this time was easily within my capabilities, but for Group 9, it was 7 minutes 47 seconds. I knew this was completely beyond me. I had been trying to maintain 30 seconds a length, therefore the whole distance in 8 minutes, but had failed abysmally. So I knew the Group 9 time would be totally and unequivocally impossible. Blast it!

I then looked at the 200 metres, and thought I may like to compete at this distance as well. Especially if I failed at the 400 metres. The time for this, was 4 minutes 10 seconds for Group 8, but for Group 9 it was 3 minutes 24 seconds.

I had not as yet, attempted timing myself over the shorter distance. This was going to have to change.

Just after my 41st birthday, I tried a time trial. Gosh, I'm now getting old. Fancy even contemplating competing at my age, especially at National level, am I nuts, or what????

The chosen distance was 200 metres, 8 lengths of Tenterden pool. I do not trust my watch, so I use the minute timer on the wall. It is very conveniently placed, as I can glance up at it with my right eye. I went flat out, for the whole distance, or at least I thought I did. The time, being 4 minutes 10 seconds. I've made the qualifying time for Group 8 just. There was no possibility of me reducing it for Group 9. This was totally beyond my reach. I realised whilst I was swimming lengths 3, 4, and 5, were slower than the others, if I can eradicate that, then my time will be about 5 - 10 seconds quicker. Still not good enough for Group 9.

Towards the end of the month, my body started to react. It was being argumentative. It was telling me it did not want to swim. My brain was having the row, I was just carrying on as normal, or as near normal as possible. I was constantly getting pain in the right leg, just below the hip, cramp in the right foot, and the constant feeling of kicking in mid-air. I ignored all the aches and pains.

361

Whether I was right, I do not know, but I'm not one to be dictated to completely, by the body. It was having its own way enough of the time; it was not going to take over entirely. On these occasions I was pissed off, fed up, frustrated, and knackered.

Towards the end of the month, things started to improve, and on one occasion I managed 50 lengths, yes, 50, straight off, no gaps, no rests, no changing strokes. When I started, I did not feel I could achieve any distance, let alone 1250 metres. After about 15/16 lengths, I found my rhythm and timing. I have no idea where it was hiding. I do not think I bumped into it whilst I was ploughing up and down, it just sort of materialised. For the last two lengths I speeded up to such a pace that I sprinted them, and achieved them in under a minute. I can still do it.

If ever I went out for the day, especially at the weekend, or for lunch in Maidstone, I knew this would greatly affect my performance for the next 24 - 48 hours. There was absolutely no chance of me achieving anything. The brain had at last come out in sympathy. It was on strike.

On these occasions, I still insisted on swimming, but I restricted it to about 10 lengths. Vicky [one of the life guards], could not believe it.

"You've only just gone in," she observed.

"Yes I know," I replied, "I'm being very self-disciplined today."

"Hear this everybody, for the first time in her life, Sue, is at long last being sensible. Shall we chalk this one up for posterity?"

I replied, "I should, it may be the one and only time!"

I had been informed the next training session was to be held on 17th February, and my profile would be worked out on that day. Ahhhhhhh hell, it has finally come to crunch time. Would all the work I have put in over the weeks and months, at long last pay dividend? What would I be allowed to swim for? Would it be my chosen distance, or something I have not thought of? If I end up in Group 9 I shall be struggling, but if it is Group 8, I should be okay, depending on how the body reacts.

I try to take it as easy as possible during the week. This is not easy, as my mind keeps thinking about the trials. I swim only on Monday, Tuesday, and Wednesday, averaging between 40 and 50 lengths on each occasion. Perhaps to many this is not taking it easy. Not at speed, but very casually. I explain to Irene, I have the trials, on Saturday, and therefore I will be unable to help her in her lessons on the Wednesday. She does not mind, and wishes me luck.

I do not swim on the Friday. I manage to keep my resolve, and not let the temptation drive me to the pool.

However, I meet up with Jan, and we have a shortened walk. I do not think Shassie, Tara, and Purdey, really noticed, they were too busy playing in the woods, and getting wet, and dirty, and chasing imaginary squirrels, to think much about anything else. Jan drives me home, and I retire half an hour earlier than usual at 19.00 hours.

I had one hell of night. I could not settle down, neither could I relax, I think the body was in overdrive. Of all the times to behave like this. Any other night, but this, please. I wanted a long peaceful, relaxing night. I was not going to get one. The brain was active, thinking about the trials. Why, oh why, does it have to be tonight? Hell! Hell! And Shiiiiiiiiit!

Saturday arrives, and I'm all bleary eyed. Blast and dam. Mum and Dad pick me up, and we all travel to the session. This is the first time Dad has been able to attend, and he is terrified he is going to be made to get into the water. He hates the water, but hates swimming more. I casually ask him if he has got his cossie, as the coach may ask him to get in the water. I do not think he realises I am only joking.

He is all serious when he replies "No."

It was only a 'wind up', to try to lighten the atmosphere. I am so nervous, on this morning. I do not know what to expect, or whether I shall be good enough. My nervousness is compounded because of the failure of a decent nights' sleep.

The first thing that occurs is my profile is worked out. Jackie has an A4 sized card to complete. It covers the whole range of movement, together with strength and power from the top of the head to the toes'. This covers every joint, and muscle in the whole of the body. Also, ability to stand, balance on one foot, walking, use of stairs, running, and co - ordination. The abilities in each section are valued between 0 to 5. 0 depicting none, as would seem logical.

My strength and power in the whole of the right side was 0. The range of movement in the right side was between 1 - 2 for the right leg, and 2 - 3 for the right arm. There was a spasm in the right arm, as well as the right leg. My left side was an improvement. Not much, but a bit! My range varied between 3 - 4 for the leg, and the arm. The power in the left leg was between 2 - 3, whilst the arm showed between 3 - 4.

For the co - ordination test I had to try and touch each of my fingers with my thumb corresponding for that hand. I was unable to do this, with either hand. My fingers just looked at me, and seemed to be saying 'Get knotted'. 'We are not interested'. 'You want that, get stuffed'. The more I concentrated, the worse it became. The fingers were locked, and they were not going to move, for love nor money. I am unable to run, also, unable to use stairs, unable to stand on one foot, without falling over, although, it is easier on the left foot, and now have difficulty holding a pen.

Jackie now refers to her magic book of words, and it transpires that I am Profile 12. FOUR LIMBS REDUCED IN FUNCTION. Severe paresis, [diminished activity of function], spasticity, [tendency to spasm], athetosis [involuntary movement of fingers and toes due to a lesion of the brain] or deformity in all four limbs. Able to walk in an unorthodox way, balance and co-ordination grossly affected. Oh, boy, I'm worse than I thought. What am I allowed to do? I hope it's the 400 metres. Profile 12 is in Group 5. Oh, sod it. That means I am only able to swim in either 50 metres, or 100 metres. Seems hardly worth my while getting into the pool. I'm nearly in tears. Well, if that is all that I can do, and then do it, I must. I am not a sprinter, and never will I be. I was in athletics though, as all I could manage, was the 100 metres sprint, and the sprint relay. Just a 1/4 of the way round a track, and after that I was knackered.

Mike ushers me into the pool and tells me to do a few casual warm ups before my time is taken. I share the lane with Sarah, who suffers with cerebral palsy. After about 15 lengths, Jackie comes over with the stop watch. This is it! OOOOOhhhhhhh. Why do I do it? Sarah very kindly stops swimming, to allow me to have the whole lane to myself.

Mike says, "You have to go flat out for four lengths, Sue."

"Ohhhhhh, I thought that I had to go as fast as I can."

Jackie sets me off, "Ready, steady, go."

I'm off. Going like a hare out of the gate at the dog track. God, this is hard work. 2 minutes later and it is all over. I'm shattered. Jackie tells me my time was 1 minute 58 seconds for the 100 metres, and my split time for the 50 metres was 58.76 seconds.

Mum and Dad hear my exclamation of Oh shit, and say to one another "I don't think Sue's made it."

On the contrary, I'm surprised it was so quick bearing in mind the sort of night I had. The qualifying time in Group 5 for the 100 metres is 2 minutes 27 seconds, and for the 50 metres is 1 minute 12 seconds. This means I'm quick enough. I've done it. Not what I want, but I've done it. Be thankful for small mercies.

The profile and grouping has to be ratified by the Officials of the British Sports Association for the Disabled, so I still do not know if I'm going. Although the times submitted, have qualified me almost to Group 8, in both the 50 and 100 metres.

As I look so different in the water, Jackie is going to endeavour to have me entered as a guest for the 400 metres, and I submit a time of 8 minutes 40 seconds and for the 200 metres a time of 4 minutes 10 seconds. She is fully aware of the reasons why I must go, and will do all she can to get me there. She wants the officials to see me in the water.

She and Mike, now try to convince me I'm a sprinter. They both have an uphill struggle on this. There is no way, I am a sprinter. The brain is equally convinced. She keeps telling me these are sprint times. *I am not a sprinter.* She informs me, with these times, and in this group, I'm about the 3rd / 4th fastest in the country at the moment on current information. I am not a sprinter. I am a long distance swimmer. The longer the better. I wish there was an 800 metres event as I would feel far happier.

She then says, "All right, you're a long distance sprinter."

Chapter 58

It was now in the lap of the Gods, as to whether I would be swimming in the Nationals. I had done all I could. There was nothing else that could be done, especially by me. There is a possibility the Officials might say as M.S. is such an unstable disease, there is not a category which is suitable. I hope they do not. That would defeat all the hard work I have done, together with all the determination, dedication, and the single mindedness. As Linford Christie states, P.M.A. Positive Mental Attitude. I think I may have that.

Jackie has informed me there is another swimmer who has M.S. and is swimming at National as well as International level. So perhaps there is hope for me yet. I would have to patient. Which is something very difficult for me. Dammmmmmmn. I wanted to know, and I wanted to know now. Was I being unreasonable? Jackie has further told me if the Officials do not let me swim, I am not to take it as a rejection, and she would enter an appeal on my behalf. As I have been relatively stable with the occasional blimp, for nearly a year, there is a very good case to be made out if an appeal is required.

My times are good enough. They should accept me. But will they?

I'm glad I only manage one stroke at that level, as I could have 2 different profiles, and groups for each stroke. As the strength and range required for each stroke is different.

Jackie has also invited me to attend a meeting which she is organising, on behalf of the Kent County Council. One of her tasks is to set up a workshop/study group for the way forward for disability in sport. She wanted me to be present. She was looking for people who were not afraid to voicing their opinions. As I'm now one of the noisy ones, and no longer afraid, it was yet another boost for my ego. I never used to be backward in coming forward. So much is now happening. My life has completely changed, and for the better.

As it was in the evening, I was worried about transport. I knew I could not drive myself, as my experience showed me, when I returned from the Office Party at Christmas. I could not possibly ask Mum to take me as she would not get home till past midnight. This would obviously be too selfish on my part, and too inconsiderate. The newspaper report had had some effect. The Volunteer Bureau, who I did not know existed, contacted me, and stated if I needed any help, they were there to assist.

For this occasion, I asked for a lift. My travel expenses were met by the Kent County Council. I was introduced to Lynne, my driver for the evening, who also attended the meeting. She found it very interesting, and deep, and offered her assistance for the future.

Meeting so many disabled sportsmen and women, was a revelation. I was glad I was not the only one who had a poor opinion of the medical profession.

It transpired one of the most fundamental bones of contention was the attitude of able-bodied people. I had come across this aspect myself.

Whilst I had been in the pool, waiting for the lessons to start, there had been some mentally handicapped people present. I was dumbstruck at the comment I overheard.

"They should not be allowed in here whilst we're in here."

I asked, "Why not?"

Their response was, "Because they're disabled."

So what, I think to myself, does it really matter -- how narrow minded some people are.

I replied "So am I!"

The retort I received was "Well, you don't look it!"

Taking this comment further, does it mean if you don't look disabled you are allowed to use the facilities, but if you do, then you are not. Stuff and nonsense! The education of able bodied people, is, we thought paramount, but this cannot be achieved overnight. It is a change of attitude which is required. Why should we not be given the same opportunity as able bodied people?

They tend to have a fear, of what we might do and achieve! Is it, they could be jealous, because we may be better than them? Even having to contend with a disability.

I do not see why disabled people, no matter how severe, should just be confined to using the pool for one hour every week.

With Jackie's help, and with the co-operation of the Leisure Centre I am going to try and organise an Open Day just for disabled people. I want to take over the whole of the centre, with the exception of the Health Suite, and give the opportunity for as many people as possible, to try their hand at, as many of the activities as possible. They may find talents they did not know they even had.

Sport for disabled people is less about 'disability', and more about sport. This was the philosophical thinking in 1995, and was being carried forward into the new year of 1996.

Lynne drove me home at the conclusion of the evening, and I was completely knackered. My vision was now completely blurred. Although I was home by 23.00 hours and in bed by 23.30 hours, this was approximately 4 hours after my usual time to retire. No wonder I was knackered. I could not put one leg in front of the other, and knew a swim in the morning was totally and completely out of the question. I felt I had gone 10 rounds with Frank Bruno! It took me 48 hours to recover. Even then I was not at my best.

Chapter 59

My Physiotherapy, has now commenced. My first appointment occurred during January, and Mum had to drive me to the hospital, as I was unsure of what to expect, or how much it took out of the body. I did not know if I was going to be pulled and stretched into positions I did not think possible. Especially with my body. I am not a contortionist, neither am I a gymnast, nor likely to be. I was always called a 'Fairy Elephant' when I was younger. This was only because I was in the 'Fairy Six', at Brownies. Surely this is a misnomer??? I know I was hockey mad, but did that make into an elephant?

The first thing she notices, I use my stick in the wrong hand. It is in my right hand. I maintain, as my right side is the weakest, and my right leg is likely to collapse, when, and if, it feels like it, at least my 3rd leg is there to prevent me from falling over. Going base over apex! I regard my stick as my 3rd leg. My 'peg leg' if you prefer. This, however, is all wrong. I have got to become accustomed to using it in my left hand. It is supposed to be used on the opposite side to the problem. Funny, ha, ha, joke, joke! This is not going to be easy.

At least when I used it in my right hand, I was able to carry a small carrier bag in my left hand. This was now totally impossible, as I do not have the strength to carry items in the right hand.

She also gives me some exercises, which are so simple and straightforward. I have to sit, with my legs outstretched, with my back supported, and stretch the thigh muscles, with the feet pointing upwards, this ensures the calf muscles and the hamstrings are taut, and hold for a slow count of five. Performing each stretch five times.

Still seated in the same position, I then have to move my right heel towards my bottom, thereby stretching the thigh muscles again, hold for a slow count of five, and for five times. This is repeated alternatively with each leg. Whilst I'm in the same position, with my legs outstretched in front of me, I then have to reach down as far as I can, below the knee, to stretch the hamstrings. Again for a slow count of five and for five times.

Turning onto my front, I have to stretch the legs, and bend the knees, bringing my feet towards the bottom, again stretching all the leg muscles, for the same count and the same number.

She did not need to work with me in the hydrotherapy pool, as my swimming was enough exercise in the water. I expect I would have confused her anyway.

Stating "What stroke would you like me to do, I can do all four!?"

After the first appointment, I drove myself, and informed her about the pain in the right leg, I was experiencing every time I was in the pool. It transpired as I was not walking properly, and not distributing my weight correctly, and evenly, the muscles, were rubbing against each other in a discordant fashion, and were therefore forming lumps, in my leg.

These were dispelled with over the weeks that followed, by rubbing a metal object, which had an electric current going through it, over the offending part of the body, which had first been coated with a gel like substance. I was informed it did not have any banned substances contained in it, and was made basically of water. The reason I was concerned about banned substances, was, as I was attempting to swim at National level, I would have to make myself available for the random drug testing scheme. I did not want to be positive, or radioactive. Yes, it is now in every sport, even for disabled people.

When all the lumps had been squashed, burst into smithereens, and finally dispelled with, she said she was recommending me to be taught how to walk properly. I immediately burst out laughing. Me, a 41 year old being taught how to walk. I thought it would be like going back to school. After all these years, of walking, I'm not doing it properly. She then realised I had a perverse sense of humour, and laughed with me.

These classes are held either in the morning or in the afternoon, and we are present at the hospital for the whole period of time. The reason for me to attend these classes was obvious. If I carried on in the same manner, then I will be in a wheelchair fairly quickly. As I have no intention of ever having to rely on one of those, I will attend the classes. She was looking at it in a long term capacity. If I carry on in the short term as I am, then it will not be beneficial to me.

Towards the end of March, I received my first appointment. It was on a Monday morning, and transport had been arranged for me. It meant I would not be able to have a swim in the morning. I resented this. I thought my swimming was more important. I did not relish the idea of going back to school.

It was not like anything I had imagined. I was treated as an intelligent human being. It seems this how we are all treated in the Physiotherapy Department, irrespective of how serious or minor the problems are. We are not a waste of time. We are made to feel as if we are someone special, or important.

I was now beginning to learn about the limitations of the disease. The fact I had such a positive attitude helped. She asked me what exercises I was doing, and what I had been given to do by the previous physiotherapist. The fact I was swimming to a level I was trying to achieve, amazed her.

I took the view, correctly it seemed, that all my bits were present, all the ligaments, muscles, tendons, and the blood flow, working normally. The problem was, the messages from the brain were not getting through. If I looked at what I was doing the right leg operated almost correctly, but as soon as I looked away, it was misbehaving, as normal. Ha, Ha, you are not looking at me, so I'm going to do what I like, the leg seemed to be saying.

She informed me my gait was too narrow, and I should widen it slightly, and place the heels of my feet on the ground first. I had been placing the whole of the foot on the ground, as I thought this would give me more balance, but I was wrong. The objectives she gave me was to improve my balance in standing, increase the strength in the lower limbs, and improve the mobility with the assistance of the one walking stick.

Also on this occasion I was seen by the Occupational Therapist. As I maintained my independence, and improvised whenever and wherever I needed to, I informed her there must other more worthy people who may require more assistance than me. One of my problems was with turning on and off the kitchen taps, and was informed these could be adapted, but I said it was unnecessary, for although I swore each time the problem arose, I just grabbed the tea towel and used that. I managed for the time being.

However, when and if, I should deteriorate I now knew where to come for assistance. When my pen falls out of my right hand, which it is now prone to do, I then transfer it to my left hand, and then continue. Although it looks like a child's handwriting, and as if a spider has crawled over it, but at least it is fairly legible, even if written very slowly.

I refused the transport, for the second appointment, as I wanted, and needed a swim. I did not feel the necessity to give it up.

I was in the pool at 07.30 hours, and completely confused the staff, as they all thought it was later than it really was. I managed 50 lengths on this occasion. When I was working I was in the pool at 06.30 hours, so this was not difficult. I'm still waking up as if I'm going to work. My built in alarm clock still switches itself on, even though I've tried to turn it off. Why won't it believe it does not need to wake me up at this god forsaken hour? It is still the same at weekends.

Upon my arrival at the hospital, she noticed my walking was an improvement, and then put me on the bicycle, then the walking machine. Also, to try and use steps.

I had to stand in between two beds and hold on to them, with my hands, and standing on one leg, now that's a joke, and lift the other leg. When it came to standing on the right leg, and lift the left foot, it would not obey me. Even with me looking at it, it still refused to obey. This was because the left leg knows I do not have the confidence in my right side. When I changed to the other side the right leg lifted a fraction, but would not manage the step. She wants me to eventually have the confidence in the right side.

When I was fit and healthy all the movements undertaken, where taken for granted at the time. She is going to endeavour to achieve that scale of confidence again. Even to the extent of hoping that I might run again. I think this may be wishful thinking. Still, you can always live in hope. I may yet be surprised!

All the while answering my questions. Why can't the Specialists do that? Why are they so dismissive and flippant? All we require are answers. The messages were getting through somehow, but because of the damaged nerves, they were being diverted, and taking a longer curvative route. Perhaps they came across all the road works, traffic cones, and temporary traffic lights, on their detours. Does the leg and the arm on the right side, start to shake, when I become tired, because the messages are getting scrambled and confused? Is it because there are so many messages, they do not know where to go? Why is it I become tired so quickly?

All the answers are now forthcoming. The nerves get tired far quicker, because they are damaged, and the ones that are not damaged have to work far harder, so tire just as quickly. When the muscles tire, under normal circumstances, the body then resorts to nerve functions, so enabling the body to carry on at the same pace, but in M.S. because the nerves are injured this normal bodily function will not continue. There it is, in a nut shell. Why are the specialists unable to explain, in ordinary language.

The next week I am faced with the weights. I am glad that I have started weight training in the gym at Tenterden Leisure Centre, so this prospect is not so daunting. I find the arms and shoulders are relatively strong, but this is due to the swimming, but the legs are so weak.

For someone who is supposedly so fit, I should be able to move more than 5 kilogram's. But I can't. The cardio vascular system is very strong. Heart and lungs, to the uninitiated. My hamstrings, [the muscles at the back of the thighs] are so taut, they will hardly lift or move anything. I have got to work on them. To loosen them up. That hurts, but then I have pulled and yanked them, whilst I was playing in badminton matches.

I have had more injuries, playing badminton, than ever I did playing Hockey. I am a glutton for punishment.

If I wish to succeed, at the level to which I have chosen to compete at, then I am going to have to endure a little pain. As the saying goes 'No pain, No gain'. Although I have not as yet had confirmation of my acceptance, for the Nationals, I have to work on the assumption I'm going to be in attendance. They sure know how to keep someone in suspense. I feel as if I'm in suspended animation.

Chapter 60

Since Switzerland, last year, at the World Badminton Championships, I had kept in touch with Kai. He had rung me on several occasions, and we had swapped letters and cards. It was pleasant to keep in touch, with those who looked upon me as someone worthwhile.

In his Christmas Card, he had asked if I was attending the All England Badminton Championships, to be held in Birmingham at the National Indoor Arena. Home of the Gladiators. This was where I met 'you know who', in 1993. Nothing like a Gladiator! And never will be!

I had no idea when it was being held, or if there was anything I could do. I explained in a letter, I was endeavouring to qualify for the National Swimming Championships, and hoped to take part in the Swimathon, as a member of a team. I hoped the tournament would not clash with any of my few commitments, and interfere with my training.

Kai sent me a postcard, from Switzerland, as he was Line Judging at the Swiss Open, and also asked Ken to sign it. Ken was also someone I met in Switzerland.

They both stated they hoped to see me. I knew there were at least two people who would be glad to see me. Who wanted me to attend. Who thought I was worthwhile.

I then had the task of finding out when it was. As I no longer have the Badminton Gazette, because it reminds me of happier times, I was not any the wiser as to when the event was occurring. I communicated with the Badminton Association of England, to ascertain the dates. As they would be organising the event, on behalf of the Sponsors Yonex, they would surely know when it was occurring. If they did not, then no one else would know.

After realising it would not clash with anything, I then thought about how to get there. Also, was there anything I could do? It would work out cheaper to attend as a volunteer, rather than as a spectator. As I would not need to pay any entrance fee, neither would I need to pay to park the car.

I knew I could not line judge, this was now totally out of the question, but I could do the scoreboard. Couldn't I? After all, you only have to follow the umpire, and if they cock it up, then that's not your fault. After deliberating and cogitating for some time, I knew time was short, so I decided to take the bull by the horns, and go.

How the hell could I get there? Could I possibly drive? I had not been that distance, or anything like it, since March 1994. Some 2 years ago. This was the last time I had had anything to do with badminton in this country.

Barbara was of the opinion I could, Jan was of the opinion I could, and so was Chris. If they all thought I could, then I can. Can't I?

I telephoned Dr John Alexander who is the Manager of the line judges, and scoreboard operators, to ascertain if there was a job I could do. I hoped he had not retired, or if he had, then he would know who had taken it on.

He said, after I explained what I wanted "I was told you couldn't do anything."

I replied, "Well you've been given duff information, because there is something I can do."

We all know who thinks I'm useless and stupid, don't we. Is he in for a shock! I explained further it would need to be a sitting down job, and I would need to leave about 16.00 hours, so I could be in bed and resting by about 17.00 hours. John thought for a few minutes, and suggested I could assist on the numbers and the name plates. He then gave me the name of the official who would arrange my booking for the hotel.

When it was all finalised I wrote to Kai, hoping my letter would reach him between tournaments, informing him I would be attending.

I was planning to leave home on Monday 11th March at about 10.00 hours. Although the qualifying tournament started on the Monday, the tournament proper began on the Tuesday evening.

On the Friday before, Kai rings me. He states he will come over on the ferry on Monday morning from Calais, drive down to Tenterden, and pick me up, then drive to Southend, to collect Ken from his parents', and then proceed to Birmingham, and be there by 12.30 hours.

Unless he has aspirations of leaving at the crack of dawn, or flying, he'll never make it. He obviously does not know our roads. All full of road works and cones. I try to give him directions to find Tenterden, but either I did not know where I lived, or else Kai's road map was strange. Perhaps it was a bit of each. I managed to persuade him I would drive, as I did not want to be without the car in Birmingham, in case I needed to leave the arena early. Also, I did not want to cause problems for others, and, neither would I be able to use the official buses, as I could not get on them, and neither could I walk from the drop off point to the hotel.

It transpired we were all staying in the same hotel. I would not be on my own. There were at least 2 others who I knew. Kai understood, and said he would see me there, and wished me luck for the journey.

I did not swim on the Monday, but had a leisurely time to get ready. Chris and the family were looking after the cat, so I did not have any worries on that score.

I left at the time I wanted, only to realise it was thick fog. Oh, hell, how long am I going to have to put up with that. First time on a long journey, and I've got to face that hazard. There are so many idiots on the roads, who do not use their lights in these conditions, and overtake even though they cannot see. I did not want to be involved in any major pile up, as this would completely blow away any confidence I may have. I'm only just beginning to feel I'm capable. If I cannot see, then surely they cannot either.

When I had done the journey previously, it had taken me three hours door to door. I was in a larger car then, but knew this time it was going to take longer. I did not know how much longer. I also knew if I could not manage the distance in one day, I would stop off overnight. I did not want to do this. I wanted to make it, in the one day if at all possible. Me and my determination. Why am I like this?

The road works started at the junction of the A21 and M25. It was then one continuous cone and deviation, almost to the junction of the M40 and M25. Do the traffic authorities enjoy causing delays? Do they enjoy digging up the roads? Especially when there is no work being carried out. The person who designed these cones, sure has made a mint, providing he holds the patent. The fog was now thinner, but I was near Oxford, and had not yet had to stop. It was coming up for lunch, so at the next services, I took a breather.

These services cater for people in a wheel chair, or able bodied. If you use one stick it is near impossible, but if you use two sticks then it is entirely impossible. All I wanted was a salad, and a drink. Was I asking for too much? I know it is a good idea to be self-service, as this cuts down on staff requirements, and we can at least have what we want. But, trying to balance a tray, use one stick to prevent you from falling over, fill your plate with food, and then stand in a queue, and being jostled, is more than I, or my precarious balance and body can tolerate.

I nearly went flying, and my salad with me. Perhaps I should have done, then maybe the Service Organisers would realise they have to rethink their strategy. I nearly did what I did in Waitrose, Tenterden, one morning, at the so called Express checkout, when I sat down, on the floor, but then there is the problem of getting up again.

However another lady customer saw my plight and directed her husband to find a table for me in the non-smoking part of the seating capacity, set the table for me, and then carried my tray to the table and helped me to my seat. If it had not been for that helpful couple I do not know what I would have done. Probably fallen on the floor. Gone base over apex! The staff now realised there was a problem, but put the blame on me for not asking for assistance. How dare they! Should I have to rely on other people for everything. Am I not entitled to any independence? Surely they should have seen the problem, and offered assistance.

After an hour's rest I set off on the final leg to Birmingham. All the while wondering about the reaction from *him*. He had not had the courage to ring me, after having spoken to Mum, before Christmas. It was now almost three months later. Would he be all over me, as if nothing has happened, as he was when I arrived in Switzerland? If this was the situation then I may vomit all over him. This sort of behaviour makes me so nauseous. It is a such sham. Or will he ignore me all together? Will he have the guts to speak? I knew he would be there, this was a badminton tournament, and nothing must ever come between him and a badminton tournament. Where badminton is concerned he is very single minded.

I drove straight to the Arena, negotiated Spaghetti Junction successfully, and realised it had been about four hours since I left home. I did not consider this as too bad. I felt rather pleased with myself, although absolutely knackered. I had to keep going just a little bit longer. I had done it. I HAD DONE IT!

I reported to John, upon my arrival, and as I waddled onto the Arena floor, the first thing I noticed was *HIM*.

He was in conversation with Beverly, a fellow line judge, and she spoke, and said hello, asked me how I was, but he finished his conversation with her, and just turned and walked off in the opposite direction. As fast as he could. He completely ignored me. I know I was tired, and Mum had told him I did not want to have anything more to do with him, but surely he could have acknowledged I had arrived. Could have said Hi, if nothing else.

After being given my Red Yonex Jumper, as per all the line judges, I then reported to the Office and paid for my hotel bill, and left.

After having checked in at the hotel, and unpacked, I went for a swim. I was in need of stretching my muscles, and getting them moving. I was at this stage almost unable to walk.

The pool was situated in the hotel's sister, and we were given free use of their facilities. Being a typical hotel pool it was tiny. I could glide across the whole length, and not need to take a stroke. With five people in it, it was crowded.

Within the complex was a sauna and steam room together with a Jacuzzi. I knew I would be walking again after my session. I was able to follow the same treatment as back in Tenterden, although my swimming would be seriously curtailed with the constant turning.

Upon my return to the hotel, I bumped into Kai and Ken. They were just on their way to the Arena, to report for duty. It seems they did not make it for 12.30. I'm not in the least bit surprised. All that fog, and the road works. Kai, it seems, overslept, or forgot to set his alarm clock. I don't think he's got a built in one like me.

They were pleased I had arrived safely, and in one piece. I thought this was a good opportunity to tell him the real reason why I needed to have the car with me.

Before I could explain fully, he said, "I know, you wanted to see if you could do it."

How perceptive of him.

"Yes, that's the real reason."

He explained further that he and Ken had discussed this on the journey. His command of the English language still amazes me. We arranged to meet for breakfast the next morning.

As it was nearing 18.00 hours, it was time for my bed. I knew I would get at least 14 hours rest. I was reckoning, though, without the behaviour of my next door neighbours.

At 22.00 hours the row started. I was disturbed from my sleep. He had such a deep voice and it was so loud, and foreign, I think he could have been the fog horn for the liner the 'Queen Mary'. I had hoped the racket would die down soon and quickly. As I had a communicating door, which was locked, thank goodness I hammered on it with my walking stick at about 23.00 hours to tell him to *be quiet.*

I had by this stage had enough. Was I being unreasonable? Should I have put my head down, and ignored it? I could not though, it was too loud. It had some effect, as the row did die down, but not for long.

I tried to determine the language, as well as try to sleep. It was not French, neither was it German, but it had a guttural twang to it. I did not recognise it. I knew it could not possibly be Italian or Spanish. So what was it?

When I awoke the next morning and drew back the curtains the world was covered in a mass of white. Oh, no, not that stuff again. I thought we had seen the last of it about a fortnight ago. The snow was everywhere, but fortunately not very deep.

I wondered about the roads, as to whether they would be clear. As on the last occasion in Tenterden it prevented me from getting to the pool one morning, as I could not get the car out of the garage, neither could I walk. I was so determined to make it. I was going to walk, come hell or high water. I did not wish to miss two sessions. I managed to get there, but of course after my swim I could not walk home again.

I have this stupid little habit of getting somewhere but never actually thinking about the return journey. After my session I procrastinated about the journey home. Hugh very kindly gave me a lift home and then his car proceeded to slide sideways down my road.

Upon looking out of my window from the hotel I realised the roads were clear and I would be able to drive to the arena as planned.

At breakfast I met up with Kai and Ken. We discussed who my neighbour could be. As they were in another part of the hotel, and on the 3rd floor, they had no idea who he could be. There were several National Teams staying in the hotel, and Ken thought that the voice may be Russian. As I had not heard the language before, I was still unsure. Upon leaving the hotel, my car was covered, totally obliterated in white, and both Ken and Kai cleared the car for me. Imprinting some rude suggestions in the snow! We then left to drive to the Arena.

As I was walking along a corridor which lies alongside the playing area, *HE* was coming towards me. I was just about to open my mouth and say good morning, when he speeded up, turned his head away and walked off. He is still unable to acknowledge me. What is it with me, have I developed two heads, or grown two more arms? Am I that much of an eyesore he can't speak to me? Still that's his problem, not mine. Whatever did I see in him?

I reported to the control desk, on the Arena floor and was given my duties. Several of the old gang saw me and spoke to me, asking me how I was. I was to work with Marilyn Bray.

Who together with her husband Allen, had been in Switzerland, and were so helpful. Also on the desk was Dave. Dave, I knew from having been at the All England before. John asked me if I could work a computer keyboard, and I said I could, providing it was a normal size. This one, however, was a pocket book size, and very tiny, and I could not possibly get my fingers round it. Fortunately Marilyn could, she has such tiny delicate fingers. It's bad enough holding a pen now, yet alone trying to get my fingers on the right keys. I'm all fingers and thumbs now.

All the players, no matter where they come from, and irrespective of whether they are in the main draw, or the qualifying tournament, all have to be registered with the I.B.F. [The International Badminton Federation], and given a number. Their numbers and names are fed into the Computer. This makes it easier to track down, as there is a two way check.

For the qualifying tournament, which was still being played, the players' names were not displayed on the courts. All that was displayed was their respective number in the draw. These numbers were then hung upon the underside of the electronic score cubes. Each court has two cubes, one at each end. The numbers are taken onto court by the line judges and score board operators assigned to the respective courts.

It was our job to have the numbers ready, for each match. Upon the numbers I placed a Post-it note stating the names of the players, what the match was, which court, whether, ladies or men's, singles or doubles, or mixed, and the time. Towards the end of the day my writing deteriorated to such a degree it was virtually illegible, and on some occasions I had to resort to using the left hand. Nobody complained about the illegible writing, I'm pleased to say. They all seemed to be able to decipher it.

The numbers were a heavy duty blue plastic, about 8 inches square, with a single digit embossed on it.

We had a rota system for lunch, so the desk was manned all the time. When I entered the staff canteen, he was seated at a table with another gentleman. They were not eating at this time, as they had several, what appeared to be computer printouts in front of them.

There was also a queue. I hate queues, as I cannot stand, for long. I joined the queue behind two gentlemen dressed in tracksuits. They were not players, but officials of some description. I was right near to where he was seated. They asked me if I had sustained some injury, as it is generally assumed if you are at a sporting event using a walking stick you have had an accident of some sort, usually sporting. I explained it was now a permanent disability, and my body had now become diseased.

I further stated "There are of course, those who think that as soon as you become like this, you lose your marbles."

I knew he heard me, as I was only about two feet from him.

After having got my meal, I sat at the nearest table to the door, which was directly behind his. When he had finished, to avoid coming anywhere near me, he bolted for the other door at the far end of the canteen and was in such a hurry he tried to go through a locked door. He hurriedly unlocked it, and went out, again managing to ignore me. Is he just childish, scared, or plain rude? I know not which. No wonder he made me feel so stupid, useless, and insignificant.

The qualifying tournament finished about mid-afternoon, and the main tournament was not starting until 18.00 hours. I knew I could not last any longer, so I made my farewells and left.

As it was still quite early, I decided upon a swim before retiring.

At 22.00 hours the row started next door. I hammered so hard on the door with my stick, I'm surprised I did not damage it. I had this same problem every night, he did not seem to listen or care about the discomfort caused to his neighbours.

393

I knew if I turned my light out at about 19.30 hours, I would get in the region of two and a half hours uninterrupted sleep, before the row started. Perhaps I was being unreasonable, in wanting to sleep, and not enjoy his foreign conversation. His was the only voice I heard.

I did not make any formal complaint to the hotel management, as I did not wish to harm Anglo - Russian relations. I did not know his Official standing with his Government, and me, only an insignificant little cog, who wished to sleep at night. Perhaps I am being thoughtless, perhaps I should just grin and bear it.

On the Saturday I had to be moved from my room, due to a very noisy night. The hotel was having a disco, at least, I think it was music, but I have my doubts, as all I heard was thump, thump, thump.

Upon my return to my room at 06.00, my neighbour was singing. I hammered on his door and told him to *SHUT UP*. This was as much as I could take. If he sounded like Plácido Domingo, I may have put up with it, but he did not, and I did think there was a time and place for everything, and this, to my way of thinking was neither the time, nor the place.

At breakfast, on the Wednesday morning, Kai and Ken gave me the biggest surprise I could ever hope to ask for.

As there was no play during the day on Friday, because it is semi - finals night, they asked me what I was doing. I stated, I had not planned on doing anything, as I would take the opportunity to have a rest all day, and a casual swim. They were not prepared to accept this, and invited me to be with them, and Olivier, [a French line judge,] on a visit to Shakespeare country, and notably Anne Hathaway's cottage. I adore Shakespeare, although I do not know all the plays, and did not need any persuading. I could not believe it, they wanted me with them. Me, of all people.

At the Arena, I almost drove straight into Yunis. He was the one who came with me to the hospital in Holland, with *HIM*, and could not understand *HIS* behaviour in Switzerland. He greets me with a kiss, and escorts me into the Arena, with his arm around me. It was so nice to be remembered.

Yunis, is not line judging now, as he has been promoted or elevated to umpire. His grading is such that he is entitled to officiate at International events. It seemed so strange to see him in his umpire's uniform, of dark blue jacket and trousers, white shirt and tie. Any cock ups are now his fault, when he is in the chair. He was still not able to umpire the latter rounds though, as his grading was not senior enough.

Marilyn, Dave and myself, realised we were going to have our work cut out today. We needed the name plates as well as the numbers. The tournament was well under way now.

We had nearly 200 matches in the day, to be prepared for. With some of the names we wondered what the matches were. It was impossible to tell whether they were male or female. One such match was Qin Yiyuan and Tang Yongshu against Chung Jae-Hee and Park Soo-Yun. China against Korea. I came to the conclusion they were a men's doubles, as there is Park Joo Bong of Korea, who is a men's and mixed doubles player. I was, however totally wrong, as the match was a ladies doubles. How silly of me, of course they were ladies, it is obvious!

I'm glad they were not in ear shot, as I may have insulted them, if they could understand English, calling them men! Marilyn and I wondered why the name plates were kept in I.B.F. [International Badminton Federation] numerical order, as we thought it may be easier to be in alphabetical order, as per the norm with the English Language. This was quickly dispelled, when we had so many oriental names. What was the surname, and what was the Christian or Forename name, we did not have a clue.

Marilyn knew I was totally fed up, with his inability to speak.

When I said to her, after I had seen him stride down the arena floor, "Whenever I see him now, I wonder what I ever saw in him."

We both realised instantaneously I was now completely over him.

I had not heard if he had taken up my challenge to him in Switzerland, when I suggested he takes the Official Referee's course, as to succeed, he would need to communicate, and I do not think he has any communication skills.

The Quarter - Finals started on Thursday, and as such we were down to four courts. This made our task easier, as we had fewer matches to prepare.

I was unsure if we were using four score cubes per court, and if so, did we need more numbers. There was one person who would know, and that would be *HIM*.

I called him over, and he said, "Yes."

I replied, "Oh, it does speak then, does it!"

He gave me the same lame crap excuse I was accustomed to hearing, "Oh, I've been busy."

I did not say any more about this, as this was not the place. It was now obvious to me, everything I had said to him in the past fell on deaf ears. He did however manage to give me an answer.

This was my first opportunity to let him know I had qualified for the National Championships.

All he managed in reply was "Oh."

I did not tell him I had not yet been accepted. Marilyn, was almost beside herself with mirth. She happened to mention every time she touched something she was getting an electric shock. This was due to the carpet. *HE* heard this comment, and with a childish grin on his face started to wipe his feet very hard on the carpet. She asked what he was doing.

I replied, "Oh, he's just being childish, and filling himself with electro static energy, so he can give an electric shock to anyone who comes near him."

He stopped immediately, turned and walked off. Is he now shocked I'm beginning to stand up for myself?

With all the badminton that was being played, neither Marilyn nor I managed to watch any. All we could do was glance at the various scores, on the Courts and ensure the next batch was ready. I had hoped as we were now down to four courts this may have been easier, but there was so much to concentrate on, this was impossible.

I realised at the end of the day, I was absolutely knackered. I could hardly walk. My legs were really being objectionable. I was so tired, I was unable to have a swim, and even a casual dip was out of the question. I was now having to have about 16 - 17 hours rest. I did not wish to miss out on my day out on Friday, so I left the Arena at about 16.00 hours, and was in bed by 16.30 hours. This ensured me 16 1/2 hours complete rest. I was now ready for Shakespeare, but was Shakespeare ready for me!

Ken drove us all to Stratford Upon Avon, and parked the car, with the assistance of my Orange Disabled Parking Permit. It still surprises me how many other drivers who do not display the orange permits, will insist on parking in the disabled bays. As it keeps on occurring, and they keep on getting away with it, there cannot be any checks made by any of the Authorities.

Why are some drivers so thoughtless of others? Although it was still very cold the snow had at last disappeared.

They had arranged we would take the official tour called 'Guide Friday', which uses open topped double decker buses. They had to be very patient with me, as I had great difficulty in getting on and off. Still I managed. As it was so cold, there was no thought of going up top. Even now it was still trying to snow.

The first stop was Anne Hathaway's cottage. A beautiful thatched residence. Upon walking to the front door, we saw several umpires.

"Oh, God," I exclaimed, "look who's here, there's no getting away from them, and they follow you everywhere."

Richard retorted, "Today it's SIR, if you don't mind, tomorrow its God!"

Upon entering the cottage, I realised immediately I was in trouble. There were steps to negotiate. I could not go up.

"Oh, yes you can," Kai states, "Ken will go up first, and pull you up, if need be, whilst I will follow, and push if necessary."

They had worked out between them, how to get me around. They were not going to be defeated. If they were not, then neither was I! Why is it, some men are so thoughtful, without having to be asked, whilst someone else could not give a dam?

At the end of the tour, we all sat in the gardens, waiting for the next bus to appear. We followed the tour round, to the various houses, notably Mary Arden's residence [Shakespeare's mother,] and his birth place, and various other properties.

Sue and Kai

In Stratford itself, we were so cold we all decided to have some lunch, and try to get some heat into our weary bones, then make our way home. By this stage I could hardly put one foot in front of the other, so Ken decided to get the car and pick us up. My vision was also blurring, and by the time we reached the hotel I could hardly move. I had done too much, but I had enjoyed the day out. Kai helped me out of the car, and I promptly fell straight into his arms. What a lovely soft landing! I suppose someone would say I did this on purpose, but I did not have the control over the lower half of my body, so I could not possibly contrive this.

In my room, I started to cry, because I realised the limitations of my bodily functions, and I would not be able to see the semi - finals, which are notably of a far superior play than the finals. I wanted to go to the Arena, but my body would not let me. How dare it continue to dictate to me!

I was still feeling the effects of my exertions, on the Saturday morning. I had had 17 hours in bed, and considered this was quite enough.

My right leg was disobeying me, even though I was looking at it. I had to drag it along. Rather like pulling the vacuum cleaner.

I met up with Kai and Ken, who realised my plight, but did not make any mention of it, thank goodness, for we discussed the previous night's play. I said I was going to have a swim, although not too strenuous, and follow with my treatment. After my sojourn in the Sauna and Steam Rooms, I was walking again. At long last, my right leg started to behave itself. I do not know how it works, but it does, so who's to argue, certainly not me.

As it was finals day, there was only one court to consider, and five matches. We knew the order of play, and were prepared accordingly.

At long last I was able to watch some badminton. The worst final was the Ladies' Singles. Ye Zhaoying [China] v. Bang Soo-Hyun [Korea] The Chinese player was seeded 1 whilst the Korean girl was seeded 3/4. The Korean won with a score of 11 - 1, 11 - 1. I am of the opinion that the World's no.1 player should not, and could not lose by that extreme margin. She was wooden, and not moving at all. Leaving shots that were clearly in, and hitting shots way beyond the base line, at the other end. The so called World's no.1 player should not make fundamental basic mistakes like the ones she was making.

I think I could have done better, even in the state I am now reduced to! It was absolute crap! Was it political? Was it fixed? Had they come to some arrangement? Was it done, so that Susi Susanti [Indonesia] the World's no.2 would not be seeded 2 at the forthcoming Olympic Games? I did not know, but there had to be a reason. Surely if it was fixed, then the two participants could have at least tried to make it a spectacle for the paying public. I am glad I had not paid to see such rubbish. I would have felt cheated. When they went to be presented with their respective medals I felt like booing.

The best final, after the men's doubles, was the Mixed. This featured an English pairing of Simon Archer and Julie Bradbury, against a pair from Korea. Park Joo-Bong and Ra Kyung-Min. Both pairs were seeded 3/4. Although the English pair lost in two straight games 15 - 10 and 15 - 10, the Koreans did not have it all their own way.

The public now had a spectacle to watch. They were behind the English pair all the way, in their struggle, and we thought at one stage the match may go to three games, but the Koreans had other ideas. Julie gives the appearance of a lady who is so feminine, and petite on court, it amazes me she can smash and retrieve as hard as she does. She reminds me of the American Tennis player Chris Evert.

The organisers, on behalf of the Sponsors Yonex, were holding a Reception for all the volunteers, at the close of play. After having been given my Blue Body Warmer, which was a gift from Yonex, I went to the reception. I did not stay long, as I was tired, especially after Friday's exertions.

As I was leaving, *HE* approached me and said, "Take care."

I was astounded, he had actually found his tongue and spoke. It is difficult to look down one's nose when the person opposite is 6 foot 4 inches, but somehow I managed it.

"I do."

I wondered if he was going to try and make a big thing of showing he cared, as when I returned from lunch during the Men's Singles Final, he made a big scene of pulling out my chair and allowing me to sit. Then I waddled out of the room.

I was escorted to the car by Kai and Ken, and we said our goodbyes.

On the Sunday, I left Birmingham, and drove home, again stopping just the once. Contemplating all that had happened and been said. All the umpires, who knew me, from previous events, were all pleased there were some tasks I could still do, and offered their assistance in any way they could, for my future efforts, in trying to get disabled badminton started in Kent.

I see no reason why they should be precluded, from any sporting activity. One of the nicest comments was from Doug. He and his wife, Anne, had taken me under their wing in Switzerland, as had Marilyn and Allen.

They all noticed a big change in me.

Doug said "You are so different from Switzerland, it is like the Sue we first met three years ago. You are much more positive now."

Chapter 61

Upon my return from Birmingham I had hoped I would have received confirmation as to whether I had been accepted to swim in the Nationals. It had now been over a month since I had had my trials, and my profile worked out. Surely this was enough time for the Officials to have made their decision.

On looking through my post, there was no confirmation; neither was there a rejection slip. Was it applicable, no news was good news? I was being ignored. This seemed to be a fact of life with me. I always seemed to be ignored. I thought I was once seen never forgotten!

I telephoned Jackie to inform her I had returned from Birmingham, and had not heard anything. She confirmed she had no further information, but would chase it up.

Meanwhile, my pussy cat had missed me. She could not make up her mind, whether she wanted to stay in, or go out. Chris said she left the door open on several occasions, whilst she was over, but the moggy just looked at her, and scuttled behind the curtain and hid.

Her attitude was, 'My Mum is not here, so I'm staying put. You're the Mum of that great big golden demented dog, I now have to tolerate every day, if I go out, I may find she's taken over completely!'

Whenever I had Shassie over she would not be in the same room as my cat. She was terrified of her. I know the cat has the tendency to walk on Shassie's nose, but is that a reason for her to be terrified of such a small, old, ball of fur and fluff, with claws, and teeth!

I knew after having had such a busy week in Birmingham, I had to write the following week off. I could not go anywhere, neither did I do anything. I tried to maintain my swimming schedule, but this failed abysmally.

For the first three days I was lucky if I managed 10 or even 20 lengths at the most. It was a real hard slog. I do not think it was because I was now in my usual-sized pool.

I did however manage to help Irene in her lessons, but only the one. Just for 30 minutes, that was all I could manage. I was so tired all the time, but as I had enjoyed myself, I did not mind too much. Well, I did mind; but not to the degree I would have had I had an appalling, unmemorable, and boring week. If that had occurred then I would probably have gone mad or stupid!

I did not find I needed 15 - 16 hours in bed, I was now glad to get back to some semblance of normality and needed only about 12 hours in bed. I found 30 minutes swimming, four mornings a week, and 30 minutes in the gym one day a week, was more than enough for my overtired, conked out, decrepit body.

The swimathon was due to take place towards the end of March, but unfortunately we were not able to form a team. One of the Margarets was in Birmingham for a conference. [I leave, she goes! Was it something I said??] Jean did not wish to commit herself, in case a problem arose, which was likely, and she would have to let us down at the last minute. The other Margaret, and myself were faced with contemplating the 200 lengths between us. A tall order.

Although we both felt there was a strong possibility we could make it, and manage the 100 lengths each, we realised it may cause more harm than good to me. We felt it may upset my training, and cause irreparable harm to my delicate system. We decided we would give it a miss this year, and take part next year.

If only I had not got this bloody awful disease then I could have contemplated the 100 lengths with ease, and then some more. Might even have completed the whole distance, as had been achieved in the past. Then Margaret need not have worried about her 100. Oh, sod it! I hate being like this, not being able to lead my life the way I want to lead it.

It seems to me I am going to have to get accustomed to my body dictating to me what I can and cannot do. I do not like it, but I suppose if I am going to get anywhere in this life, then I am going to have to get accustomed to being dictated to. Ahhhhhhhhh!

The week before Easter revealed that the British Sports Association for the Disabled, [the B.S.A.D.], had no record of ever receiving my profile test. Oh, hell, would I have to go through it all again. Jackie, fortunately had kept a copy, and faxed it through, for immediate attention. She was still of the opinion I would be attending, but until I see it in black and white, I will not believe it. I do not believe anything unless it is written down. A throw back from the job, I suppose.

Something materialised in their offices, it was my profile test! They had at last found the original, and were going to forward it to their Physiotherapist for immediate attention.

I still kept up my swimming, just in case, and of course my weight training. I knew all the other competitors would be training hard, so I had to keep at it. I wanted to know, what races I would be swimming, as I would have to gear my training accordingly. As they say 'No pain, No gain'! I needed to be certain as to whether I would be sprinting, or long distance. Although the long distance is outside of my group. I want to show the Officials I am capable of a long distance although I'm not supposed to be able to. I am not a sprinter! I am still not a sprinter!

A week after Easter, Jackie received a message on her answering machine, the B.S.A.D., had agreed my profile and I was entered for all four distances.

That is the 50, 100, 200, and the 400 metres. Bloody hell, all that lot, they've got to be joking, haven't they?

408

They were going to confirm in writing. I will really have my work cut out now. There is no possibility I can possible swim in all 4 distances in 2 days. If the competition was over 10 days, then I possibly could. As this would allow me to have enough recovery time between events. It now depends on the schedules.

I hope the 400 is on the Sunday, as this would then enable me to swim in either the 50, or the 100, on the Saturday. I hope it is the 100 metres on the Saturday, as I'm not a sprinter it would enable me to attempt the longer distance, although flat out. I want to do one that's in my group, and one that's out of it, to give me two reasonable chances of being spotted by the selectors.

There is still the faint outside chance of being selected for Atlanta, as a member of the British squad, for the Paralympics. Providing I do well, and there is a space available in my group, and at my distance.

I'm going to Sheffield. I've done it! I'm in the Nationals. Me, at my age of 41 now swimming competitively. Who says swimming is for the youngsters? Baloney! The commentators are going to have some fun with me around. Defying all the odds!

For the first time in my life I've got to face a 50 metre Long Course Championship size pool. What a daunting prospect. Not bad for someone who was made to feel so useless, stupid, and inadequate. That should show him! *I'VE DONE IT!*

The nearest I have ever been to a Long Course Championship size pool was whilst I was visiting

Canada, in the early eighties, with my Parents, and we had a tour of the Montreal Olympic facilities. As I was not swimming in those days, I did not appreciate what I was looking at. My photographs are a reminder, but even those do not convey the true splendour, or the atmosphere of the complex.

Whilst I am having my tea with all the regulars, at the Leisure Centre after we have completed our swim, I happen to mention I have no experience of racing. Neither am I likely to get any.

I have been sent an application form for the 'Federation Games' being organised by the B.A.L.A.S.A. games. [British Amputee and Les Autres Sports Association]. This event occurs in mid-May, in Swindon. Before the Nationals. I enter for the 100 metres only. As the swimming is on one day only, I really cannot do any more. I will look upon this event as nothing more than another training session, to give me some idea of how I'm progressing, and also some much needed experience of racing. I chose this distance rather than my preferred distance, as this is officially within my category.

Two weeks before the Swindon event, the organiser telephones me, to inform me the swimming events have had to be cancelled. It transpired only 8 swimmers had entered out of all the distances, and in all the groups. It meant there was not enough interest. I had expected there would have been a great deal of interest as this would have been the last event before the Nationals.

He asked me if I was interested in any of the other activities, but I said since the onset of the disease I was incapable of participating in any of the other activities. Normally, I would have jumped at the chance to try my hand in competition at any other activity, especially in my old sports of badminton, tennis, squash, and hockey, but not now. I just love being competitive! I'm not going to get any racing experience from this quarter. It would appear I shall be racing in Sheffield blind, metaphorically speaking.

To help in this problem all the people I have met over the months, are going to form themselves into a relay squad, and take me on for one length at a time. They say they could not possibly do any more, as one length for them flat out is more than they can manage. Even then they do not hold much hope of keeping up with me, but at least it will help me in racing.

They even volunteered Charles, who is now 89 to take me on. I declined this specific offer, as I do not think it would be very beneficial to Charles.

I am unable to attend the swimming club, as this is held on a Monday evening, at 21.00 hours. I am therefore, unable to gain any experience from that quarter, more's the pity. I would have had nearly 2 hours in bed by then. Also, I would miss out my swim on the Monday morning, as well as the Tuesday morning, and probably the Wednesday morning, together with my lessons. This would mean 3 sessions lost to one, and also my casual walks in the afternoon with Shassie, when she looks after me. I am now unable to do anything on a social basis in the evening, if I wish to be functional for the next 48 hours.

I suggested to Dave, the maintenance manager, after an idea from Hugh, if a hare could be fixed up to coincide with me starting off, and I could swim after it rather like the greyhounds chasing the hare, at the dog track. I could come out of the starting gate all guns blazing! The only problem would be it would get terribly soggy and squelchy, and probably sink.

The nearest Long Course Championship-sized pool to Tenterden is situated at Crystal Palace National Sports Centre. Near the site of the Crystal Palace, which burnt down in 1936. It was originally erected in Hyde Park for the Great Exhibition of 1851 and moved to its new site at Sydenham, before the catastrophe. Dad remembers visiting it, before the electrical fault engulfed it in flames.

As Jackie was convinced I was attending Sheffield, I wrote to the centre at the beginning of April to request details of facilities, and pricing, this was before I knew I was attending. Having not received a reply, after 3 weeks, I telephoned and complained about the lack of response. This geared them into some action, as in the post the next day I received a price list, details of facilities, maps of the grounds, and approach roads. Mum agreed to take me, as it would be impossible for me to drive there, and swim, and then drive back again. I have to rely on others for so much now. There was no sauna or steam room, neither was there a Jacuzzi. I would therefore be unable to complete my treatment.

At the beginning of May, Mum drove us both there. Dad was unable to attend as he was in hospital yet again, but this time, having the replacement knee joint replaced It had now become completely infected, and his body had decided to reject it. As dad was still in hospital he was not going to be cajoled into having a swim, something which he would hate.

The journey to the centre was easier than finding one's way in. There was no sign for disabled parking, only a sign for permit parking. I know I hold the Orange Disabled Parking Permit, but I did not think it entitled me to park in that specific car park. We then left the car as near as possible to what we thought was the entrance. There were steps everywhere. I tried to get in one door, but was told it was not the entrance, and they then showed me to another set of steps. They do not cater for any form of disability here.

At the next set of steps, I noticed there was no hand rail, so I walked down the grass embankment. I knew it would be a soft landing if I fell. Then at the bottom, another set of set of steps. Oh, sod this, not again. To hell with all this. Again I walked down the grass embankment. They are not going to get the better of me, no matter how hard they try. I will swim in that pool, even if it's the last thing I do! This building will not beat me!

Upon entering the centre I complained bitterly to the receptionist, about the inadequacies of just getting to the door. She agreed that when the place was built the designers and planners did not consider disabled sports people. They were hidden away in a corner, and never allowed to see the light of day, it seemed to me.

I said I would need to use the hoist.

"Oh, there isn't one, neither are there any lifts, anywhere in this building," she remarked.

When you are all worked up for an argument, it is very deflating when the recipient agrees without any form of a challenge. She did show me on a plan the best way to come in, and the nearest place to park, on another occasion. I was astounded. This, I thought, was the National Sports Centre, I assumed it would have had them.

She rang through to the life guards, and warned them I would need assistance. She then said it was originally built for elite swimmers, and was not envisaged to be used by the general public. Disabled people were thought to be incapable of any sport or activity in those days. I wondered, as I had qualified for the National Championships, would that not make me into an elite swimmer, although disabled.

Having found the changing rooms, and given up with the battle to get my bag into the tiny lockers, we were faced with another two flights of steps. Oh, shit, not again.

No wonder they did not reply to my letter, they do not want disabled people here.

On reaching the pool, I was not as astounded as I thought I would be. Although it is 50 metres long, and 8 lanes wide, it did not look daunting, especially when looking down upon it. I was by this stage knackered.

I was helped in, which was relatively easy as I was moving with gravity. I sat on the side of the pool, with the steps on my right, and took hold of the nearest rail with my right hand, and tried to reach the far rail with my left, but it would not reach. The life guard took hold of my hand and placed it on the rail, and in the process I swung my body round, and then descended down the steps, and began my swim.

Once in, I realised that it seemed a bloody long way.

"Oh shit, what have I let myself in for," I exclaim.

I thought I would be able to swim like I do in Tenterden, length after length after length. I found I could not. I could only manage it in bouts of two. I could not put two and two together to make four. I was annoyed. I put it down to the journey, apprehension, the difficulties in getting in, the psychological aspect of facing a 50 metre pool for the first time, and the fact I was knackered before I even started.

In the end I managed a total of 14 lengths, but only 3/4 length of back stroke. I did not attempt the butterfly, as I can only just manage 25 metres of that stroke, in one go. I was very disappointed in my effort, but then, was I possibly expecting too much on my first attempt? Mum was rather more pleased with her effort as she managed four lengths, but then as she is not a swimmer, this was something to be proud of.

When it was time for me to get out, I again requested assistance. This was going to be harder, than getting in. I was now going against gravity. The life guard who helped me in, got in the water with me, and whilst I was hanging onto the steps for dear life, he was pushing up against me, so I would not fall. Another life guard came over and took hold of my shoulders and heaved, whilst the other one pushed. Together they eased me up, until I was kneeling on the top, and then I managed to get up. If only I was not like this, and much younger! I thanked them both for their assistance, it would be so much easier if there was a hoist.

Sheffield has one, thank goodness. I then took a well-deserved breather, and sat on the wall alongside the pool.

In lane seven a female swimmer was at work with her coach. She had a beautiful freestyle [front crawl], so easy, with split second tumble turns. She was a joy to watch. The more I watched, the more my bottom lip dropped in admiration. I was gob smacked! As she was so professional, I thought she must be a member of the British squad. I wish I could do it like that. I thought I recognised her, but I was not certain. I hoped she would be in swimming the next time I went, because then I could discover her identity.

Upon leaving the centre, I noticed how tatty and scruffy it was. It was also terribly shabby, dark, dirty, and dingy. It would need millions spending on it to get it up to scratch. It needs the insides ripping out and starting from scratch, if at all possible.

I hope they apply for National Lottery money, because of the extensive improvements needed, and to encourage more International sporting fixtures. I often wondered why the National Championships were held in Sheffield. Now I know.

The gym was, it looked to me, in a very dilapidated state. Tenterden could knock spots off that one. If Tenterden had a 50 metre pool it could be head and shoulders above the facilities at Crystal Palace, although it would be missing the Athletics Track.

We just do not appreciate how lucky we are at Tenterden. If Crystal Palace National Sports Centre, is a prime example of the equipment and facilities for our best International Athletes, for both disabled and able-bodied, and I am not just referring to Athletics, then it is no wonder we do not achieve much. Anything that is achieved, is won against all the odds. The only decent part, it seemed to me on first glance, was the Athletics track, but I think a vast amount of money has already been spent on it .

We will have to return, as I want to ensure I can swim long distances in a 50 metre pool, and to perfect my turns, but at least I will know what to expect, and where to park for ease. I hope I will not have the psychological problems again. I said to Mum it was a bloody long way, just for 30 minutes in the water.

Following my disastrous attempt at a 50 metre pool I ensured I could still swim a long distance on the Friday following, and on the other two days in the week following. I easily convinced myself that in a 25 metre pool I have no problems, but a 50 metre, seems to take on a whole new meaning.

As Dad was still in the hospital, grumbling that he has now got to use crutches instead of a Zimmer, Mum took me again to Crystal Palace on the Wednesday of the next week.

We followed the directions given by the receptionist, and used one of the two disabled parking spaces, near the entrance. This made my task so much easier. The building and the facilities had not improved during the week. Perhaps this was too much to hope for! The staff were, as proved on the previous occasion, just as thoughtful, and helpful. If only the building was like the staff!

I wanted to aim at 20 lengths non-stop. This would have been the equivalent of 40 lengths in my pool. I knew this distance was well within my capabilities, as I had managed it on the previous Tuesday.

Having got in, I set off. It did not seem quite so far this time. It did not feel like 50 metres, but then I do not know what 50 metres feels like! I did in fact complete 16 lengths non-stop, then completed another 8 lengths of various other strokes. I have now conquered a 50 metre pool. At long last! All in all, it was 24 lengths, 10 more than the previous week, and a complete length of back stroke. I think this is a first! It was so much like hard work. I left it at that. I did in actual fact complete the equivalent of 48 lengths.

I've done it! I've done it! I felt very pleased with myself. Sheffield will not be such a daunting prospect. All I need now is race experience, and my tumble turns working out. These are still uncontrolled. Arms and legs everywhere. I'm still not satisfied. That's the problem of being a perfectionist! Dammmn!

One lady remarked to Mum, she was amazed I managed at least three lengths to her one, and was even more amazed when she learnt I was disabled. Mum, this time, completed six lengths, which was two more than the previous week, so she again felt pleased with herself.

In lane seven, next to mine, the professional was back. I saw her before she got in the pool and immediately recognised her as Sarah Hardcastle, who has recently qualified for Atlanta. The Olympic Games, 1996.

I wonder if I could be there for the Paralympics? There is always a faint possibility. Think positive, woman! It is always easy to differentiate a professional from the ordinary swimmer. Even in heavy training they make it look so easy. She is a tall girl, very long legged, just like Karen Pickering who I met last September, at Whitstable, again another British Olympian.

There was absolutely no chance of me even attempting the butterfly, with Sarah next to me. I would not like to splash her from lane seven into eternity. She swims two lengths of front crawl in just above 60 seconds, and I can do it in just under two minutes. She is therefore twice my speed. My locals think I'm quick, but compared to Sarah I'm like a snail. Plodding along in the slow lane.

I remarked to Mum, upon leaving the pool, what she thought would have happened if I had started swimming at a young age.

If I can manage to get to National level within five and a half years, and at my age, never having swum before August 1990, just splashing about in those days, would I have made international level at a much younger age?

How much would my life have changed if I had swum instead of playing hockey, and athletics? Would I have gone down with this bloody disease? However sport was an alien concept to both of my parents, as they were only really interested in academia. I was not academic. I think, though, I would probably have excelled at any sporting activity, as that was what I enjoyed the most at school.

After my diagnosis mum wanted me to move to the coast near them. This was not agreeable to me, and I think she now realises I'm better off where I am, in Tenterden, in my little bungalow which I adore. We can always look back, but now I'm looking forward. Here's to Sheffield. I'm almost ready.

Chapter 62

The week of the Nationals was now upon me. I decided not to swim during the week. This, I thought, would make me suffer with withdrawal symptoms, so when I eventually got in the pool at Sheffield, I would do well. I decided I would concentrate on the gym, and therefore the weights. Hoping at the last minute this would build me up into Miss Universe, some hope, if it had not worked by now, it never would.

My resolve did not last. I swam once during the week. Still, perhaps I can still suffer with withdrawal symptoms, when I eventually splash into the pool, I can't say dive as this is impossible now.

My parents were picking me up on the Friday morning. My Dad said he was coming, and he would not miss it for the world. He was at this stage in a wheelchair. My biggest surprise was Kai had decided to come over from Holland, and watch. I collected him from Dover Hover port on the Thursday afternoon, and we had a leisurely evening together.

Upon our arrival at the hotel in Sheffield, I discovered when given my entry documentation, I had been entered for the 50 metres, 100 metres, and the 200 metres, all front crawl or freestyle. Apparently my time for the 400 metres was too slow. Three races in two days; I was really going to have my work cut out, I hope my body does not give out on me. I hope I can make it last through two days of competition. I only had one race on the Sunday, and that was the 50 metre sprint. Ohhhh hell, I am not a sprinter. What have I let myself in for??

This was an international meeting. My first competition, and I'm racing against foreigners. What *have* I let myself in for? Talk about being slung in at the deep end, figuratively speaking. There is no going back now. I'm here, so I might as well make the best of it, and try to do the best I can. I had the opportunity to meet many other disabled people from all parts of the globe as there were teams from Australia, Germany, Poland, Sweden, and the Netherlands, staying at our hotel.

We were taken to the pool on the Saturday morning, by busses, which had been especially hired and adapted to accommodate wheelchairs. There were many different styles and sizes of machines. I was by now beginning to get nervous, but I tried not to show it.

The pool was magnificent. So different from Crystal Palace. We went from street level straight onto pool side. No steps to negotiate. The changing facilities were again on pool side. Again no steps. This was a dream. I found a place to perch, by the diving pit, and behind the diving boards. I was completely out of the way.

I was joined by a couple of blind girls who were both representing Great Britain in Atlanta, at the Paralympics. Janice Burton, who is classed as B1 [totally blind], a member of the C.O.S.A.C.S.S. club, and Kirsty Stoneham, who is classed as B2 [partially sighted], a member of Dartford District club. There are three groups for the blind. Next to us were the Hungarian team, and further along the bench were the Dutch team.

My first race was the 100 metres, which was event 117. We had to report to the stewards at least three races before.

I knew I needed some time in the main pool, just to get accustomed to the 50 metres again, so I had a short warm up. It was beautiful. It was great just to feel the water around me. I was immediately put more at ease. This sense of euphoria did not last however.

When I reported in, I was a complete and utter nervous wreck. I did not want to do it, but at the same time I did not want to let the squad down, they had invested a lot of time and effort in me. Jackie saw my plight, and came over and put her arm round me saying it would be all right, and just to try my best.

I had already spoken to Duncan Goodhew, [former, Olympic Gold Medallist 200 metres breast stroke]. He has now retired from competitive swimming, and uses his immense knowledge and experience in helping others not so fortunate. He had encouraged me to 'go for it'.

I had some stiff opposition. Margaret McEleny, and Jane Stidever, both selected for Atlanta, were in all of my races. I was also up against representatives from Spain, Sweden, Netherlands, and Germany.

Having given permission to get in the water, the bleep went and we set off. I thought once I was in the water I would feel more at ease, but I was still nervous. I put everything I had into it, but in the last five metres my body decided to give out. It had had enough. I struggled on, and hit the wall at the end. When I looked up at the electronic scoreboard, I was confused, I could not see my name, and then upon squinting through my goggles I thought I had come 6th. I had failed.

When I heaved myself out of the pool, I just laid along the side panting for all I was worth. The officials were quite worried and thought I needed a doctor, but I just said it was okay, and I would get myself together, eventually.

What have I done? I've failed. I've let them down. I've let myself down, and my parents down, and I've still got the 200 metres in the afternoon to do. I did not want to do it. How on earth could I tell Jackie? I couldn't. I then decided to take part, but I was going to enjoy it, and just take it casually.

During lunch, I managed to speak to Jackie, and she was over the moon with what I had achieved. I was surprised at her reaction, as I thought I had failed. She told me coming 4th in the time of two minutes, was remarkable, bearing in mind I had world class opposition. It transpired I was only one second behind the Bronze medal winner, who was representing

Sweden. If only the body had not given up when it did, I might have won a medal in my very first race. Perhaps I'm not as bad as I thought. This did not change my resolve, however, about the 200 metres. I was still only going to enjoy it and take it casually.

I noticed my body was rebelling. It was doing the usual. 'I've worked for you, and now I'm giving up', it was saying. It had ceased up completely. Nothing wanted to work. Kai suggested I have a massage, and this seemed to ease out the limbs, but it took nearly two hours of pushing and pulling by the Physiotherapist, to get my limbs mobile again.

I used the diving pit to warm up in. I knew it would need to be deep, but I had no idea just how deep, it seemed to go on forever. Although there were black lines upon the base to enable you to swim in a straight line, it seemed such a long way down.

This of course upset the exact precision for the tumble turns. I knew how to keep in a straight line, and I also knew where the wall was. I could see it.

But how do the blind swimmers keep in a straight line, and how do they know where the wall is? I had to ask. I hoped Janice and Kirsty would not mind me asking. They informed me they managed to keep in a straight line by following the lane rope. They keep to the side of the lane, and can then feel the rope, and by counting the strokes they know how many it takes from dive in to the wall. There is a problem with this, however, as when you start to get tired the arms shorten

425

and therefore you do more strokes per lane and this could upset the timing for the tumble turn, so as they approach the wall an official then hits them on top of the head with a long stick which has about 9 to 12 inches of polystyrene at one end. This then indicates how many strokes they each need to do before going into the turn.

Upon looking around me, I was surprised there were no officials who I recognised. I kept remembering my days as a line judge, at all the International Badminton Tournaments I used to officiate at. I think it was this experience of international competition that helped me through the week-end.

Event 220 was my next race. The 200 metres freestyle. I kept my resolve and enjoyed it. I again had Jane Stidever against me, but also representatives from Spain, Australia, Sweden, Germany, and Poland. I came 5th. My time of 4 minutes 16 seconds, was only six seconds slower than my submitted time, and this time I was casual. I wonder what the result would have been if I had tried?

I was not as tired as I was in the morning, I was at last satisfied. I felt I could hold my own in such illustrious company, and I had not let the squad or anyone else down.

As I was racing again on the following day, I did not attend the championship dinner on the Saturday night. Kai was me! He went in my place. I was in bed by 19.00 hours. Knowing full well I had to sprint in the morning. UGH!

Sunday loomed. This was it. My last race, and it has to be a sprint. 50 metres. One lap, that is all. No turns to do, just one lap.

Event 350, and I was again up against the two British girls together with representatives from Hungary, Germany, Sweden, Scotland, and Spain. I had no aspirations of doing very well, except I was not going to come last. I did not care where I came, except I WAS NOT COMING LAST.

I heaved myself into the water, in my lane three, with the Hungarian girl in lane four. I looked to the wall at the far end and said to myself 'That is what you're aiming for'. 'That's all'. 'Think positive, woman, just like Linford Christie, P.M.A.'. [Positive mental attitude].

The bleep sounded, and I set off. I could see the Hungarian girl in my sight all the way. She was not going to overtake me. I was not coming last. Again the body decided five metres out it had had enough, but it had reckoned without the brain. I pushed it, that girl was not going to overtake me, I was not coming last. I hit the wall ahead of her. I had not come last.

I looked up at the electronic scoreboard and was totally confused. My name was there, but I could not ascertain my position, nor my time, I was in lane three that much I knew, but the rest was a complete blur. I looked up to where my parents were sitting together with Kai, and they were waving frantically. I just waved very nonchalantly back. I had not come last.

The Scoreboard

We were given permission to get out, and upon heaving myself out of the pool, being in much the same state as the previous day.

I was approached by one of the Officials, who said "If you would like to go and wait outside the stewards' office you will be presented with your medal."

"What medal?" I retorted.

He continued, "You came 3rd, you have just won the Bronze medal."

"Don't be stupid, I don't win medals."

He was by now a little confused, "You were in lane three?"

"Er, yes."

"You are Sue Pepper?"

"Er, yes," beginning to sound even more wary.

"Well, you have come in third, and won a Bronze."

I still did not believe him.

"But that's ridiculous, I didn't, I don't win medals."

I thought to myself medals are for really good swimmers, not for the likes of me. He confirmed it with another Official, and I had to accept I had come 3rd, I had won a Bronze medal.

Oh, bleeding hell, I've done it, me at my age, in that company. So much for me not being a sprinter.

As the realisation began to dawn I fell back into the pool, with a mighty big splash. Alan Cook, one of the squad's coaches and Chairman of B.S.A.D. South-East, was waving and shouting at me saying it was great swim.

When I reported in at the stewards' office, I asked what my time was. I managed it in 54.25 secs over some 4.5 secs quicker than my submitted time.

To enable me to get anywhere further up the medals I have got to improve by about 10 seconds. Margaret won in a time of 44.98 secs, with Jane second in a time of 46.48 secs.

At the medal ceremony, I still could not believe what I had done. No wonder my parents and Kai were waving at me like demented idiots. My very first competition, an international competition at that, and I come away with a Bronze Medal, at the age of 41 years. Nearly all my fellow competitors were old enough to be my daughters.

Although I managed to win a medal, 480 miles is a bloody long way to drive, although Mum drove, just to spend approximately seven minutes swimming in the main pool. I spent more time in the diving pit warming up and cooling down than ever I did in the main pool. Still I think at the end of the day it was worth it.

I have now given Jackie and the coaches at the Squad some ammunition, to try and convince me I am a sprinter. But I am still not a sprinter!

I may possibly be selected for the Paralympics in August, [a very outside chance], also the Open Day for the Disabled, at Tenterden Leisure Centre, to organise, and to attempt to start disabled badminton in my area, and to extend it to all of Kent hopefully. Hopefully to extend my contacts with the Kent Sports Development Unit.

I do not come from a sporting family. It is not in any of our genes, so I do not know where my fitness and sporting fanaticism materialises. Perhaps it has lain dormant for generations, and decided to explode with me. It has certainly come out with a vengeance!

My life has turned a complete full circle, I do not suffer with M.S. I live with it. I listen to what the body tells me, which is something I never did in the past. I feel healthier, fitter, and leaner.

There is no such word in my dictionary as can't, if something is difficult, I find the best way round it. I improvise. Just because I have an incurable disease, no matter how minor at the present time, does that mean I should just sit at home and vegetate? Of course not!

Although someone who was at one time very dear to me, who made me feel so useless, stupid and inadequate, proved himself to be stupid, useless, and inadequate.

I am still the same person, as I was before this happened. As Diana said, if I had not been competitive at swimming, I would have found something else, as I am that type of person.

If I was to work, either full time or part time, this would preclude me from having any form of social life, neither would I be able to keep mobile, and therefore I would deteriorate that much quicker, and be in a wheel chair by the turn of the century. I have no intention of so doing. I will get into the next century standing, as best I can on my own two legs, or perhaps three if you include my peg leg.

As M.S. attacks everybody differently, I am unable to advise other sufferers to do as I do. My treatment works for me. If someone else is attacked in the same way as myself, especially in their legs and/or arms, then I would strongly recommend them to swim and keep as mobile and active as possible.

The use of the gym is essential to keep off the onset of osteoporosis, and by keeping the body toned, this maintains the victim's well-being. If you look good, then you feel good.

The heat from the Sauna and Steam Rooms, seem to get into the muscles and ease the flow of messages through. Together with the massage from the Jacuzzi, my body tends to work as I want it to work, although for not nearly long enough.

I still wish I could run down the street, swim marathons, go out for an evening, go dancing, sing and attend concerts, umpire and line judge badminton, umpire hockey, go sailing, play tennis, and squash, work, and live a perfectly full and normal life.

I have at long last accepted all these activities are beyond me now, but I have the future, and it is as full as I can make it.

If you should find yourself in a similar position, do not be put off by being second best, or by playing second fiddle. You are a human being after all, just the same as anybody else.

Do not tolerate being told there is nothing you can do, because there is always something that can be achieved, no matter how minor. It may take some time to find, but you will find it with perseverance, with me I was lucky.

I have always been sporty, so therefore it seemed natural to me to turn to that pastime.

I have lost the ability to sing now, but I can still listen to good music. Being like I am, does not prevent me from having the radio on.

You always find out who your true friends are, when adversity strikes, and you always manage to find new ones, who did not know you before it happened, so they are unable to compare what you are now to what you were then.

The ones who did not want to know you after, were not really friends at all.

There will always be some ignorant moron who laughs at you because of the way you waddle down the street, or struggle with the car.

They would be laughing on the other side of their face if it happened to them. Also, they should be thinking, 'there but for the Grace of God, go I'. Those persons are just treated with the contempt they deserve, nothing more and nothing less.

I would like to pass on my good wishes to you all, and to those who may find themselves in a similar position, I express my hopes you manage to have as full and as meaningful life as that which has happened to me.

THE END

Thank you.

Chris and Ollie Johnston, with Kai and Sue